To Jim,

Fasten your seat
belt & enjoy the
ride —

David

Economic Warfare

Economic Warfare

*Secrets of Wealth
Creation in the Age
of Welfare Politics*

Ziad K. Abdelnour

with Wesley A. Whittaker

WILEY

John Wiley & Sons, Inc.

Published by John Wiley & Sons, Inc., Hoboken, New Jersey.

Published simultaneously in Canada.

For general information on our other products and services or for technical support, please contact our Customer Care Department within the United States at (800) 762-2974, outside the United States at (317) 572-3993 or fax (317) 572-4002.

Wiley also publishes its books in a variety of electronic formats. Some content that appears in print may not be available in electronic books. For more information about Wiley products, visit our web site at www.wiley.com.

Library of Congress Cataloging-in-Publication Data:

Abdelnour, Ziad.
  Economic warfare : secrets of wealth creation in the age of welfare politics / Ziad K. Abdelnour with Wesley A. Whittaker. – 1
      p. cm.
  Includes index.
  ISBN 978-1-118-15012-2 (cloth); ISBN 978-1-118-19765-3 (ebk); ISBN 978-1-118-197646 (ebk); ISBN 978-1-118-197639 (ebk)
  1. Investments–United States.   2. Global Financial Crisis, 2008–2009. 3. Wealth–United States.   4. United States–Economic policy.   I. Whittaker, Wesley A.   II. Title.
  HG4910.A615 2011
  330.973–dc23

                                                          2011032044

Printed in the United States of America

10 9 8 7 6 5 4 3 2 1

A return to first principles in a republic is sometimes caused by the simple virtues of one man. His good example has such an influence that the good men strive to imitate him, and the wicked are ashamed to lead a life so contrary to his example.

—Niccolo Machiavelli (1469–1527)

This book is dedicated to Nadia, Karl, and Mark.

I couldn't have been luckier than having such a family.

Contents

Foreword

by Marc Rowan

While the financial crisis or Great Recession that began in 2008 dominates our financial consciousness, it strikes me that the events that began in December 2010 and will no doubt continue through the U.S. presidential election in November 2012 may have more of a lasting impact on our collective economic futures.

In December 2010, a mere day apart, rioters in London protesting cutbacks in tuition aid attacked Prince Charles's car carrying the prince and Camilla, while the next day in Tunisia economic frustration set off a protest that has engulfed the Middle East and has already resulted in three Arab leaders being deposed.

In the rest of the world, protesters have since taken to the streets in Greece, Iceland, France, Portugal, Ireland, Israel, China, and elsewhere to vent their rage at aid cutbacks, food inflation, lack of economic opportunity, financial destruction caused by major banks, changes in retirement age, or government austerity generally. At their core, these protests are about economic policies or at least changes to existing economic policies.

The year 2011 represents a turning point where governments around the globe are finally realizing that the promises that have been made to voters may no longer be able to be kept and that an endgame of sorts has been reached where spending in excess of current receipts may no longer be able to be financed.[1]

Certainly, the weaker and more heavily indebted economies around the globe are already experiencing a painful austerity and an abrupt change to the social contract. On a projected basis the total of all of the promises made by politicians of all parties to a generation of voters now exceeds that which many countries can afford to pay without the destruction of their underlying economies.

It wasn't until the riots in the United Kingdom in the summer of 2011 that I began to warm to the title of Ziad Abdelnour's latest book, *Economic Warfare: Secrets of Wealth Creation in the Age of Welfare Politics*.

I found myself trying to explain to my teenagers why the streets in London near where we lived for a few years had erupted in riots and anticipating their next question as to whether or not the same thing could happen in the United States. I explained that, while there was certainly an element of hooliganism underlying the riots, the United Kingdom was going through a difficult economic period and that this was particularly difficult given significantly less economic and social mobility throughout the population in the United Kingdom when compared to the United States. It sounded so mundane when I said it that it took a while for my teenagers to appreciate that we were having an important conversation about the true nature of America and how we differ from much of the rest of the world. America does not have a tradition of class warfare.

The vast majority of Americans have never believed the concept that one must fail in order for another to succeed. In fact, we have celebrated those who have achieved economic success in our society whether in industry, Internet, medicine, fashion, music, finance, or otherwise, and our system allows for significant economic and social mobility based on ability and hard work. Further, what happens in America ultimately influences what happens in the rest of the world.

America is still roughly a quarter of worldwide gross domestic product and is a beacon for the young and ambitious around the world. Was I wrong? Is our great tradition at risk? As the United States confronts its economic challenges, the debate is no longer about *if* we have a problem but rather *how* we address the prospect of future deficits and government spending given the ripening of the entitlement promises made by a generation of politicians from both sides of the aisle to the past 80 years of voters.

With partisan politics at high decibel levels in advance of the presidential election in 2012 and a fundamental debate taking place between the "reduce the size of the problem" crowd and the "raise more money from those who can afford it" crowd, I worry that certain fundamental premises of our collective economic success are in jeopardy. Sometimes when the debate is all around us, it takes an outside observer to make us appreciate how unique our economic model really is and how privileged we are to live in a country where we have economic liberty.

Ziad Abdelnour comes from a successful and prominent merchant family in Lebanon and relocated to the United States in 1982 as that country was going through a civil war. Ziad is an accomplished businessman in his own right and has become a trusted adviser and confidant to many successful families throughout the United States and the world. Ziad's passion in defense of the case for individual economic liberty in the United States is exceeded only by his contempt for those who have abused the system to the detriment of all.

Conservatives and liberals will each find much to agree and disagree with in Ziad's book. *Economic Warfare* is a timely addition to the debate and a good history lesson in advance of the next election of how our modern financial institutions came to be and how far from the founding fathers' intent many of them have strayed.

Ziad argues forcefully that much of what we have come to accept as "progressive" ideas needs to be looked at through a different prism—a prism of economic liberty. Traditionally, we are taught to judge the success of a society by how it deals with the least able, most vulnerable members of that society. *Economic Warfare* challenges us by asking whether it is not the reverse that should be true. Shouldn't we judge a society by how they treat the most successful? Do we vilify, tax, expropriate, and condemn those who have succeeded, or do we celebrate economic success as the engine that propels our society toward greater collective well-being?

Economic Warfare's timing could not be better. As protesters fill the streets in cities around the globe, and as the United States begins to frame the solutions to our deficit issues, Ziad takes a refreshing look at the U.S. system and offers some strong advice as to how not to destroy that which has made our country unique.

Many of Ziad's concerns are reminiscent of a recent quote from the *Financial Times:*

> Given the concentration of savings among a minority of the population, soaking the rich will be easier than slashing entitlement spending. But paralysis in Washington and the Fed's dual mandate could result in a third path equally devastating to the wealthy: allowing inflation to debase private savings while easing indebtedness. Either way, America's outnumbered savers may succumb to the tyranny of the majority.

I have known Ziad for more than 25 years since our time together at the Wharton School and as a coworker at Drexel Burnham Lambert in the mid-1980s. I truly admire Ziad's passion as well as his ability to see events and trends for what they are. Ziad's outsider's perspective on what is great about the United States and what we are in danger of losing is timely and informative and an important contribution to the debate going forward.

Marc Rowan
Partner
Apollo Global Management, LLC
www.agm.com/Home.aspx
August 2011

Note

1. John Maudlin, *Endgame* (Hoboken, NJ: John Wiley & Sons, 2011).

Foreword

by Herman Cain

The natural state of our economy is prosperity. Freedom guarantees that. The only force capable of undermining it is government. *Economic Warfare* tells that truth.

We are stuck in the worst economic recovery since the Great Depression. It is so bad that at this point into the recovery, we are 8 million jobs short of being tied for last place with the previous worst recovery. Our gross domestic product is a trillion dollars or two short of where it should be, and a multiple of that in terms of wealth has dissipated. Our economic weakness has now become a top national security threat.

Did the market fail or did the government fail? If so, how? I have made my business career by asking the right questions. Are we working on the right problem? Do we have the right people? Are we close enough to the action? Ziad Abdelnour's strong suit is to ask questions until the bottom line is found. He has surrounded himself with outstanding people and an unmatched network. You can't get closer to the action than he, particularly at the level at which he operates.

Abdelnour lays out in detail that even the most well-meaning government policies have unintended consequences that have harmed the economy. If government policies were held accountable the way private businesses are, the scoreboard would say government is failing to help people.

This book makes one of the strongest cases yet that to have a warm heart, one must have clear eyes. Abdelnour sees clearly, and his vantage point is the front line of battle over the future of our country.

There are few problems in the world that economic prosperity cannot help solve. Yet the engines of that prosperity are under fierce attack. The forces that seek power over others have gained the upper hand against those that seek freedom. By harming wealth creation, they cause even more strain on society. Historically, this is nothing new. State domination over its subjects has roots that connect statism, totalitarianism, communism, and socialism to more modern-day variants of liberalism and progressivism. It is a constant fight and we must win.

As Abdelnour illustrates, the forces against wealth creation accelerate when the Progressives are in power. They forced Obamacare and "Dodd Frankenstein Financial Deform" upon us. Unlike the elected representatives who voted for those bills, Abdelnour actually read them and offers us his chilling dose of reality.

It speaks volumes of the resiliency of the American economy to still be standing after the onslaught of economic policy termites eating away at the foundation for so long. We now face a perfect storm, but we will fight back. One only needs to observe the unrest across the world to imagine what life will become here if we don't get our economy turned around soon.

But how? It is not as though people lose sight of simple principles in a complex society as much as it is a Progressive tactic to confuse people. For example, if the world consists of two farmers, and one is paid government benefits, who pays? Exactly. The other farmer pays. Redistribution is a negative-sum game, and people understand that.

In another example, if one farmer raises cattle and the other grows vegetables, they are both better off through voluntary trade. Making other people better off is the only way to satisfy your needs. Is it bad that some people make many people better off? Do you deserve a special attack by government if you make millions of people better off? Voluntary exchange is a positive-sum game.

Abdelnour uses great skill explaining how a complex global economy still boils down to a few of those core principles. He reveals tactics used by the Progressives to confuse people through victimhood, race baiting, and preying on the compassionate sensibilities of most, and shows how to defeat them.

A great example is Abdelnour's investigation that uncovers the true underpinnings of the mortgage crisis. It may be the best diagnosis you will read. As you will see, it was a colossal failure of government, the remedy of which is not to bail out and subsidize failure.

But trade and wealth creation is not all upside. It is failure, too. Failure is a necessary component to growth and success. Babe Ruth struck out 1,330 times but also hit 714 home runs. We need to let failing entities fail. Only then will successful people turn these enterprises back into wealth-creating vehicles again. "Too big to fail" is a concept that perpetuates failure and saps vitality from the rest of the wealth creators to do so.

Wealth creation is not a business suited to those whose skill set consists of voting "present." It requires decision making, risk taking, hard information, discipline, insight, and intelligence. Abdelnour is generous with his valuable insight. He offers a range of opportunities so that each of us can find our role in the battle. He shares lessons for all of us to absorb.

In true nonpolitician, business-like fashion that makes me proud, Abdelnour focuses on commonsense solutions. We have gotten away from the 10th Amendment. The only equal outcome for all that can be achieved by the federal government is misery for all. It is not that people shouldn't be helped. It is that in most cases, it is not the role of the federal government to do so.

He gives us a penetrating look at each major department and shows how a return to the 10th Amendment will reduce spending, limit the scope of government so freedom expands, and ultimately how that will lead to improved wealth creation, which is the only demonstrated way to help people. We know what happens when Progressives have full control and no opposing forces to draw battle lines. It's called Detroit.

Join me in support of his prescription to reassess all regulation against a standard of whether it creates more entrepreneurs. Then install a Fair Tax and sound money, and the economy would boom for a decade or more. By adding more engines to the train, it increases the number of cars that will be pulled along.

In whose hands should you place your trust for improving the economy? An entrepreneur, whose job it is to solve problems for a profit? Or a bureaucrat, whose job it is to cause problems for a profit? I know where I put my trust, and I'm sure 90 percent of us agree. We outnumber them, so let's act like it.

Ziad Abdelnour is a shining example that immigrants make our country stronger. He came here legally, and he came here to produce. He used freedom to pursue his dreams. God bless him for having big, big dreams. For as much wealth as he has created for entrepreneurs worldwide, he has generated a multiple of that for society. He's a reminder that the American Dream isn't a house, or any property, or the consumption of any good. It is to be productive creating wealth.

Get ready for a no-holds-barred attack on the forces aligned against prosperity. As a person who gets accused of flunking Political Correctness 101, I have to admit his candor and bluntness will send a wake-up call to some. I find it refreshing that he not only is willing to take many tough stands, but never once leaves you guessing where he stands.

This could indeed be the most important book you read all year.

We all must find in *Economic Warfare* what we can do to be part of the solution. For some, it may be expanding your investing or operating horizons. For others, it may be picking up the weapon of knowledge and defeating the enemy by casting a crucial vote.

The very people whose policies unleashed the attacks on our economic foundation are waging a full-blown assault on the true wellspring of business formation, innovation, and job creation: the wealth creators.

When you see how the Washington–Wall Street corridor, which I call the Chaos Industry, profits at the expense of average Americans, you will want to take action. He pulls back the curtain and reveals who is stealing our birthright. Progressive policies have failed. Their "throw sand in the gears, then blame the engine" approach to running the country is running it into the ground. The time to go along to get along is over.

This is for those who aspire to be rich the old-fashioned way, by understanding that consumers ultimately have the say over who becomes rich.

The turnaround must come from outside of the Washington establishment. It must come from you, Ziad Abdelnour, and me. Battle lines have been drawn. Now is time to rise up, band together, and use knowledge as our ammunition and our votes as weapons.

On one side of the battle are the fakers and takers. On the other side, there is Abdelnour and all of the wealth creators. Who offers you more opportunity?

The Founding Fathers did their job. We must be the Defending Fathers. Consider *Economic Warfare* as a modern version of the *Federalist Papers*. When you're done reading it, you will join me in hoping Ziad Abdelnour soon makes good on his promise to keep writing more.

I am up to his challenge of creating 50 million new millionaires. As some of you may know, this book is scheduled to be published at a time when I am running for the office of President of the United States of America. My private-sector experience tells me the government doesn't create wealth, jobs, or prosperity. I am confident that by getting the government off your back, out of your way, and out of your pocket, you will do the rest. Fifty million is a lot, but I will give it my best if you do the same.

Abdelnour does society a great service in laying bare the destructive fallacies of Keynesian economics. For that, he earns an honorary doctorate in "CAIN-sian" economics: the economics of growth, opportunity, and wealth creation.

One of my favorite political lines on the campaign trail comes from former U.S. Senator Everett Dirksen. He once said, "When they feel the heat, they will see the light." It is no coincidence that Ziad Abdelnour's name translates into "one who brings light to the world in abundance." He shines light on what we all need to know so that we can bring heat to those elected to represent us.

The Cold War was won without firing a shot. Armed with Abdelnour's insights, perspective, and wisdom, victory will be secured

at the ballot box in support of policies that pay respect to the fact
that the true American Dream is wealth creation.

Renew wealth creation and renew the American Dream.

Herman Cain
2012 Republican presidential candidate
http://www.hermancain.com/

Prologue

I t was a lazy, hazy Sunday morning, late in the summer of 2010. I had just brewed myself a cup of coffee and was browsing through the paper while my computer booted up. It was routine for me to check in with my social networks every morning, just to stay in touch with my family, friends, and business associates. A message popped up on LinkedIn. It was a message from Ziad Abdelnour to the members of the Financial Policy Council group. The message said:

> I need a ghost writer to help me put the zillion ideas running in my head in a clear and succinct fashion in a book that will totally "revolutionize" the financial world from a real Shock and Awe perspective. I already put most of my thoughts on paper and in blogs. Need though a real smart and reliable person who can help me accelerate the process; given time is of the essence and I don't have much time on my hands these days. What do you guys say?

I had met Ziad online in 2006 when I was looking for someone to handle a deal that my firm couldn't. Ziad ran a private family office in New York called Blackhawk Partners Inc., which was a recognized player in private equity finance. I was working for a funding consultant out of Montana. Ziad had a blog on his web site and I often commented. He seemed to like my comments. We'd talked a few times on the phone on financial topics. I would ask him questions, and he would always answer them promptly and diligently.

I had a strong respect for Ziad and was honored when he invited me to join his LinkedIn groups for Blackhawk Partners and the conservative fiscal think tank, Financial Policy Council. Still, I felt comfortable enough to privately reply to his query, asking if he needed someone to write his Christmas cards. I thought it might start off his Sunday with a chuckle and thought nothing more of it. Less than 15 minutes later, my cell phone rang. It was Ziad.

"If anyone else had sent me such a flippant response as this to my serious request," he said in a measured and deliberate tone, "I would have sent them back a searing reply that would have set their screen on fire."

He paused.

"But you, sonofabitch, you can write."

Thus began what can only be described as a powerful and magical journey into the world of a very smart, focused, and gracious man; a Machiavellian "iron fist in a velvet glove" kind of man who wears his power with a comfortable awareness and a confident humility. He is an extremely astute and very successful businessman who operates on the principle of utilizing the best, most comprehensive intelligence in order to achieve flawless and ruthless execution. He is feared by some, respected by most, and admired by many.

I hope I have been able to paint an accurate portrayal of Ziad Khalil Abdelnour. His name literally translates into "One who brings light to the world in abundance." That is truly his mission. I believe this book will bring the Light of Truth to the many people who have been kept in the darkness for far too long. Maybe it will even spark an open and honest debate about economics and free market enterprise.

I am honored to have played a part in its creation.

Wesley A. Whittaker
July 2011

Preface

For the last several years, I have been urged by many friends and colleagues to write a book encapsulating my business and political philosophies spanning 25 years in the eye of the storm.

Well, here it is.

Economic Warfare: Secrets of Wealth Creation in the Age of Welfare Politics is not about lamenting the current economic malaise with which the United States is still struggling. It is about solutions.

Although I don't have all of the answers, I can humbly confess that I have surrounded myself over the years with an unparalleled global network of sources of wisdom, expertise, and intelligence that have been instrumental in helping me fully monetize on the political trends shaping up.

There is no secret recipe for success. It begins with having an honest and realistic approach to life. I am not here to paint you a rosy picture or to provide you step-by-step instructions on how you can become a millionaire. There are still a vast number of ways for a person to reach that level of personal net worth. I am more interested in what happens after you get there, showing you a few of the options available for multiplying that investment many times over. I am not into job creation, saving the rain forest, or building democracy in Kazakhstan.

I am into creating wealth, lobbying for just causes, and empowering the best and brightest to do more of the above over and over again. Because of that, I have been called Machiavellian. I consider it a compliment.

What I am sharing in this book is what I have learned on the way to succeeding in spite of the best efforts of the anticapitalist radicals who have temporarily seized control of our government. I have done it without compromising basic business principles like risk management and ethics. I believe I speak for many of my professional peers when I say that I am appalled that a very few have nearly destroyed our economy because of their greed and corruption.

I believe we are at a crossroads in this nation. More than 235 years ago, we declared ourselves independent from an economic system that chose winners and losers based on patronage and heredity. We fought to free ourselves from a market model where the government dictated how successful we could and would become. We chose instead to have a free-market system in which a man could become whatever he dreamed as long as he was honest, faithful, and provided value. From the beginning of this republic, we have been told that government had the power and the authority to achieving economic stability and assure our business success. For nearly 100 years, we have been assured, in election after election, that if we just give the government a little more power and a little more control, our economy will always be solid and our business climate will be vibrant.

As I look around today, I believe the time has come to pull back the curtain and reveal the fact that we have not only been robbed of our birthright, we have very nearly been sold into slavery by our government in order to support their unquenchable lust for power. We are a nation that was built upon the rule of law, but we have allowed our leaders to become so compromised and corrupt that a small number of the financial and political community think they have actually become too important to be allowed to fail and too rich or too important to be held accountable for their hubris and incompetence. A nation that was once described as a city on the hill, shining the beacon of freedom and liberty to the rest of the world, has been reduced to a weak, indolent, broke shadow of her former self; the subject of scorn and derision around the world because of the corruption in our system.

It is time to sound the trumpet and arouse the citizens! To paraphrase Walt Kelly, we have met the enemy and he is among us. In this book, I reveal the true nature of the enemy that threatens to destroy the free-market capitalist system that made this nation the most exceptional country that ever existed. I will show where the weakening of our system began, how it was accomplished, and by whom. I will also give you some strong and serious solutions for routing this traitorous faction once and for all while creating wealth in the process.

We are in an economic war. It is a war between those who create wealth and those who believe they have some sort of divine mandate to appropriate wealth. They don't have such an authoritative command. I don't think they ever did. We have tried their command-and-control methods for nearly a century because they said they knew better. It is now obvious that they didn't.

My intention with this book is to incite the American people to rise up and assert the fact that this is our nation, our government, and our way of life. If this book is successful, a vast number of Americans will emerge who are ready, willing, and able to fight for this nation and all that it was created to be. And they will discover that there are more of their friends and neighbors who share their morals, their ethics, their hopes, and their dreams than there are of the so-called elites; the Takers and Fakers who just want a free ride.

Enjoy one of the most inspiring and educational books you will ever read. It is my hope that this book will change your life forever. That is change that I can believe in.

Ziad K. Abdelnour
July 2011

Acknowledgments

This book could not have been written without my friend, Wesley A. Whittaker, a writer of many talents whom I mentored at an accelerated rate on the fundamental workings of the financial world. In the process, he had to read every blog post I ever made, every magazine interview I've ever given, and everything I've ever published. To ensure that what I was saying could be substantiated, he did pains-taking research and read more than 30 books on various aspects of the topics of finance, economics, and constitutional law.

Wes has done a remarkable job of helping me put my thoughts and experiences on paper. I am tremendously grateful to him and hope this will be a long partnership together, empowering more wealth creators, activists, and entrepreneurs worldwide by utilizing the synergy of our combined talents.

I am also grateful to Victor Sperandeo, another man of many talents, a great friend and my key to the esteemed publishing house of John Wiley & Sons. This led me to Kevin Commins and his great team including but not limited to Pamela Van Giessen, Judy Howarth, and other Wiley team members who were instrumental in publishing and promoting this work to the world.

I am equally grateful to my good friend Mark Minevich, who opened up many doors to me to practically every publishing house across America and pushed my book on all of them as well as any agent could ever have.

I can honestly say I have been very blessed throughout my life with an amazing group of friends, influencers, and supporters—"world citizens" who have provided me with insight and expertise second to none in the process of building my "political and business war machine." They have influenced me, they have shaped me, they have humbled me, and they have made me a much better person.

I acknowledge the contributing influences of my larger-than-life role models, especially Carlos Slim Helu, Michael Milken, Marc Rowan, and David and Charles Koch; world-renowned academics, thinkers, and philosophers F. A. Hayek, Milton Friedman, and Arthur Brooks; the common sense, wisdom, and inspiration of the great political figures Ronald Reagan, Murray Rothbard, Ron and Rand Paul, Herman Cain, and Scott Garrett; and many more who have reinforced the notion of the American Dream.

Although it would not be humanly possible to mention all, I would like also like to particularly thank the following friends whose invaluable insights and feedback not only inspired me but thankfully held me to very high standards of quality and authenticity while producing this great manuscript.

This exclusive group includes but is not limited to: Burt Abrams, Elias Araktingi, Zeina Awad, Robert Ayan, Porter Bibb, Tom Blinten, Sharon Bush, Wael Chehab, Christopher Driscoll, Ferris Eanfar, Yaron Eitan, Joseph Farah, Robert Fay, Gil Feiler, Susan Finston, Marwan Forzley, Michael Friesen, Daniel Galvanoni, Richard Gonda, Patrick Kedziora, David Kopp, Sampath Kumar, John LeBoutillier, David Loeb, Herb London, Michael Luther, Joe Mancuso, Bobby Menonn, Ali Mogilner, Allstone Moore, John O' Callaghan, David Pohndorf, Frank Pons, Thomas and Penny Power, Muhannad Qubbaj, Michel Renirie, Wayne Allyn Root, Robert Savage, Victoria Silchenko, Ira Stoll, Bart Stuck, Ted Virtue, and Barbara Winston.

I must not forget my partners, board members, and other friends who have been associated with the different organizations I have been instrumental in forming or in which I have held a leadership position over the past two decades. These include:

- Blackhawk Partners, http://blackhawkpartners.com/.
- Financial Policy Council, www.financialpolicycouncil.org/.
- U.S. Committee for a Free Lebanon (USCFL), www.freelebanon. org/.
- Arab Bankers Association of North America, www.arabbankers.org/.

They say a man is as good as the "brain trust" around him. I can humbly say I have assembled, over the years, one of the smartest and most empowering brain trusts around. It goes beyond borders and encompasses all ethnicities and religions. These exceptional men and women have one thing in common: a genuine pursuit of excellence and a sense of mission second to none.

Finally, I wish to acknowledge the writers whose work inspired me and provided enormous resources for this book: Thomas J. DiLorenzo, Nick Humphrey, Bill McBride, and Dr. Astrid S. Tuminez.

Thank you all for making this journey an adventure.

Ziad K. Abdelnour
July 2011

Introduction

In my 2005 book, *The Raising of a President: The Mothers and Fathers of Our Nation's Leaders,* I talk about 14-year-old Franklin Delano Roosevelt arriving at the Groton preparatory school, bound by family tradition to the school's motto *Cui servire est regnare,* "To serve is to rule."

This motto was exemplified best by Franklin's distant cousin, Theodore, who devoted all of his energies to making America the Land of Opportunity. Franklin was, unfortunately, burdened by an ever-present and overbearing mother, which no doubt greatly influenced his policy formulation when he rose to the presidency in 1933. The nation was reeling from the Depression, with unemployment reaching a staggering 25.2 percent, or 31.6 million people. The Nationalist Socialist Party had effectively seized the German government and elected Adolf Hitler as chancellor. And the League of Nations was showing itself to be grossly ineffective at stemming the global rise of militant nationalism as Japan joined Germany in exiting the organization.

In Franklin Roosevelt's mind, leading by being of service was best expressed by the maternal instinct of providing recovery and relief through his New Deal programs of agricultural and business regulation, inflation, price stabilization, and public works. New organizations were created and given extraordinary power and latitude. These included the National Recovery Administration (NRA), the Federal Deposit Insurance Corporation (FDIC), the Agricultural Adjustment Administration (AAA), the Civilian Conservation Corps (CCC), the Public Works Administration (PWA), and the Tennessee Valley Authority (TVA).

The Nanny state was born, and in the decades since, every Democrat-controlled Congress has devoted itself to building upon this foundation. The international communists and socialists saw an opportunity to ingratiate themselves with the new liberal movement that had seized upon the crisis by expanding the role and power of the federal government in America.

By infiltrating the media, the universities, the labor unions, and the globalist organizations that were springing up on both sides of the Atlantic, they repeatedly pounded the message that the only way to salvation for the common working man was by way of Washington, D.C.

By the 1960s, the generally accepted belief was that there were only two political parties of any significance in America. The Republican Party represented the wealthy and the Northeast elites, and the Democratic Party was the champion of the working man and the underdog in our society. If you voted Republican, you were elitist, cruel, and probably racist. If you voted Democrat, you were caring and supportive of your fellow man and believed in a fair share for everyone. The message has been so thoroughly indoctrinated into the American people that some Republicans have felt the only way to govern effectively was to "go along to get along."

In *Economic Warfare*, Ziad Abdelnour has stripped away the rhetoric and cultural mythology to reveal how America has been taken over by anticapitalist wolves in sheep's clothing. There is no righteousness on the banks of the Potomac River, only greed, ignorance, and corruption. The myth of Big Government benevolence and altruism is blown away to reveal naked greed, class envy, and lust for power at any cost. The professional political class has been co-opted by international banking interests and globalists to destroy, once and for all, the free-market capitalist economy of the United States. They have allowed the economy to be openly assaulted and have attempted to blame the resulting misery on "the Rich." Abdelnour is having none of it.

As the progeny of international wealth and power in pre–civil war Lebanon, Abdelnour has an intimate knowledge of who the rich are and how they live. As the head of a private family office in New York City, he deals with the wealthy on a daily basis and shares the intimate details that only an insider would know as to who the rich are, how they became rich, and what they really do with their money. The truth is a far cry from the daily drumbeat of class envy and economic equality coming out of the Washington establishment and parroted by propagandists in the mainstream media.

Chapter 1 examines who the rich are and what that means in America. It then reveals how the system has been gamed to prevent you from becoming rich and why you should be upset about how the successful people in this country are maligned on a daily basis. Abdelnour strips back the veneer to reveal the true agenda behind our expanding central government and why you should be demanding answers from Congress, not more programs. It is impossible to separate politics and economics because they are interlinked.

Chapter 2 opens with a description of the damage that has been inflicted on the American economy in the past few years, making the indisputable charge that we are involved in an economic war for the survival of America. Drawing upon a wide array of sources, Abdelnour gives a concise history of how the recent economic bubble began, how it burst, and who was responsible. The facts are clearly stated, and the names have not been changed to protect anybody. More than just the criminal acts by a few nefarious characters, the 2008 collapse of our economy was the result of a series of avoidable actions and bad decisions made by people who should have and often did know better. It was the "perfect storm" of hubris, incompetence, and greed, and it never should have been allowed to happen.

From the very beginning of our republic, there has been an ongoing debate between those who believe the original intent of the founders was a small, limited role for the federal government and those who believe the central government is the nexus of all economic and civic life in the United States.

Chapter 3 reveals the truth about the American War for Independence and corrects some long-held myths about why this nation broke free from England. It also reveals the fact that not all of the founding fathers were necessarily on the side of Freedom and Liberty, but actively campaigned to bring America back into alignment with the European establishment, much to the detriment of this nation's original intention. The seeds of our current malaise were planted in our infancy.

We are in a battle in this nation over what constitutes sovereignty and who has the right to partake of and control the economic benefits gained from our unique system. America was created to be an exceptional Land of Opportunity where the individual could take an idea, develop it, and create wealth in the process. The capitalistic free-market economy gave everyone the opportunity to gain financial freedom and independence. Not everyone was pleased about this, and an enemy has arisen in our midst who has single-mindedly worked to subvert and even destroy this opportunity.

Chapter 4 reveals exactly who the enemy of free enterprise is and how they operate, while Chapter 5 gives a glimpse into the violence and chaos that could lie ahead if this enemy is allowed to triumph over the American way of life.

With Chapter 6, Abdelnour begins to lay out a plan for restoring economic freedom, not just in this country, but around the world. We are in a global marketplace now. If we are to prevail against the enemy within and once again compete against the other nations of the world, we must have a knowledge of what constitutes wealth, how to attain it, and what to do with it after we have. This is a book about solutions. Chapter 6 deals with the philosophy of wealth creation.

Chapter 7 reveals Abdelnour's personal strategies and vehicles for wealth creation, and in Chapter 8, Ziad gives the reader an inside look at specific investment tactics and why traditional investments may not be good bets in today's economy. This is no-nonsense straight talk from a man who has been there and has the track record to back up what he is talking about. There is a major difference between theoretical knowledge and experiential knowledge; Ziad gives no quarter to the academics and economists who "believe" this or that theory about how the process of wealth creation should work.

Chapter 9 discusses how all of this wealth creation knowledge and all of the tools can be applied on a global scale, giving his personal evaluation of which foreign markets are good bets for future investment, which markets should be avoided, and why.

Finally, Ziad Abdelnour issues a call to his fellow Americans to rise up and participate in dumping the Nanny government once and for all by participating in a voter revolution that will restore America to its rightful place as the home of liberty and economic freedom in the world.

For nearly 100 years, Washington has claimed that they had all the answers and could solve all of our social problems. The federal government has taken every opportunity to expand its reach and control of our lives while sticking us with the bill for its incompetence and bureaucratic shortsightedness. The federal government has not been able to solve the problem because they *are* the problem.

Chapter 10 gives a rundown of areas in which we, the people, should demand accountability and effectual change in the next administration that moves into the White House.

We are at a crossroads in our history. We can either repeat the same mistakes that we have made over the last 100 years or we can call an end to the nonsense.

Economic Warfare gives you the information and the tools you need to make an informed and rational choice. It isn't about party labels or basic political philosophies. It is about America and restoring our birthright as Americans to enjoy life, liberty, and the opportunity to pursue happiness, all of which can only be secured by the creation of wealth.

This book will educate and reveal. Much of what Ziad Abdelnour writes will be reassuring and give one hope. But much will give one pause. To chart the dangerous waters in the coming years, you need this book at your side.

Doug Wead
Presidential historian, *New York Times* best-selling author, and
adviser to two presidents
Northern Virginia

Prelude

The President
The White House
1600 Pennsylvania Avenue
Washington, DC 20500

Dear Mr. President,

I am writing to express my deep concern over the quickening pace at which one of the fundamental principles upon which this great nation was founded is being steadily and purposely undermined and eroded. It has become undeniably apparent to me and many of my professional peers that there are, within your administration, certain elements who have initiated policies and programs whose sole aim is to expand the command and control of the federal government over the natural and inalienable right of the individual to freely create and build personal wealth.

When you campaigned for the office of the presidency, you offered the American people an opportunity to choose a different path from those taken by previous administrations. The watchword was *change,* and you told us that you were a candidate who was going to break the "business-as-usual" cycle that has put Washington at odds with the rest of the nation. From the moment you took the oath of office, you belonged to all of the people, regardless of their political persuasion, not just Democrats or Republicans or Independents. You do not represent union members over white-collar workers. You do not stand with African Americans against Asian Americans or support Latinos over Caucasians. You are not to elevate the poor people at the expense of the rich or to appropriate the wealth of the middle class to distribute to those who have no class at all. You are supposed to be president for ALL of us.

That you and I may have differing political philosophies is really a moot point. Political labels no longer have any relevance in this discussion. What does matter is that we are both Americans and we must work together to preserve the republic. As president and CEO of Blackhawk Partners, I run a private family office attending to the investment needs of a very sophisticated and discerning international private and corporate client base. I was born into a family of power, money, and influence. My father, Khalil Abdelnour, was an industrialist and former member of Parliament in Lebanon for 8 years. My uncle, Salem Abdelnour, was also a member of Parliament in Lebanon for over 20 years and a masterful commodities broker. He amassed a substantial fortune and became an accomplished networker and power broker in the Middle East.

I came to America in 1982 to seek my own fortune. Following graduation from Wharton Business School, I became a citizen of this great nation and had the amazing good fortune of coming under the mentorship of some of the most powerful financiers this nation has to offer. In the past quarter of a century, Mr. President, I have been personally involved in structuring and completing over 125 financial transactions worth in aggregate over $10 billion; so when I offer my insights concerning the health and well-being of this economy, I am not just giving my opinion. I have skin in the game.

This letter is written with the hope that you will consider an alternative point of view as you seek answers and guidance for resolving this current crisis. Although I don't have all the answers, I strongly feel these suggestions work as they have been tried and tested over time again and again. The demands of your job require that you seek wise counsel. The evidence suggests that you are, to this point, being ill served. I am asking for a meeting at your earliest convenience. I wish to share some practical financial guidance as a balance to the counsel of the learned academicians who have presented recycled and conflicting theories. I would like for you to consider the thoughts and insights of a Wall Street veteran who has made a career of empowering entrepreneurs and creating opportunities. You may feel that some of my thoughts are pretty controversial. I strongly feel that you need to hear wisdom gained from experience, not theory deduced from subjective analysis or biased by ideology.

In my opinion, Mr. President, you need an alternative to the advice of those who actually have some complicity in the current situation and, therefore, a clear conflict of interest. I wrote this book with that in mind. I hope you find it helpful.

Sincerely,

Ziad K. Abdelnour
President & CEO
Blackhawk Partners, Inc.

Chapter 1

The War against the Rich

There is only one class in the community that thinks more about money than the rich, and that is the poor. The poor can think of nothing else.
—Oscar Wilde (1854–1900) Irish writer, poet, and playwright

I am normally a very private person. As a global deal maker and financier attending to the investment needs of a very sophisticated and discerning international private and corporate client base, my work requires the utmost discretion. When hundreds of millions of dollars may be involved in a single transaction, wisdom dictates that I not broadcast my movements nor forecast my intentions in the realm of finance. But I am also a warrior. When I see injustice, when I see abuse of power, when I see a bully throwing his weight around and terrorizing innocent people just because he thinks he can get away with it, I am compelled to take action.

The majority of the American people are still grappling with what happened to them and their economy in the fall of 2008. The predominant media, comprised of little more than talking heads who read the daily dominant social theme dished out by their corporate masters, repeat the mantra that while bad things were done by men who behaved inconsiderately, nothing actually illegal took place. It was just an unfortunate and untimely chain of events.

"Yes," they smile with a look of genuine concern "A few people made outrageous sums of money while the overwhelming majority of the American people lost their entire financial nest egg, and that's unfortunate, but that's just the way the market works. You win some. You lose some."

Really? As they say in Beirut, "Kalam Tafeh!"

What happened to this economy was, at the very minimum, a violation of the fiduciary trust and relationship that supports the capitalist free-market system. In the case of a few highly placed individuals, it was a clear conflict of interest, professional malpractice, political malfeasance, fraud, and theft by conversion. In the case of people like Henry Paulson, Ben Bernanke, Timothy Geithner, and several senior managers of the top New York banks, they should be indicted for conspiracy to defraud the American people on a massive scale. These men are, in the opinion of many, financial outlaws who arrogantly believe themselves to be above the law. Until we have a Justice Department that understands and applies the basic concept of rule of law and upholds the U.S. Constitution, this will be an open wound in the collective psyche of all Americans. We will become a nation full of anger, resentment, cynicism, and skepticism. We will cease to be the greatest nation in the history of the world.

That is exactly what I am seeing happening today in America. The public servants who are supposed to be working on our behalf, paid by our tax dollars and charged with working to ensure domestic tranquility and promotion of the general welfare, seem to be alternating between an apparent ambivalence and an adversarial position where our fiscal inquiries are concerned. In the name of correcting the weaknesses in the financial system, these agents of the state have launched a full-blown assault on the true creators of wealth in this nation, while the small group who actually participated in, promoted, and profited from the latest economic crisis have walked away with millions of our dollars in their pockets.

Just Who Am I?

I have dual citizenship and am proud to be an American, but I am of Phoenician lineage. Trading and deal making is in my DNA. The Phoenicians are the ancestors of the modern Lebanese people. Power, money, and influence have been in my family for decades. My uncle, Salem Abdelnour, became a masterful commodities broker. He amassed a substantial fortune and became an accomplished networker and power broker in the Middle East. My father, Khalil Abdelnour, was an industrialist and financier. Both men served as members of Parliament in Lebanon.

Lebanon in the 1950s and 1960s was known as "the Switzerland of the Middle East," a very calm oasis with not a single shred of trouble. Beirut was nicknamed "Paris on the Mediterranean." It was a center for international trade, finance, and education. My family lived in the fashionable, affluent neighborhood in Ashrafieh, later to be known as the heart of the Christian quarters.

During the Lebanese Civil War in the mid-1970s, my younger brothers, Wissam and Hicham, and I were sent to the prestigious Ecole des Roches, a 148-acre estate in the Normandy region of France. I developed many relationships there, which still make a tremendous difference in my life. These friendships have allowed me to experience the true measure of success: being able to have a positive impact in someone else's life for purely altruistic reasons. Many of my fellow students from those days have risen to places of significant power and wealth and have remained my close friends. I am humbled and grateful for the opportunity to play a small but important advisory role in the lives of men whose decisions today shape the world tomorrow.

I returned to Beirut in 1978 to start my graduate studies at the American University of Beirut (AUB). I chose economics as my field of study because I had reached a point in my life where I realized that the whole world revolves around those who control the money. If I was going to succeed in life, I knew I had to get out from the shadows cast by my uncle and my father. I was very popular among my classmates and almost single-minded in my focus to gain knowledge. All of that changed in the spring of 1981. That was when I met Nadia.

Over the next year, I became a changed man. I had come alive and discovered many new and varied interests as my relationship with Nadia grew. I was confident that I had found the love of my life. My father did not share my enthusiasm. We were not a traditional family that believed in arranged marriages or other such customs, but it had been assumed by almost everyone that I would marry a certain young lady who was from one of the most prominent banking families in the Middle East. When I announced to my parents that it was my intention to marry Nadia, it became clear that I had derailed a master plan that had been years in the making. My father informed me, in a very calm and matter-of-fact tone, that it was my life and my choice to make. I was over 21 and free to live my own life—but I would do so living in my own home and on my own money.

I graduated from AUB in early 1982 with a BS in economics. In the fall of that year, I purchased a one-way ticket on a flight bound for the United States with less than $10,000 of my personal savings to my name. There was the possibility of a job in the Credit Management program of Chase Manhattan Bank in New York City. I look back now and am amazed at the audacity of that 22-year-old kid from Beirut.

My first years in New York City were filled with wonder and amazement that I had finally arrived in this place, the center of the financial world. As I worked and learned the business, I pursued my graduate degree. In August 1984, I graduated from the Wharton School of Business with an MBA in finance. Two years later, after a stint with the Wealth Management Group of American Express Bank, Drexel Burnham Lambert hired me to work in its high-yield bond department. After learning all that I could from working at Drexel and spending a decade arranging the financing for and putting together the deals of over 50 private companies in both the United States and emerging markets, I finally formed Blackhawk Partners, Inc., my private family office.

The Richest Man I Know

Forbes magazine has identified Carlos Slim Helú as the richest man in the world. His estimated net worth is more than $74 billion. How did he get this wealthy? He started very young and he earned it. Slim's father, Julian, immigrated to Mexico from Lebanon in 1902 at the age of 14. By the age of 23, he had opened a store in Mexico City selling fabrics, sundries, and simple clothing items. His goods were of good quality; he sold his merchandise at a fair price and always treated his customers with respect. As his business grew, Julian began taking his profits and investing in real estate in downtown Mexico City, anticipating that the business district would be growing. By 1926, he had accumulated enough wealth to be considered affluent. He taught all of his children three basic business principles. The first was to always have a business that provides goods or services that the majority of the people need. Second, always provide good quality at a fair and reasonable price. Finally, tenaciously manage your income and expenses so that you can reinvest your profits into your business.

Carlos has always been adept at multitasking, always looking to leverage his time and always seeking to fully maximize an opportunity. At age 12, he used his allowance to buy shares of stock in a local bank and made money. While attending engineering school, he also taught classes in algebra and linear programming and made money. This technological aptitude led to the formation of a subscription service that provided up-to-the-minute company information to stock market investors. By age 26, Carlos was worth $40 million on paper. He parlayed that into investments in construction, real estate, and mining companies, always striving to fulfill a need while providing quality service for a fair price.

In 1982, when the Mexican economy nearly collapsed, Slim stepped in and used his fortune to purchase a variety of companies that provided basic goods and services and had good management histories. His gamble paid off when the economy rebounded. He was able to buy the Mexican phone company Telmex, combine it with a mobile phone company called Telcel, and expand both to eventually provide dependable, affordable telephone service throughout Latin America. By continually placing his personal wealth at risk and utilizing a disciplined investment strategy based on his father's basic business philosophy, he eventually found himself listed as the richest person in the world.

I happen to know Carlos Slim Helú. He is a humble, sincere, caring man who does not think of himself or his life in terms of how much money he has made. He is more concerned with what he can do with his wealth to improve the world. He has taken a quote by Albert Einstein and made it his life's Mission Statement:

Only a life lived for others is worth living.

I share these two examples with you not to impress you, but to illustrate that even those who are born into affluence sometimes must risk it all to pursue their dreams. It is also important that you understand that wealth creation is a process that takes place over a period of time, and it can be learned and put into practice by anyone.

Why You Are Not Rich

My intention with this book is to not only shine truth on some of the misconceptions that have been taken as gospel regarding America's economic legacy, but to also provide some insights into ways you can protect and grow your personal wealth and turn around the current situation to your advantage.

The fastest transfer of wealth in the past 20 years was due to a lack of pertinent regulation, artificially low interest rates, and no risk management. Regulators did not pay sufficient heed to the warnings that were raised more than a decade ago. First Greenspan and then Bernanke kept the interest rates low while a new breed of mathematical whiz kid gamblers lured Wall Street into an "easy money" mentality with their algorithms and super computer arbitrage programs. Add to that shady mortgage originators, politically motivated securities underwriters, and sloppy credit rating practices, and you have the perfect conditions for a financial tornado. In the end, they all worked together unknowingly to turn Wall Street into an international casino underwritten by the American taxpayer.

A large and probably unavoidable part of the challenge in today's technology-driven marketplace is that the velocity of money is fueled by such techniques as high-frequency trading, front running, credit default swaps, and collateralized debt obligations (CDOs).

Traditionally, a home mortgage was a loan made by a local banker, and it stayed in the community until it was paid off. The Rule of

Threes was the inside joke in the banking fraternity: borrow money at 3 percent, lend it to home buyers at 3 points higher, and be on the golf course by 3.[1] That all changed in 1970 when the Government National Mortgage Association, now known as Ginnie Mae, introduced the concept of securitization—purchasing mortgage loans from local banks and bundling them into bonds that were then sold to investors through investment banks.

The next step was the development of the collateralized mortgage obligation (CMO), which was created in 1983 by the investment banks of Salomon Brothers and First Boston for U.S. mortgage lender Freddie Mac. The CMO is a stand-alone special-purpose entity that owns a pool of mortgages. Investors buy bonds representing different classes of risk called *tranches*. Return of investment is determined by the structure of the deal, which could be "high risk–first payout" or "first in–first out" or some other arrangement that dictates how money received from the collateral will be distributed.

This led to the development of collaterialized debt obligations (CDOs), a form of structured asset-backed security (ABS) whose value and payments are derived from a portfolio of fixed-income underlying assets, not just mortgages. CDO securities are split into different risk classes, or tranches, where "senior" tranches are considered the safest securities. Interest and principal payments are made in order of seniority, so that junior tranches offer higher semiannual or coupon payments and interest rates or lower prices to compensate for additional default risk.

A CDO is a sophisticated form of an IOU against the cash flow that the CDO collects from the pool of bonds or other assets it owns. If cash collected by the CDO is insufficient to pay all of its investors, the junior tranches suffer losses first.

The financial crisis of 2007 was fueled by the fact that many CDOs were backed by subprime mortgage-backed bonds. When mortgage defaults became a widespread problem, the drawback of CDO investors contributed to the collapse of certain structured investments held by major investment banks and the bankruptcy of several subprime lenders. It also did not help that global investors began to discover that the AAA-rated bonds in which they thought they were investing were really a bundle of BBB investments with the patina of an AAA rating. In other words, wholesale institutional fraud facilitated in large part by the same ratings agencies who so piously downgraded the nation's credit rating.

Historical safeguards like regulatory agencies and credible rating agencies that were created to protect the integrity of the financial system have been compromised by the large Wall Street firms and their drinking buddies in the federal government. The swift prosecution of fiscal malfeasance and political corruption, which used to be the expected response to such bait-and-switch con games, has apparently been sidelined. The federal government and the largest financial institutions seem to have been totally co-opted by a group of elitists running an open larceny ring, seemingly oblivious to the pain and suffering they are wreaking upon the public and ignoring any fiduciary responsibility they had to their investors. It is like the old spaghetti western where the gang of banditos has taken over the village and is laughing while they loot the bank, drink all of the booze, and bully the villagers. What we have now is definitely not free-market capitalism. It is a reign of financial terror.

The Federal Reserve was created to prevent banking panics and wide swings in the economy by holding inflation in check and protecting the value of our currency. It was given autonomy to protect it from political influence; in other words, politicians couldn't give away economic perks just to get reelected. The Fed has strongly resisted any effort to apply any kind of oversight to its activities by claiming they are attempts to politicize the Fed, but let's look at the record.

Almost every Fed chairman in the past 60 years has manipulated interest rates to brighten the economic outlook for incumbent presidents or newly elected presidents who won by large margins. The purchasing power of the U.S. dollar has fallen 94 percent in the past 100 years. The only way you can create inflation is by creating more money that is backed by the same reserve assets; the Fed is the only entity that can create more money. Ben Bernanke's quantitative easing (QE) programs have pumped billions of unfunded dollars into the economy, thereby setting us up for massive inflation in the very near future. If this isn't a form of financial terrorism, it is incompetence of the highest order.

A body cannot function properly nor experience its full potential when it is laboring under the growing infestation of parasites. In the same way, America will never reach the zenith of freedom and prosperity that is the birthright of every one of its citizens as long as we allow ourselves to be governed by those who feel they have a mandate to take what isn't theirs and to appropriate what they haven't earned.

When you combine unrepentant bankers, incompetent politicians, and the legion of special-interest moochers who could not operate without a government stipend, you end up with a national economy that has been beaten, abused, and depleted of all vitality.

We are on the edge of economic collapse unless we wake up and forcibly take back control of our government and economy. Over the past 100 years, the game has been rigged, slowly and piecemeal at first, always in the name of serving the greater good, preventing the next bubble or providing greater transparency and security. It is as if the American people are suffering from battered spouse syndrome; the politicians, the greedy bankers, and the Fed all lie to us while they steal our wealth and our liberty. Every time we call them on it, they promise to never do it again if we'll just give them one more chance. So we let it slide and then act shocked when they do it to us again. Maybe we should have our collective head examined.

Who Are the Rich and Why Should You Care about Them?

It is an oft-repeated axiom that a person can learn a whole lot about a society by how it treats its poor; but just as much may be learned by looking at how that same society treats its rich. Indeed, the economic future of the poor—and our nation—will be determined in the coming decades by how we treat the people in this country who create great wealth. It will be determined by our understanding of the so-called rich and by our need to foster and protect this minority of true wealth creators.

It is an unpopular thing to say, I know. Rich people need help? Rich people need to be protected? Rich people a minority?

"Give me a break," people say. "They just seem to keep getting richer!"

I am talking here about the entrepreneur who risks all of the capital he can muster from his family and friends to build a company that fills an underserved niche in the market, provides a needed service, or develops a new technology. These are the people the plundering bureaucrats and career politicians have deemed "the rich." These are the people they have targeted for appropriation to support their unsustainable way of life.

In their narrow view of the world, rich people become "rich" by either inheriting their money or appropriating wealth through manipulation of the system with their cronies, or are self-made entrepreneurs. The first group is so small that they don't really matter. The second group is easy for the bureaucrats to intimidate and the politicians to plunder with ever-widening regulations and more oppressive oversight; but, again, there are not that many people who fall into the crony-capitalist category. The overwhelming majority of people I refer to as "the rich" are independent-minded, maverick entrepreneurs and business owners who risk their own capital, sweat, and tears to provide a good or service of value to the world around them.

Regrettably, too many Americans, and far too many of the intellectuals and politicians, understand neither these people we call "the rich" nor the methods they have used to become rich in the first place. Did hedge fund managers and investment bankers game the system and walk off with a lot of money? Yes. But, again, having a lot of money no more makes you rich than growing up next door to the Greenwich Country Club gives you class. The rich are people like Bill Gates, Warren Buffett, Larry Page and Sergey Brin, and Michael Dell. They have provided value to the world and been rewarded for their efforts. They also know, better than the federal government, how they should best utilize that wealth.

Most people don't think they actually know anyone who is truly rich. Not really. They experience them in the abstract, through magazine articles, newspaper stories, or *Lifestyles of the Rich and Famous* clips. They catch a glimpse into their psyches through statements they make in the media or interpretations of their latest business maneuver. They try to quantify their importance in their own lives by studying policy statements and annual reports or poring over ratings and statistics that rank their net worth and their influence; but the study and the analysis is always through the prism of someone else's ideological lens. In that respect, our opinions about the rich are a sort of societal inkblot test, revealing more about ourselves than anything else. Our analysis of the raw data confirms our deeply held notions about the rich and, in the end, has more to do with our views on capitalism itself.

Those who are vested in the philosophy of the Left, believing capitalism creates unfair outcomes, have statistics to confirm their outlook. It seems absurd on its face that the top 1 percent of American families control 90 percent of the nation's wealth. Wouldn't it be possible, they ask, to contrive an economy that is just as prosperous but with a fairer distribution of wealth? Couldn't we cap the earnings of the rich at $50 million? Or even $100 million? The defenders of capitalism and free markets on the Right say "no." They contend that the bizarre inequalities we see are an indispensable part of the processes that create wealth. They imply that capitalism doesn't make sense, morally or rationally, but it does make wealth. So don't knock it, they say.

What nonsense! It has very little to do with the reality of the rich. It is really quite sad that defenders of the rich or even the rich themselves can't come up with a better economic or moral case! Quoting Adam Smith and supply side economists just doesn't cut it.

American novelist and homespun philosopher Mark Twain reportedly noted that a person can lie with the numbers but the numbers don't lie. The rich have most of the money. That's why they are called "the rich."

So who are the rich? Having spent a lifetime working with some of these people to create and preserve their wealth, I believe I am qualified to explain who they are, where they come from, and why you should care about preserving their wealth and protecting their desire to hold on to it.

The Millionaire down the Street

To begin with, you probably won't find many rich people in the Who's Who or Most Likely to Succeed lists compiled during their high school or college days. They probably didn't get the highest SAT or ACT scores in high school, and they probably weren't considered a member of the popular clique by their classmates. They are certainly not the best looking, and they probably didn't get where they got through the force of their personalities, charisma, or celebrity. A great number of the richest among us never finished high school, and many who did manage to get into college never graduated. That's because the rich in this country are chosen not by blood, credentials, education, or service to the establishment. The rich become rich based on their performance and their relentless desire to serve the customer. The entrepreneurial knowledge that is the crux of wealth creation has little to do with glamorous work or with the certified expertise of advanced degrees.

Great wealth rarely comes from speculating and creating nothing. The John Paulsons of the world are a very small and very lucky group. Most major wealth creation comes from doing what other people consider insufferably boring: navigating the tedious intricacies of software languages, designing more efficient garbage collection routes, or designing a system for stocking fresh products on the shelves in grocery stores is not glamorous. These people don't immediately conjure images of mansions, limousines, and vacations in the hottest spots of the world in Gstaad, Monte Carlo, or Cabo San Lucas. Improving the speed and efficiency of butchering livestock, customizing insurance policies, or tramping the wilderness in search of petroleum leases seem far removed from the glamorous life. Memorizing building codes, speeding up the delivery of a hot pizza, or hawking pet supplies all seem like mundane and tedious tasks, but these are all paths that individuals have taken up the mountain of accumulating wealth in America. In short, America's best entrepreneurs usually perform work that others overlook or spurn. They do it better, faster, and at a better price than the competition. For that, they become the rich.

Because these men and women often overthrow rather than embrace established norms, the richest among us are usually considered rebels and outsiders. Often, they come from places like Omaha, Nebraska; Blackfoot, Idaho; or Mission Hills, Kansas—places usually mentioned in New York either with a condescending smirk or as the punch line of a comedy routine. From Henry Ford to Apple cofounder

Steve Wozniak, much of America's greatest wealth creators began in the "skunk works" of their trades, with their hands on the intricate machinery that would determine the fate of their companies. Bill Gates began by mastering the tedious intricacies of programming languages. Sam Walton began with a nickel-and-dime Ben Franklin variety store in Newport, Arkansas. Larry Page became the first kid in his elementary school to turn in an assignment from a word processor because his parents were both computer science professors at Michigan State University. Familiarity with the core material, the grit and grease, the petty tedium of their businesses liberates entrepreneurs from the grip of conventional methods and gives them the insight and confidence to turn their industries in new directions.

The truth is that great wealth is often created by the launching of great surprises, not by the launching of great enterprises. Unpredictability is a fundamental part of great wealth creation, and, as such, it defies every econometric model or centralized planner's vision. It makes no sense to most professors, who attain their positions by the systematic acquisition of credentials pleasing to the fraternity of their peers. By their very definition, innovations cannot be planned.

From the outside looking in, one would assume that once wealth is acquired, life becomes one endless vacation full of idle play and relaxation. One would be quite wrong. The richest among us are faced with another equally daunting task once they have accumulated great wealth. Just as a pot of honey attracts flies as well as bears, it doesn't take long for a seemingly endless stream of bureaucrats, politicians, raiders, robbers, relatives, short-sellers, long talkers, managers, missionaries, and manipulators to come calling. They all have this strange notion that they can spend your money better than you can and are somehow entitled to a portion of your money for granting you the privilege of their expertise. They are, for the most part, leeches, con artists, and moochers.

Leading entrepreneurs in general consume only a tiny portion of their holdings. They are often owners and investors. As owners, they are initially damaged the most by mismanagement or exploitation or waste of their wealth. Only the person who created the wealth has a true appreciation of its value and what it represents. As long as Steve Jobs was in charge of Apple, it grew in value; but put some random manager in charge of Apple, and within minutes, the company would be worth significantly less than its present value. This was proven most effectively when Jobs was replaced by John Sculley; the Apple board could not get Jobs back fast enough. As companies such as Oracle, Lotus, and Google have discovered, a software or tech stock can lose most of its worth in minutes if fashions shift or investors question management decisions.

A Harvard Business School study recently showed that even when you put "professional management" at the helm of great wealth, value is likely to grow less rapidly than if you give owners the real control. A manager of Google might benefit from turning it into his own special preserve, making self-indulgent "investments" in company planes or favored foundations that are in fact his own disguised consumption. It is only Sergey Brin and Larry Page who would see their respective wealth drop catastrophically if they began to focus less on their customers than on their own consumption. The key to their great wealth is their resolution not to spend or abandon it, but to continue using it in the service of others. They are as much the servants *to* as the masters *of* Google.

This is the other secret of the richest among us and of capitalism itself. Under capitalism, wealth is less a stock of goods than a flow of ideas. Economist Joseph Schumpeter set the basic parameters when he declared capitalism "a form of change" that "never can be stationary." The landscape of capitalism may seem solid and settled and ready for seizure, but capitalism is really a mindscape.[2] Volatile and shifting ideas, and the human beings behind them, are the source of our nation's wealth, not heavy and entrenched establishments. There is no tax web or bureaucratic net that can catch the fleeting thoughts of the greatest entrepreneurs of our past or our future.

The Socialist Fallacy

Socialist regimes try to guarantee the availability of material things rather than the ownership of them. They use such terms as *distribution of income* to introduce the ridiculous notion that everyone should be paid "fairly" instead of rewarded for the amount of risk they are willing to take with their own capital and resources. Today's college students are being indoctrinated with the notion that socialism can succeed this time if everyone just works together. This is in spite of the overwhelming historical evidence that socialism has never worked beyond a small, tightly controlled community of either like-minded or fully coerced participants. They are not being told that socialism had its roots in an authoritarian regime.[3] That is the only way socialist policies can succeed on any scale.

British statesman Winston Churchill said:

> Socialism is a philosophy of failure, the creed of ignorance, and the gospel of envy, its inherent virtue is the equal sharing of misery.

Socialism tends to destroy wealth. Socialism does this by draining its vitality away. It does this by destroying the desirability of wealth as a wholesome value. Socialism kills the chance that any community can survive by browbeating the concept of vested ownership, on which community survival is always dependent in the end.

In the United States, the government has traditionally guaranteed only the right of people to own property, not the worth of it. The belief that wealth consists not in ideas, attitudes, moral codes, and mental disciplines but in definable and static things that can be seized and redistributed is a materialist superstition. It made the works of Marx and other prophets of violence and envy seem childish, even silly. It betrays every person who seeks to redistribute wealth by coercion. It balks every socialist revolutionary or union organizer who imagines that by seizing the so-called means of production he can capture the crucial capital of an economy. It baffles nearly all aggregators who believe they can safely enter new industries by buying rather than by learning them. Capitalist means of production are not land, labor, or even the capital itself. They are ideas and inspiration. Unless we are ready to enter Huxley's *Brave New World,* talk of redistributing wealth is nothing more than fantastic nonsense. Do the fantasy; give the employees or government or union the factory or hotel or restaurant, and in five years everything will be a mess and most of the jobs will be lost, forever.

The wealth of America isn't an inventory of goods; it's an organic, living entity, a fragile, pulsing fabric of ideas, expectations, loyalties, moral commitments, visions, and people. To slice it up like an apple pie and redistribute it would destroy it just as surely as trying to share Stephen Hawking's intellect by sharing slices of his brain would surely kill him. As Mitterrand's French technocrats found early in the 1980s, the proud new socialist owners of complex systems of wealth soon learn they are administering an industrial corpse rather than a growing corporation. That is why the single most important economic issue of our time, one that directly impacts the poor and middle class alike, is how we treat the very rich among us.

If the majority of Americans smear, harass, overtax, and maliciously regulate this minority of wealth creators, our politicians will be shocked and horrified to discover how swiftly the physical tokens of the means of production collapse into so much corroded wire, eroding concrete, and scrap metal. They will be amazed at how quickly the wealth of America is either destroyed or flees to other countries.

This book will hopefully prevent such a disastrous end to the Great American Experiment by not only revealing where and when we have gone off track, but also provide some real-world solutions for restoring the hope for a better tomorrow and reviving the willingness of people to believe that they have the ability to make their lives better.

There is a scripture that says, "My people perish for lack of vision." The socialist influence that has turned our education system into an indoctrination process with its emphasis on political correctness over political science and economic justice over economics is slowly but relentlessly producing a nation of drones, unable to dream, incapable of embracing individuality, and abhorrent of acting upon such basic instincts as self-interest and individual sovereignty. I hope to provide an alternative argument that will persuade you to take the actions necessary to preserve American exceptionalism and liberty.

Can We Separate Economics and Politics?

Some people criticize the injection of politics into economic discussions, but economic historians tell us that economists used to understand

and accept that economics is wholly interrelated with politics because politics and economics are mutually inclusive and reactive.

Progressive economists have artificially tried to somehow separate the two, like Descartes tried to separate the mind from the body. Adam Smith, the father of modern economics, talked a lot about politics in relation to economics. The reality is that mainstream, neo-classical economists preach that politics is an irrelevant and separate topic because they are either emotionally and intellectually vested in wholly discredited models or locked in the paradox that it is difficult to get a man to understand something when his livelihood depends on his not understanding it.

It is fairly obvious that we cannot discuss our economy or make investing decisions without addressing politics. In the real world, political decisions determine who gets bailed out and who doesn't, who stays afloat and who goes under, who gets rewarded and who gets prosecuted. That is an acceptable process as long as it occurs in an environment of truth and justice, supported by the rule of law. Unfortunately, there currently seems to be an aversion to prosecuting anyone who commits a financial crime, especially if they are part of the small gang of greed-driven bankers who nearly took the system down. Even then, when there are prosecutions, punishments seem to be very arbitrary; some get hit hard, while some get just a slap on the wrist. Some even get a pat on the back, like Paulson after screaming, "The sky is falling!," and then using the Troubled Asset Relief Program (TARP) to bail out the bad bets that his buddies had made in the market. The thugs of the Service Employees International Union (SEIU) brutally beat up a bystander who voiced opposition to their demands to the nonexistent right to collective bargaining. It is captured on camera and shown on the nightly news, but the ineffectual Justice Department looks the other way. The New Black Panthers get captured on video intimidating voters at a polling place in Philadelphia, perpetrating voter intimidation in open and notorious violation of the Voter Rights Act, while the feckless and racially biased attorney general decides it is inappropriate to prosecute. This has led, unfortunately, to an alarming rise in national cynicism and a growing lack of trust in the veracity and fidelity of the federal government.

To say we are on the verge of an economic meltdown is not a wholly inappropriate analogy. While the media cheerleaders would like everyone to believe that the current indicators are suggesting, as of this writing, that the American economy is recovering from the Great Recession of 2007–2008, the Average Joe on the street knows it isn't true. The recession, which started in 2007, is ongoing. The underlying fundamental causes of the meltdown have not been addressed. Banks are still not lending. Companies are still not hiring. Congress has still not seriously addressed the growing debt. Neither has Congress checked its own out-of-control spending. The much lauded reforms installed by Frank-Dodd are nothing more than another expansion of federal government control over the engines of wealth creation.

What is going on here?

Notes

1. Scott Patterson, *The Quants: How a New Breed of Math Whizzes Conquered Wall Street and Nearly Destroyed It* (New York: Crown Business, 2010), 186.
2. George Gilder, "The Enigma of Entrepreneurial Wealth," *from Recapturing the Spirit of Enterprise* (Richmond, CA: ICS Press, 1992). Retrieved from www .inc.com/magazine/19921001/4341_pagen_5.html.
3. F. A. Hayek and Bruce Caldwell, eds., *The Road to Serfdom* (London: University of Chicago Press, 2007), 76.

Chapter 2

Report from
the Battlefield

*Pride gets no pleasure out of having something; only out of having
more of it than the next guy.. . . . Pride is spiritual cancer; it eats up
the very possibility of love, of contentment, or even common sense.*
— C. S. Lewis (1898–1963), British novelist,
essayist, and Christian apologist

It is the twilight of the first decade of the twenty-first century as
I write this. The world has changed in many ways in the past 10
years; yet, in many ways, nothing has really changed at all. The
age-old conflict between right and wrong still rages, but the differ-
ences between the Good Guys and the Bad Guys seem to have
become less definite. I am sure that some media jackal with an agenda
or some book critic on the Wall Street payroll will probably accuse
me of being too simplistic, but that is because we have allowed them
to frame the argument. We have allowed them to say that the concepts of right and wrong are dated and not sophisticated enough for
the complexities of modern society. Don't let them blow their relativistic smoke up your pant leg. There is a growing segment of our

society who does not want anyone to be able to distinguish between right and wrong because they don't want to be exposed. They have substituted "sophistication" for lack of integrity, fortitude and morality. As much as I love the work that I do, I find myself growing increasingly hostile toward the direction of the industry in general, as do many of my colleagues and business partners who have been in the financial world for over two decades now and have seen it all.

We are a nation of more than 310 million people and our national debt has grown to over $14 *trillion*. That's about $45,000 for every citizen; however, every citizen is not a taxpayer, and this debt will be borne by the taxpayers in this country. When distributed among the taxpayers, the amount equals more than $126,000! And what do I mean by distributing the national debt? This is the amount that you are responsible for paying whenever someone casually throws out a phrase like "the *government* supplies" or "the *government* provides." There is no separate autonomous entity known as "The Government." This is the pipe dream of those professional politicians who lust for power and control over other people's lives and fortunes. We, the People, are the true government, and the time has come for us to take back control of that which was initially created to serve our best interests.

Current unemployment is officially over 9 percent. Unofficially, it is generally agreed that it is at least twice that when you factor in the number of people who have fallen off the government's rolls by either exhausting their benefits or simply giving up the search for meaningful work. Forty-five million Americans now receive government assistance just to purchase food, nearly two million have filed bankruptcy, and more than a million, including close friends of mine, have lost their homes in foreclosure proceedings. As of September 2010, 23 percent of U.S. homes are worth less than the mortgage loan.[1] Homeowners across the country have lost an average of 39 percent of the value of their properties over the past three years.[2] Commercial real estate values have fallen 40 percent since their peak in 2007, according to a recent Reuters article.[3]

It is this loss of equity and value in real estate that troubles me most. It wasn't because of normal market forces like supply and demand. Many of the subprime mortgage loans should never have been made; we have become a nation incapable of living within our means. We seem incapable of accepting the reality that owning a home is not and never was intended to be a right. It is a reward for working hard and saving up enough money to not only purchase a property, but to maintain and improve it.

This crisis was the direct result of the financial blitzkrieg that has ransacked our economy over the past three years. It was an orchestrated pilfering of the wealth of this nation by private global bankers and financial institutions in league with elements within the government. There is no doubt that these people have committed a series of crimes, the least of which are abuse of their fiduciary responsibilities and compromising established business ethics; but nobody has been convicted. No one has been indicted. The greatest economy in the world has been callously brought to its knees, millions of people have seen their life's savings evaporate, and the crime is not even being investigated. How could this have happened in America?

An Inside Job

In September 2008 we witnessed one of the most brazen and daring transfers of financial assets ever to take place in recorded history. Certain large Wall Street banks pumped up the subprime mortgage bubble, made billions of dollars by securitizing the mortgage debt, and when the bubble inevitably burst, they transferred their losses to the federal government and received bailouts because they were deemed "too big to fail." This con job was pulled off, for the most part, in broad daylight and in full view of the whole world. In the space of a few days, this nation was the victim of an orchestrated theft of nearly $6 trillion. That's six million stacks of a million dollars each or $54,000 for every taxpayer.

This crime did not just happen; in fact, it didn't start out as a criminal activity at all. It had its genesis 34 years ago as a noble gesture on the part of a man who, history has shown, had more compassion than common sense. It was yet another example of the best intentions of the federal government not only exacerbating the problem, but creating even worse conditions due to the principles of unintended consequences and ignorance of basic human behavior—in this case, pride and greed.

The Community Reinvestment Act (CRA) was signed into law by President Jimmy Carter in 1977 with the lofty goal of making credit obtainable and housing affordable for those who found themselves living in lower-income neighborhoods and housing projects. There was plenty of evidence in the 1950s and 1960s that banks unfairly discriminated against poor and minority people who wanted to share in the American Dream of homeownership. Practices like "redlining" or identifying entire neighborhoods as bad risks were not endemic, but were widespread enough to cause the Congress to pass a law telling banks they had to have policies that did not discriminate against lower- and middle-income mortgage applicants. Banks were instructed to operate in a safe and sound manner, and were not required to make high-risk loans that may bring losses to the institution.

Until the early 1970s, the practice of creating mortgages from real estate had been based on the "originate and hold" business model. This meant that a bank would originate a loan of money for a buyer to purchase a home in the community, and the bank would hold a mortgage against that property, collecting principal and interest until the mortgage was paid off. The U.S. Department of Housing and Urban Development (HUD) changed that process when they created a mortgage-backed security that was sold through the Government National Mortgage Association (GNMA or Ginnie Mae) and backed by a portfolio of mortgage loans.

Through the 1970s and 1980s, banks were regulated by one of four different entities—the Comptroller of the Currency, the Board of Governors of the Federal Reserve System, the Federal Deposit Insurance Corporation, or the Federal Home Loan Bank Board— depending on their charter. These regulators graded the banks on how well they had performed in upholding a "continuing and affirmative obligation to help meet the credit needs of the local communities in which they are chartered." These evaluations had increasing bearing on the bank's ability to expand through merger, acquisition, or branching and encouraged bankers to take more risks in the area of real estate financing.

This pressure to loosen credit requirements in targeted demographics, namely urban poor and minority communities, was not
significant until the Financial Institutions Reform, Recovery, and
Enforcement Act of 1989 (FIRREA) made portions of the evaluation
process public. Community organizers and advocacy groups began
using the data to press for increased enforcement of the CRA. The
Federal Deposit Insurance Corporation Improvement Act of 1991
(FDICIA) modified the CRA to give institutions more favorable   *Not*
ratings if they sponsored or set up branch offices operated by minority   *owned*
and women operators in disadvantaged neighborhoods. In 1992,
Freddie Mac and Fannie Mae were instructed, under CRA amendments contained in the Federal Housing Enterprises Financial Safety
and Soundness Act, to devote a significant percentage of their lending
efforts to support affordable housing. When the Riegle-Neal Interstate
Banking and Branching Efficiency Act of 1994 made interstate banking
possible, advocacy groups increasingly used the public comment
process to protest bank applications on CRA grounds. This led many
institutions to establish separate business units and subsidiary corporations to facilitate CRA-related lending and, some would say, made
housing affordable and accessible to many who otherwise might have
been ignored.[4]

The unintended consequence of this legislative foray into social
engineering was that the consumers in these markets were not given
the necessary education to properly utilize the financial resources that
were now available to them. They were to become the prime target
demographic for the emerging subprime mortgage originators who
would prey on their naiveté and general lack of financial acumen.

In July 1993, President Clinton had urged revising the CRA to
make it easier still for lenders to comply. This was at the urging of
his economic policy adviser and former Goldman Sachs chairman,
Robert Rubin. The then chairman of the Cato Institute, William A.
Niskanen, criticized these changes in testimony before Congress, pre-
dicting that they would be costly to the economy and dangerous to
the banking system.[5] He urged that the CRA be repealed. His warnings fell on deaf ears. From 1995 to 1998, subprime mortgage lending,
aimed precisely at the demographic served by the CRA, reached $150
billion per year.[6] The federal government officially endorsed the

subprime mortgage business in November 1997 when Freddie Mac helped Bear Stearns launch the first publicly available securitization of CRA loans. Bear Stearns, of course, then went on to issue $384.6 million of such securities, all of which carried the Freddie Mac guarantee as to timely interest and principal.

Running the Red Lights

Storm clouds were beginning to appear on the financial horizon. It cannot be said that there were no previous warnings. For years, the basic concept of risk and reward was being ignored. In May 1998, Brooksley Born, chairperson of the Commodity Futures Trading Commission (CFTC), officially raised concerns about credit default swaps. These financial instruments are traded over the counter between banks, insurance companies, or other funds or companies. Ms. Born's concern was due to the lack of transparency, and she felt they should be regulated. This brought immediate and uncharacteristically vocal opposition from Federal Reserve chairman Alan Greenspan and Treasury secretaries Robert Rubin and Lawrence Summers.[7] On May 7, 1998, former Securities and Exchange Commission (SEC) chairman Arthur Levitt joined Rubin and Greenspan in objecting to the issuance of the CFTC's concept release. Their response sought to dismiss Born's analysis. They accomplished this by focusing on an absurd hypothetical possibility—that CFTC regulation of swaps and other OTC derivative instruments could create a "legal uncertainty" regarding such financial instruments and therefore, supposedly, produce a reduction of the value of the instruments. Using their political muscle, they managed to get Congress to freeze her agency's funding, effectively forcing her out of office.

Born's concerns were validated in late September of that year when the Federal Reserve Bank of New York had to step in and rescue Long-Term Capital Management (LTCM), a hedge fund that lost more than 90 percent of its asset value over the first nine months of 1998. LTCM had been put together by mathematicians and computer geeks who were convinced that they had developed computer programs that could predict and take advantage of relative value gaps between pairs of similar securities. John Meriwether, Myron Scholes, and Robert Merton had put together what they considered to be a crack team of financial engineers, programmers, and a state-of-the-art computer system. They believed they had a formula that reduced risk to an acceptable and manageable level. They were wrong. Their formula didn't take into account the possibility of a catastrophic event such as that which occurred on August 17, 1998, when the Russian government defaulted on its sovereign debt. LTCM was leveraged at more than 100:1. This left them exposed, with no reasonable hope of recovery. Investors fled to liquidity, and $1.9 billion in LTCM assets vanished into thin air![8]

The Government Accountability Office (GAO) warned that a bailout of LTCM would just encourage firms to make risky loans on the assumption that the government would bail out "too big to fail" banks and companies.[9] Again, the Ivy League theorists scoffed at the notion that financial professionals would be anything other than prudent in the management of the nation's economic engine, and the warnings were ignored. It seemed the only consequence for the LTCM failure was a changing of leadership at one of the larger institutions. Goldman Sachs CEO Jon Corzine had been closely involved with LTCM. As a result, he was forced out in a boardroom coup led by co-chairman Henry Paulson. Corzine, thoroughly chastened for his questionable assistance to LTCM, cashed in his chips and walked away with $500 million when Goldman Sachs later went public. He then went on to become one of the U.S. senators from New Jersey.

The Joker of Gotham City

One of the main reasons that the greedy bankers were able to walk off with the wealth of this nation is that they have built up a professional image to disguise what it is that they actually do. They have also created their own language and jargon to baffle and intimidate the uninitiated. That is what you do when you are creating an illusion. Bankers and politicians are masters of illusion. They create things out of thin air and then use them to gain real wealth and real power.

When the bipartisan Gramm-Leach-Bliley Act was signed into law by President Bill Clinton in November 1999, the Glass-Steagall Act of 1933 was repealed, and commercial banks, investment banks, securities firms, and insurance companies were allowed to merge to create the "financial services" industry. The bankers loved it because they got to keep your money whether you were investing in good times or saving in bad times. The politicians loved it because they put even more clauses in that encouraged lending to underserved and minority home shoppers in support of the Community Reinvestment Act. That translated to more votes and more campaign contributions for themselves. To the subprime mortgage companies, it was like pouring lighter fluid on smoldering coals. The market caught fire and heated up rapidly.

By the year 2000, the Treasury happily reported that $467 billion in mortgage credit had flowed through CRA-approved lenders to low- and medium-income borrowers.[10] Substantial risks were being taken by the young math whizzes on Wall Street with the blessings of their elders. Average investors were being gutted by elaborate derivative schemes that were nothing more than financial shell games disguised as sophisticated computer programs and algorithms. Regulators looked the other way, and underwriters smilingly signed off on the credibility of the entire con. Truckloads of money were being raked in by Goldman, Bear Stearns, Citibank, and Lehman, while the rising real estate values across the nation began to show imperceptible signs of slowing and even flattening. It was a warning sign that was ignored.

The subprime mortgage industry's loan volume topped $330 billion by the end of 2003.[11] A year later, the subprime sharks, led by Ameriquest and funded by Lehman Brothers, were writing $529 billion in questionable mortgages per year![12] The philosophy of the greedy bankers was to let the party continue for as long as the Fed kept interest rates low and they could sell the perception that real estate was going to keep on appreciating. The more people they talked into buying, building, or refinancing homes, the better. It wasn't just the poor people who were being seduced by the easy money; the middle class and the affluent were getting into the game all across the country. It was the proverbial Golden Goose for everyone; but enough is never enough to the financial alchemists of Wall Street. Through the delusory magic of fractional reserve banking, a bank could lend $13 for every $1 held in equity. For the untutored and confused, the traditional rate ("fraction" in the fractional reserve system) of what must be held in reserve to cover losses was $1 (to be held in the bank) for every $10 lent out. The additional $3 difference, above, is a big deal.

If everyone was in a borrowing mood, why not meet the market demand and create more money to loan? More money to loan meant more money to be made in profits from mortgage-backed securities, credit derivatives, and other exotic instruments. Right?

In stepped Goldman Sachs's chairman, Henry Paulson. On April 28, 2004, this square-jawed, formerly fair-haired financial genius led a coalition of investment banks, which included Morgan Stanley, Lehman Brothers, Bear Stearns, and Merrill Lynch, in requesting that the SEC loosen the capital reserve rule and let the banks regulate themselves. To the utter astonishment of the entire financial services industry, the SEC unanimously agreed to the change after only 55 minutes of discussion. Within a few months, Bear Stearns, which was ostensibly using borrowed money to fund its mortgage-backed hedge funds, saw its leverage ratio reach 33 to 1![13] The subprime mortgage market was immediately flooded with billions of dollars in funding. This was like pouring gasoline directly onto open flames. The subprime mortgage market exploded!

Red flags began popping up everywhere as 2005 dawned. The late Edward Gramlich, appointed to serve as a Fed governor by President Clinton in 1997, had grown concerned about the appearance of predatory lending practices as early as 2000. He thought the Fed should begin a program of auditing some of the mortgage originators to ensure the integrity of resulting securities and privately broached the subject with Fed chairman Alan Greenspan. Greenspan was ideologically opposed to what he saw as unnecessary regulation, so Gramlich didn't pursue it.[14] On May 18, 2005, Gramlich tendered his resignation from the Federal Reserve Board of Governors. Gracious to the end, he only hinted at any conflict within the central bank, saying they had "met several difficult monetary challenges, and several diverse regulatory challenges."[15]

The chorus challenging Federal Reserve chairman Greenspan's reading of the subprime situation continued to grow louder. At an annual Jackson Hole retreat that was doubling as a retirement celebration for the chairman, eyebrows were raised and tempers flared when International Monetary Fund (IMF) economist Ragurham Rajan delivered a controversial paper that was critical of the financial sector and warned of pending economic collapse; Larry Summers scoffed at Rajan's concerns and called the warnings "misguided."[16]

American economist Robert Shiller repeated the theme in a *Wall Street Journal* article in August 2006 that warned of the coming "financial Apocalypse." In the meantime, *Wall Street Journal* writer Michael Siconolfi began investigating why the SEC had decided to end its investigation into the "pricing, valuation, and analysis" of mortgage-backed collateralized debt obligations by Bear Stearns, deciding not to take any action. His *WSJ* article on December 10, 2007, asked the question, "Did Authorities Miss a Chance to Ease Crunch?" and implicated then New York attorney general, Eliot Spitzer, for failing to pursue further probes into Bear Stearns's questionable dealings. In addition, Bear Stearns and other banks were known to routinely use funds from the capital accounts of publicly traded companies for prostitutes, strippers, and other immoral or even illegal services, billing them as "research" or "public relations" or "business entertainment." This has also been well documented. Although the U.S. government went after Elliot Spitzer on these kinds of issues, no one is holding the biggest investment banks responsible for this unethical and even illegal activity, which is endemic to this segment of the financial services division.[17]

On September 6, 2008, Fannie Mae and Freddie Mac were placed into conservatorship by the Federal Housing Finance Agency (FHFA) director, James B. Lockhart III, at the urging of Henry Paulson, the newly appointed U. S. Treasury secretary.[18] Federal Reserve Bank chairman Ben Bernanke voiced his approval of the move, and Mr. and Ms. U.S. Taxpayer became the *underwriters* of $5 trillion in mortgage-backed securities (MBSs) and debt owned by the Federal Reserve. This unprecedented transfer of assets to the Fed was barely mentioned by the national press. The *New York Times* painted the enslavement of the taxpayer simply as a government takeover.[19]

One week later, secret meetings were held over the weekend at the offices of the New York Federal Reserve Bank. The attendees included then New York Fed official Timothy Geithner, officials from the U.S. Treasury representing then Secretary of the Treasury Henry Paulson, regulators from the New York State Insurance Department, executives of AIG, bankers from JPMorgan, bankers from Morgan Stanley as consultants for the Treasury, and a group of Goldman Sachs bankers led by CEO Lloyd Blankfein. Everyone but Blankfein was there to head off a financial crisis that was threatening to take down AIG, Lehman Brothers, Merrill Lynch, and several other firms that had been caught up in the slice-and-dice MBS derivatives game that Goldman had been hawking. All Blankfein wanted was his money, and he seemed prepared to bring down the entire financial system to get it.[20] Following that weekend, Goldman Sachs ended up with at least $52 billion from the U.S. government via the AIG bailout, Paulson's Troubled Asset Relief Program (TARP), and Geithner's later FDIC bailout called the Temporary Liquidity Guarantee Program.

In the second quarter of 2009, Goldman Sachs posted a record profit of $3.44 billion and gave the American taxpayer the middle finger.[21] In a November 8, 2009, interview in London's *Sunday Times*, Blankfein declared, "I'm doing God's work." The state of Massachusetts disagreed and accused the delusional Prophet of Mammon of facilitating the fraud that led to the collapse of the subprime mortgage bubble. Goldman Sachs "agreed" to pay a fine of $60 million to end the investigation.[22]

Allow me to put that in perspective for the average person who doesn't toss around 9- to 12-figure numbers all day. A crackhead walks into a liquor store and takes $52,000 out of the cash register. He gets arrested but gets the district attorney to drop the charges and let him walk after he pays a fine of $60, which he pays from the stolen cash! And he gets to keep the rest of the money, too!

The extent of the criminal behavior of the greedy bankers leading up to and causing the financial meltdown that occurred in 2008 is mind-boggling when you know the facts. It includes financial fraud; self-dealing; and the pernicious synergy between compromised rating agencies, banks, and the consultants that sold marginal investments as

AAA rated, even while making money by betting against their own products, to the detriment of AIG and others.

And on the left of the political spectrum, the radicals of the 1960s who were now the heads of the community organizations and advocacy agencies created to bleed the system on behalf of the victim classes just shook their heads in disbelief. For decades they had preached about the evils of capitalism, and now these geniuses on Wall Street had done their work for them. They had been given enough proverbial rope and they had hung themselves with it. Greed and arrogance had breathed new life into the utopian dreams of the socialists.

A Crisis of Consciousness

We live in a society that is based on 30-second sound bites. We have technology that puts all of the information of humankind at our fingertips, but we have the attention span of a three-year-old at a carnival midway on the Fourth of July. We throw around a lot of words like *democracy, federal, republic, nationalist, socialist, liberal,* and *right-wing*—but do we really know what they mean?

The attractive, well-coiffed heads on television feed us the talking points of the day in small, candy-coated portions; smirking openly at the ease with which they are able to dictate popular opinion and influence policy. We dress the way a few select fashionistas dictate to the point where the color and pattern of a man's necktie signals his level of professional achievement. Our entertainment follows prescribed formats with predictable outcomes. The celebrities who pose as statesmen and politicians in our government listen to us with the same rehearsed look of concerned interest and share with us their carefully crafted "thoughts," with the strategically placed applause lines, from a teleprompter.

It is all carefully orchestrated to hide this fact: The men and women whom we have elected to represent our interests—to protect the general welfare of our nation and to defend the rights and liberties spelled out in our Constitution—in actuality have become, regardless of their political party affiliation, little more than circus monkeys doing the bidding of their unseen masters. Powerful lobbying groups actually write legislation to grant their industry favorable status, tariff protections, and tax incentives. They then shop it around Capitol Hill, pouring millions into the reelection campaigns of whichever Congressperson will sponsor the newly minted federal legislation.

Even our institutions cater to our collective attention deficit disorder, and we just accept it. Let me give you an example: According to a timeline published on the web site for the Federal Reserve Bank of St. Louis, the current economic crisis was *started* on February 27, 2007, when the Federal Home Loan Mortgage Corporation, also known as Freddie Mac, issued a press release announcing they would no longer buy the most risky subprime mortgages and mortgage-related securities. That is either an indication of incredible naïveté, gross condescension, or complete insanity! I may often have the opinion that the governors of the Federal Reserve System operate in a myopic vacuum void of logic and reason, but I don't think they are naïve. And in spite of the results of their tinkering with the economy, I doubt they are in the grips of institutional insanity. That leaves only one logical conclusion. The central bank interacts with the average American citizen from a position of cold, fundamental arrogance and condescension to the point of contempt. How else would you explain such a nonchalant and flippant statement about the current economic crisis?

Since the Panic of 1819, we have had economic bubbles burst in the nauseating cycle of boom and bust that pockmarks the image of American prosperity, but *this* is different. This is a financial meltdown that has resulted in the calculated loss of billions of dollars in accumulated wealth, numerous bank failures, massive expansion of government power for which the government has no legal right, and the near extinction of the individual sovereign freedom and liberty that made this nation the most unique and successful social experiment in human history. There are many who believe that it is not over yet! This is an act of war against the American people, and it is a war that started a long time before February 27, 2007.

Notes

1. Wells Fargo Economic Research, *Weekly Economic & Financial Commentary*, September 17, 2010.
2. Michael Gerrity, "U.S. Homes Lost $1.7 Trillion in Value in 2010, Total Value Destruction Since Market Peak Now $9 Trillion, Cost of 12 Iraq Wars," Real Estate Channel, online, December 9, 2010.
3. Nick Zieminski, "U.S. Commercial Real Estate to Bottom in 2010—Survey," Thomson-Reuters, Reuters News Service, online, November 5, 2009.
4. Ben S. Bernanke, "The Community Reinvestment Act: Its Evolution and New Challenges," speech given at the Community Affairs Research Conference, Washington, DC, on March 30, 2007. Retrieved from www .federalreserve.gov/newsevents/speech/Bernanke20070330a.htm.
5. William A. Niskanen, *Repeal the Community Reinvestment Act: Testimony of William A. Niskanen, Chairman Cato Institute before the Subcommittee on Financial Institutions and Consumer Credit, Committee on Banking and Financial Services United States Senate, March 8, 1995* (Washington, DC: The Cato Institute, 1995).
6. Michael W. Hudson, *The Monster: How a Gang of Predatory Lenders and Wall Street Bankers Fleeced America—and Spawned a Global Crisis* (New York: Times Books division of Henry Holt and Company, LLC, 2010), 125.
7. Peter S. Goodman, "Taking a Hard New Look at a Greenspan Legacy," *New York Times*, October 9, 2008, p. 3.
8. Scott Patterson, *The Quants: How a New Breed of Math Whizzes Conquered Wall Street and Nearly Destroyed It* (New York: Crown Business, 2010), 95–100.
9. Thomas J. McCool, "Responses to Questions Concerning Long-Term Capital Management and Related Events," Government Accountability Office, February 23, 2000, p. 2.
10. Robert E. Litan, Nicolas P. Retsinas, Eric S. Belsky, and Susan White Haag, *The Community Reinvestment Act after Financial Modernization: A Baseline Report* (Washington, DC: U.S. Department of the Treasury, 2000), 16–17.
11. Ibid., 217.
12. Hudson, *The Monster*, 221.
13. Stephen Labaton, "Agency's '04 Rule Lets Banks Pile Up New Debt," *New York Times*, October 3, 2008, p. A1.
14. Greg Ip, "Did Greenspan Add to Subprime Woes?" *Wall Street Journal*, June 9, 2007, p. B1. Retrieved from http://online.wsj.com/article/ SB118134111823129555.html?mod=todays_us_money_and_investing on 03May2011.

15. Federal Reserve System, Press Release, May 18, 2005. Retrieved from www.federalreserve.gov/boarddocs/press/other/2005/200505182/. PDF of letter attached.

16. Justin Lahart, "Mr. Rajan Was Unpopular (but Prescient) at Greenspan Party," *Wall Street Journal*, January 2, 2009, p. A7. Retrieved from http://online.wsj.com/article/SB123086154114948151.html.

17. United States Senate Committee on Finance, Press Release, October 10, 2008. Retrieved from http://finance.senate.gov/newsroom/ranking/release/?id=53c45ec5-d2c4-464b-8dfe-cea11d887c30.

18. Henry M. Paulson, Jr., *On the Brink: Inside the Race to Stop the Collapse of the Global Financial System* (New York: Business Plus, 2010), 1.

19. Gretchen Morgenson and Charles Duhigg, "Mortgage Giant Overstated the Size of Its Capital Base," *New York Times*, September 7, 2008, p. A1. Retrieved from www.nytimes.com/2008/09/07/business/07fannie.html.

20. Matt Taibbi, *Griftopia* (New York: Spiegel & Grau, 2010), 115–116.

21. Ibid., 120.

22. Zachary A. Goldfarb, "SEC Accuses Goldman Sachs, Fabrice Tourre of Defrauding Investors. *Washington Post*, April 17, 2010, p. A01.

23. Federal Reserve Bank of St. Louis, "The Financial Crisis—a Timeline of Events and Policy Actions." Retrieved from http://timeline.stlouisfed.org/index.cfm?p=timeline.

Chapter 3

The Seeds of Our Destruction

And I sincerely believe, with you, that banking establishments are more dangerous than standing armies; and that the principle of spending money to be paid by posterity, under the name of funding, is but swindling futurity on a large scale.
    —Thomas Jefferson (1743–1826), author of the U.S. Declaration of Independence and third president of the United States, in an 1816 letter to John Tyler

When I became a citizen of the United States, I was required to study the nation's history in order to pass my citizenship examination. I approached this task with the same focused intensity with which I approach every challenge. I wanted to be as well versed on American history as the average person who was born here. Imagine my surprise when I discovered that the average native-born citizen knows very little about their nation's history. Many people with whom I have talked think that 1776 is the date we celebrate the victory of the United States over the British. It isn't. It is the year that Thomas Jefferson wrote the Declaration of

Independence. The American Revolutionary War went on for another seven years. The American Historical Association randomly selected 400 people from *Who's Who in America* to take a multiple-choice test on a general overview of American history. They found that over 70 percent of the respondents thought Thomas Jefferson was one of the framers of the Constitution in 1787. He wasn't. He was in Paris at the time, serving as minister to France. Had he been in Philadelphia, we might have been protected from some of the economic problems that we have today.

The most common misconception is that the War for Independence was fought for *political* liberty. That is simply not true. The inhabitants of the American colonies were almost all British subjects who shared the same rights and privileges of any man or woman walking down Fleet Street in London. The Englishmen who settled in the New World brought with them charters that protected their rights and liberties as granted under the Magna Carta, the Great Charter issued in 1215 by King John and the basis for all British law.

What America fought for and won was *economic* liberty. In 1763, George Grenville became Britain's prime minister. That country was broke from their Seven Years War with France. Grenville's solution was to impose a series of direct taxes and trade regulations on the prosperous American colonies. The Americans would have none of it. On July 4, 1776, the 56 delegates to the Continental Congress adopted and signed the United States Declaration of Independence declaring that the 13 American colonies were now independent and sovereign states and were no longer part of the British Empire. In 1781, the several sovereign American States formed a "firm league of friendship with each other" codified as the Articles of Confederation and called themselves the United States of America. The War for Independence finally ended with the signing of the Treaty of Paris and the Treaties of Versailles on September 3, 1783.

The Americans knew they had created something new and different, something that had never been done before. They had established a nation whose economy was based on merit, not on garnering the favor of the crown or some royal adviser. They had created an economy in which reward was in direct proportion to effort, where the laws of supply and demand determined a man's success in the marketplace instead of the arbitrary dictates of some governmental authority. They had created a land where anyone could come up with an idea or provide a needed good or service and make as much money as they could for as long as they could.

The "Pursuit of Happiness" was understood then as a thought form and concept. It was held as an inalienable liberty. One could happily pursue the expression of any and all forms of wealth to assure the survival of one's life. And one could do this by almost any means except by employing any activity that was harmful or damaging to another's property or physical, emotional, or spiritual well-being. This personal sovereignty of the individual was likewise understood, naturally and intuitively, as being only granted by some supreme intelligence; some creator, maker, divine architect, or God, as one could imagine in one's own personal way. Man's law, and manipulations of that law bent largely upon power control, held no sway against liberty in the intuitive understanding of the Founding Fathers.

America needed a government that supported and nourished this new economic model. They knew they had the resources to become a mighty nation if they just could find the balance between freedom and regulation, but there had to be checks and balances. History had taught them that the utopian dream of communal sharing of resources and responsibilities was a beautiful vision and a lofty goal, but one that always broke down in the face of human self-interest. They reasoned that what they needed was a central government with strong but limited powers to ensure that there was fair trade between the states and protection from foreign influence and interference.

". . . In Order to Form a More Perfect Union . . ."

In the summer of 1787, delegates from all of the states except Rhode Island met in Philadelphia for the purposes of discussing ways to fix the Articles of Confederation. They wanted to have a stronger central government with powers over foreign and domestic commerce. They also hoped to find an acceptable means for Congress to fairly and reasonably collect tax revenues from the individual state treasuries.

Virginia lawyer James Madison was joined by New York banker Alexander Hamilton in convincing other delegates to scrap the Articles of Confederation and adopt a new constitution for a completely new form of government: a union of sovereign states under a central government of elected representatives—a federal republic. Madison's motives were his concerns over the fragile bonds of the Articles; Hamilton's motives, it turned out, were far more pecuniary in nature.

Alexander Hamilton was a member of the New York delegation, along with State Supreme Court Justice Robert Yates and John Lansing, Jr., the mayor of Albany. Hamilton, the illegitimate son of a Scottish prodigal and a married French Huguenot woman, had been born into abject poverty around 1757 on the island of St. Nevis in the Caribbean. He had come to Boston in 1773, presenting himself as the grandson of Scottish nobleman John Hamilton and eventually landed in New York where he attended King's College, now known as Columbia College. His intelligence, ambition, and organizational talents led him to serve as Washington's aide-de-camp during the war. He later distinguished himself in combat, attaining the rank of colonel. Hamilton married Elizabeth Schuyler in 1780, the daughter of one of the wealthiest businessmen in New York. In 1784, he founded the Bank of New York, America's oldest continuously operating bank.

The Man Who Would Be King

Hamilton was a man driven by a need for social status and a craving for fame. He was an elitist who viewed the people of the American colonies as having "the passiveness of the sheep in their compositions" and unable to be roused from "the lethargy of voluptuous indolence."[1] He disguised his true disdain for his fellow citizens with an avowed mission to serve "the public good," but held a firm distaste for anything parochial and regarded the "local attachment" to the interest of the states over that of the nation as undermining the American cause and his own ambitions.[2] Management and control of his public image was a paramount obsession with Hamilton. Defense against a perceived slur would eventually lead to his untimely death as the result of a duel with Aaron Burr in 1804.

On Monday, June 18, 1787, he rose in the Philadelphia convention to offer his opinions as to which direction the delegates ought to take regarding amending the existing Articles of Confederation. He spoke candidly because the candidates had passed a motion to conduct the convention in secret; however, James Madison was taking notes as an unofficial recording secretary. What neither Hamilton nor anyone else knew at the time was that Judge Yates was also recording statements almost verbatim, using a form of shorthand he had developed to record testimony before his court.

Hamilton supported scrapping the existing compact and writing an entirely new guiding document for the nation. Hamilton was "fully convinced that no amendment of the Confederation leaving the states in possession of their sovereignty could possibly answer the purpose."[3] Hamilton was a nationalist and an adherent of the mercantilist model of economics. His plan was for a strong central government that controlled the economy through a central bank.

Mercantilism is often confused as a preference of business and industry over agriculture. It is, in fact, the use of the government to fulfill one's personal objectives and self-interest. In other words, if Thomas the Tailor becomes the favorite haberdasher of the king, then Thomas gets to make all of the king's clothing. He also gets to produce all of the finery for the royal family, all of the clothing for the members of the court, garments for the castle servants, the uniforms for the king's army, and so on. All of the other tailors in the realm have to scramble for the leftovers. Mercantilism creates an elitist commercial monopoly that eventually corrupts the state bureaucracy and infuriates its citizens. America was founded and originally set up expressly to counteract mercantilism by diffusing power in such a way that there would be no place that a mercantilist entity could find a single patron with whom to curry favor.

Hamilton's proposal would have codified the wealthy elite as the upper chamber of a bicameral parliament, elected the president for life, and effectively transplanted the English form of monarchy and mercantilism to American soil. There were even persistent rumors that he was involved in a conspiracy to actually establish a monarchy on

America's shores by installing the Duke of York, King George III's son, to rule.[4]

He was voted down by the convention. In fact, Hamilton's continual machinations and backroom conniving so infuriated his fellow New Yorkers that Yates and Lansing left the convention in July, ethically negating Hamilton's role at the convention. As was to be the model throughout his political career, Hamilton was never one to be hindered by what he considered to be such minor technicalities. He wasn't allowed to participate in further votes, but when the final resolution was drafted, Alexander Hamilton was one of the signers of the new Constitution. He also worked tirelessly to see that the nation's new compact was ratified, writing 51 of the 85 *Federalist* essays that explained the new Constitution and have served to shape interpretation of that document ever since. New Hampshire became the ninth state to ratify the new Constitution of the United States of America on June 21, 1788, and the new federal government began operations just eight months later.

George Washington became the nation's first president in 1789, and his cabinet consisted of just seven men. John Adams was vice president, Thomas Jefferson was secretary of state, Henry Knox was the secretary of war, Samuel Osgood was the postmaster general, John Jay was the secretary of foreign affairs, and the attorney general was Edmund Randolph. Washington remembered his former aide and, on the recommendation of Philadelphia merchant and Revolutionary War financier Robert Morris, named Alexander Hamilton to be the first secretary of the Treasury. Hamilton was considered to be one of the brightest candidates for the position despite the fact that he was self-taught in the law, economics, and finance.

In his "First Report on the Public Credit," delivered to Congress on January 14, 1790, Hamilton laid out a plan for the establishment of a properly managed but ongoing national debt as the vehicle for easy credit and prosperity for all. The federal government would assume all of the old debts of the Confederation in exchange for new government bonds paying 4 percent interest per annum. He was convinced that the only path to success in any society was to tie the interests of the wealthy, the primary government bondholders, to the state in the belief that they would support his dreams of a larger, centrally controlled government.[5] He maintained that his plan would restore land values, stimulate manufacturing, lower interest rates, and "promote the increasing respectability of the American name."[6] This new scheme was widely endorsed by people all over the country, who quickly exchanged their worthless Confederation notes for new Treasury bonds. He then introduced a series of tariffs and excise taxes in order to raise the revenue to back the bonds.

It was claimed to be merely an unfortunate coincidence of the day that the news of the payoff was slow to reach the nation beyond the city limits of New York, allowing many of Hamilton's friends and relatives the opportunity to scour the countryside buying up old Confederation notes from unsuspecting holders for pennies on the dollar.[7] Hamilton scoffed at those who raised questions of impropriety and arrogantly waved off their concerns stating that "how things are done governs what can and will be done: the rules determine the nature and the outcome of the game." This philosophy became known as Hamiltonianism[8] and underscored the policies and platforms of his newly formed political party, the Federalists. Continuing his campaign for "the common good," he had the federal government assume the debts that the individual states had accumulated fighting the War of Independence.

The second nail that Hamilton drove into America's free-market coffin came in 1790 with the establishment of the Bank of the United States. This was the nation's second attempt at a central bank. The Bank of North America had been chartered by the Continental Congress in 1781 and was organized by Robert Morris. By 1783, the Bank of North America had died an ignoble death under allegations of fraud and mismanagement; however, Hamilton convinced Congress that this new central bank was going to be different.

Thomas Jefferson considered Hamilton to be dangerously ambitious and raised the point that the Constitution did not grant Congress the power to create a bank or any other entity. With uncanny foresight, Jefferson wrote, "To take a single step beyond the boundaries thus specially drawn around the powers of Congress, is to take possession of a boundless field of power, no longer susceptible of any definition."[9]

Hamilton countered in his *Opinion on the Constitutionality of an Act to Establish a Bank* that "principles of (Constitutional) construction like those espoused by the Secretary of State (Jefferson) and the Attorney General (Edmund Randolph) would be fatal to the just and indispensible authority of the United States." Then Hamilton delivered the *estocada*, or "death blow" to the free-market economic model. He claimed that the Constitution "implied" power to the federal government by the very fact that the government was sovereign and had the right to assume any power it needed to perform its duties as a sovereign entity.

"It is not denied," argued Hamilton, "that there are implied as well as expressed powers and that the former are as effectually delegated as the latter."[10]

In one swift and deliberate motion, the concept of limited government was tossed out the window and the new government assumed the authority to do nearly anything it wanted.

This plan was opposed by Thomas Jefferson, James Madison, and others as a concentration of economic power in the hands of the central government and, more specifically, in the hands of Alexander Hamilton. The proposal was defeated in Congress five times before Hamilton and Jefferson struck a deal. Hamilton agreed to support Jefferson and Madison's plan to move the nation's capital out of New York to a new, centrally located national capital city that they had planned in northern Virginia. His price was their support of his central bank plan.

Jefferson didn't believe the Congress would ever approve Hamilton's blatant grab for federal power, so he agreed to Hamilton's offer. Because of the way he had doled out the advance notices for funding and paying the government bonds on the war and old Continental debts, Hamilton knew he had the votes he needed to get his bank charter through Congress. Thus was Washington, D.C., created, as well as the establishment of the perpetual debt of the federal government and its ability to use taxation and regulation to affect political policies and social agendas.[11]

On February 24, 1791, Washington signed the bill chartering the Bank of the United States, and from that failure of vision and wisdom formalized the principle of implied powers for Congress. The new American economy was quickly introduced to boom–bust business cycles as the federal government borrowed, spent too much, and then printed money to cover its shortcomings. Between 1791 and 1796, price levels jumped 72 percent.[12]

Hamilton wasn't finished defining the new government to his own specifications. He had one more act to fulfill his dream of a New Britain; the federal government had to function in the mercantilist model, centrally controlling the economy and involving itself in every aspect of the citizen's daily life. In December 1791, he submitted his magnum opus to Congress, *The Report on Manufactures*. This report was in response to a request from Congress for Hamilton's opinion on "the means of promoting such as will tend to render the United States, independent of foreign nations, for military and other essential supplies."

In the first few paragraphs, Hamilton acknowledged the commonly held notion that "it can hardly ever be wise, in a government, to give direction to the industry of its citizens. This, under the quick-sighted guidance of private interest, will, if left to itself, infallibly find its own way to the most profitable employment: and it is by such employment that the public prosperity will be most effectually promoted. To leave industry to itself, therefore, is in almost every case the soundest as well as the simplest policy."[13] This is commonly referred to as a *laissez-faire* economic model in which transactions between private parties are free from excessive government interference in the form of regulations, taxes, or tariffs.

Hamilton then proceeded on for another 26,000 words, laying out a detailed economic policy that not only decidedly opposed a laissez-faire economy, but was firmly rooted in English mercantilist principles. He went into exhaustive detail, listing the specific industries that the government should promote and outlining the instruments the government could use to exercise economic control over these favored industries. Tariffs and bounties were to become the weapons of choice in the Hamiltonian economic arsenal.

His grand ambition blinded him to one small truth; government bureaucrats have no way of knowing which enterprises will thrive and which won't. They are usually operating on nothing but theoretical knowledge and supposition; they have no skin in the game and often have little accountability for the mistakes that they make.[14]

I have no dispute with the historical portrait of Alexander Hamilton as an intelligent and articulate man who had a smooth way of ingratiating himself with the affluent and powerful; however, the portrait of him as a champion of freedom and liberty simply isn't true in the looking glass of historical investigation. He was an ambitious and arrogant nationalist who held the notion of individual sovereignty in contempt. He was more than willing to rewrite historical fact to prove his point. On June 29, 1787, he put forth the argument that the citizens of the states had never been sovereign and that the states themselves were merely "artificial beings" that had nothing to do with the creation of the union.[15] This statement revealed an illogical sense of reality in the mere fact that the Constitution that *created* the national government had to be ratified by the individual states, each of them choosing to *voluntarily* enter into a compact with each other for the purpose of "forming a more perfect union."

The fact is the perpetual federal debt system put in place by Hamilton was nothing more than what we now know as a Ponzi scheme designed to benefit the banking establishment. In order to function properly, the federal government must constantly be looking for more ways to generate more debt. This means that it must, by design, insert itself into every area of your life, every activity in which you are involved, and control the percentage of winners it allows in the financial arena. The fact that such a small percentage of Americans now control such an overwhelmingly large percentage of the nation's wealth is the logical fulfillment of the grand scheme that Alexander Hamilton conceived at the end of the eighteenth century.

The Hamilton Legacy

When Thomas Jefferson became president in 1800, he rolled back or eliminated many of the taxes and tariffs that Hamilton had encouraged, but he was not able to kill the beast of federal debt–based spending. We were a young nation, but one that had been thrust into the international spotlight by our break from the British Empire. We were growing and expanding to the west with the admission of the state of Ohio and the Louisiana Purchase. We had a new capital city on the banks of the Potomac River in northern Virginia and a new military academy on the banks of the Hudson River at West Point in New York. All of this required money, and the government could create money only by creating debt. The charter of the Bank of the United States was allowed to lapse in 1811 under James Madison, but he was forced to charter the Second Bank of the United States due to the debts incurred by the War of 1812; a war ignited, coincidentally, by the mercantilist policies of Britain.

Hamilton's legacy was further codified in 1819 when Chief Justice John Marshall, a Federalist and self-described admirer of Hamilton, put forth his opinion in *McCulloch v. Maryland* that the word *necessary* in the necessary-and-proper clause of the Constitution didn't mean "indispensable," but instead meant "appropriate;" almost quoting Hamilton verbatim in the ruling.[16] Marshall had also concocted the power of "judicial review" in his 1803 ruling in *Marbury v. Madison* that was based largely upon Hamilton's inferences in *Federalist No. 78,* that "the authority which can declare the acts of another void must *necessarily* be superior to the one whose acts may be declared void."

President Andrew Jackson became so incensed by the loose credit policies and the currency manipulation of the national bank that he made it his personal mission to return the nation to hard currency. This caused the Depression of 1837 and a 26-year period known as the Free Banking Era, during which the money supply and price controls fluctuated wildly, causing many banks to last no more than five years.

Thomas P. Kane, former deputy comptroller of the currency from 1886 until 1922, believed that a system was necessary that offered the advantages of a centrally controlled currency but had none of the inherent opportunities for political favoritism and malfeasance that had been the bane of the Bank of the United States. In his comprehensive history of banking entitled *The Romance and Tragedy of Banking,* he noted that there may have been too much optimism for the National Bank Act because ". . . history teaches us that the public faith of a nation alone is not sufficient to maintain a paper currency. There must be a combination between the interests of private individuals and the government.[17]"

According to Kane, the first of four major bank panics during the 40-year National Banking Era occurred in 1873 and was caused by New York bankers manipulating the stock exchange by "creating and fostering the *fictitious valuations* attained at home and abroad for railroad and other corporate securities. . . ."[18]

The Congress had been so anxious to have a transcontinental railroad that they employed Hamilton's tactic of bounties in the Pacific Railroad Act of 1862, creating political entrepreneurs like Thomas Clark Durant. They chartered the Union Pacific Railroad to head west from Iowa and the Central Pacific Railroad to head east from San Francisco. For each mile of track Durant and his associates laid, they were given 20 sections of land and loans ranging from $16,000 per mile across flat prairie to $48,000 per mile in mountains. Nobody in the federal government thought to have oversight on the project, resulting in massive waste and corruption. Union Pacific ended up defaulting on $16 million in government loans, which sent the stock market into a tailspin.[19]

Fortunately for the nation, for every political entrepreneur who needed government financial grants or guarantees to launch their business, there were more market entrepreneurs who saw a need and invested their own capital and sweat equity to come up with a solution. This was the entrepreneurial spirit that had launched America and had seen it through its growing pains. By the first decade of the twentieth century, it appeared that this foundational spirit had returned in full force. Nearly 20,000 banks had been opened, and over 80 percent of them were not national banks. What was even more alarming to the tight-knit banking fraternity in New York City was that these upstarts held more than half of the nation's deposits, were maintaining a healthy balance between debt and savings, were not exceeding the reserve limits based on the gold and silver that they held, and were making profits![20] Even the federal government was using its stockpile of gold to redeem its bonds and was reducing the national debt. To the Ivy League disciples of Hamilton's principles of perpetual debt, this was sacrilege.

The Panic of 1907 was "officially" caused by a failed attempt to corner the copper market and led to a two-week period of bank runs and a near collapse of the stock market. Historical anecdotal evidence points to the crisis having been ignited when rumors were published that the Knickerbocker Trust Company was insolvent. Whatever the true cause, the Panic prompted Congress to create the National Monetary Commission. The Commission, led by Republican U.S. Senator Nelson Aldrich of Rhode Island, spent $300,000 for a year-long fact-finding tour of Europe to study European central banking methods and monetary policy. That is the equivalent of $20.2 million today. The visible result was a 30-volume report on the history of banking in Europe that was designed to make the American people think that the issue had been well researched. What was not as visible was the process used to draft the legislation that was to finally and permanently bring Hamilton's dream to reality.

Bringing Hamilton's Monster to Life

Late on the evening of November 22, 1910, six men boarded a private railcar that was sitting on a siding near the passenger rail station in Hoboken, New Jersey. These six men represented about a quarter of the nation's wealth. The owner of the car was Senator Aldrich, whose daughter was married to John D. Rockefeller, Jr. His guests were the assistant secretary of the Treasury Department, Abram Piatt Andrew; Paul Warburg, a naturalized German representing Kuhn, Loeb & Co. and the Rothschild interests; Frank A. Vanderlip, president of the National City Bank of New York; Henry P. Davison, senior partner of J. P. Morgan Company; Charles D. Norton, president of First National Bank of New York, and Benjamin Strong, representing J. P. Morgan and, privately, the interests of the Bank of England.[21] The cover story for the trip was a duck-hunting excursion on Jekyll Island. The truth was they stayed in seclusion on the island for a week hammering out the legislation that would become the Federal Reserve Act of 1913. The legislation was actually based on Warburg's 1907 white paper entitled "A Plan for a Modified Central Bank."

To illustrate the reality of how little influence political labels have over the money elite, the original legislation was written and sponsored by a Republican, Nelson Aldrich; but before he could get it enacted, Woodrow Wilson and the Democrats had been swept into power. The Aldrich Plan was picked up in the house by Virginia Democrat Carter Glass and steered through the Senate by Robert Latham Owen, a Democrat from Oklahoma. The Federal Reserve Act was signed into law December 23, 1913, with very little fanfare or public notice. Most of the legislature had gone home for the holidays, and it would be decades before the general public would fully grasp what had been done to them. This act created a publicly funded but privately owned and controlled banking cartel called the Federal Reserve System. It was really a central bank that kept the reserve deposits of all other banks, issued the national currency, and had absolute control over monetary policy.

Springtime for the Progressives

The Progressive movement sprang up during the Theodore Roosevelt administration as a reaction to "The Gilded Age." The Gilded Age is most famous for the creation of a modern industrial economy. During the 1870s and 1880s, the U.S. economy grew at the fastest rate in its history, with real wages, wealth, gross domestic product, and capital formation all increasing rapidly. A national transportation and communication network was created, the corporation became the dominant form of business organization, and a managerial revolution transformed business operations. By the beginning of the twentieth century, per-capita income and industrial production in the United States led the world. The Progressive Era in the United States was a period of social activism and reform that flourished from the 1890s to the 1920s. The main goal of the Progressive movement was purification of government. Progressives were usually white, educated, and self-righteous in the embrace of "scientific methods" as applied to economics, government, industry, finance, medicine, schooling, theology, and education.

Progressives seem preoccupied with the concept of "fairness." My observation is that they always seem to think they know what is best for everyone else. They are, in my opinion, usually self-righteous busybodies whose views are often well intentioned but misguided and almost always devoid of any critical analysis, such as consideration of unintended consequences. The Eighteenth Amendment is a good example of this; it curbed public drunkenness but gave us speakeasies, bootleggers, and Al Capone.

Other Progressive brainstorms gave us the Sixteenth Amendment of the U.S. Constitution, resulting in federal income tax. The Seventeenth Amendment to the Constitution established direct election of United States senators by popular vote and removed the only true representation that the sovereign states had at the federal level. If a senator were beholden to the state legislators who had selected him or her to serve, they would be less likely to support a federal program that appropriated the resources of their state. After the passage of the Seventeenth Amendment, the members of the U.S. Senate became a de facto House of Lords, counselors to the imperial presidency and answerable to none.

The Progressives gave us the Federal Reserve Act of 1913, which co-opted the federal government's constitutionally mandated function of managing the monetary supply and policies of the nation and effectively turned it over to a private banking cartel, which wrote banking regulations with the force of law.

Warren G. Harding was a Republican president, but he continued federal dominance for "the public good" with the 1922 Fordney-McCumber Tariff Act. It was supposed to protect American farmers and businesses from European competition. Many economists look at this tariff as the genesis of the Great Depression, which began with the Wall Street crash of 1929 and ushered in a decade of high unemployment, a 45 percent drop in industrial production, an 80 percent drop in home building, and the failure of 11,000 banks. It should be noted that the Federal Reserve stood by and did absolutely nothing to mitigate the stock market crash of 1929 despite its founding principle to "maintain long run growth of the monetary and credit aggregates commensurate with the economy's long run potential to increase production, so as to promote effectively the goals of maximum employment, stable prices, and moderate long-term interest rates."

In plain English, the Federal Reserve System is not part of the federal government. It is a private central bank that was put into place to make sure that a healthy balance was maintained between the money supply and the availability of credit so that businesses could borrow the money they needed to create the products that the market demanded at a fair and reasonable price while creating jobs in the process. Nowhere in that definition is there any mention or expectation of the federal government's creating jobs or redistributing wealth. This omission was totally lost on Franklin Delano Roosevelt, president from 1933 until 1945. His "New Deal" economic programs were the federal government's responses to the Great Depression and focused on relief for the unemployed and poor, recovery of the economy to normal levels, and reform of the financial system.

One of the first pieces of legislation FDR signed was the Glass-Steagall Act, which created the Federal Deposit Insurance Corporation (FDIC) and banking reforms that prohibited bank holding companies from owning financial companies. This particular piece of legislation, ironically enough, actually held the priests of Mammon in check until it was dismantled by Republican senators Phil Gramm and Jim Leach during the Clinton administration.

FDR also gave us the Securities and Exchange Commission (SEC) in 1934, supposedly protecting our investments on the one hand, while on the other hand seizing all privately held gold under Executive Order 6102. The National Labor Relations Act gave workers legal permission to organize unions, to engage in collective bargaining, and to take part in strikes. Thanks to World War II, continued government tinkering with economic theories, and Roosevelt's numerous national "make work" programs, deficit spending went through the roof under FDR. These and many other programs that were initiated during the so-called Progressive Enlightenment of the Thirties have served only to expand the size and reach of the federal government. In a later chapter, we will show how many of the federal programs and agencies that were promoted as being bulwarks of American freedom and prosperity have, in fact, become a pernicious cancer that threatens to destroy our very way of life.

In the 1960s, Lyndon Johnson's "Great Society" programs declared a war on poverty, illiteracy, racism, and the lack of fundamental services for the sick and elderly. Medicare, Medicaid, Volunteers in Service to America (VISTA), National Public Radio (NPR), the Public Broadcasting Service (PBS), Head Start, and the proscribed use of seat belts all came into being under this massive societal makeover. Such a vast government entitlement safety net was installed that many people were, for the first time in America, faced with a simple economic choice: continue to struggle to free themselves from poverty and work hard for little pay or just give up and resign themselves to a life on the government dole and not have to work at all. The basic economic principle of self-interest was ignored again. The result of this grand Hamiltonian scheme has been several generations of Americans living substandard lives steeped in ignorance, immorality, violence, and poverty as a permanent underclass of victims.

Other examples of unintended consequences coming from Progressive minds include the McCarran-Ferguson Act of 1945. This federal law exempts health insurance companies from most federal regulation, including federal antitrust laws to a limited extent, as long as state laws regulate the "business of insurance." This piece of legislation is responsible for your not being able to go across state lines to purchase health insurance at a competitive price. When this was coupled with the 1986 passage of the Emergency Medical Treatment and Active Labor Act (EMTALA), the seeds for our present-day health care crisis were fertilized. EMTALA requires hospitals and ambulance services to provide care to anyone needing emergency health care treatment regardless of citizenship, legal status, or ability to pay. There are no reimbursement provisions, but if you refused to participate, you were not allowed to partake in the Medicare and Medicaid payment programs. Considering that these two programs typically constitute 40 percent of a hospital's revenue stream, the Progressives had once again used the guise of "doing good" to grab more political and economic control over the lives of American citizens.

And What about the Fed?

In the nearly 100 years that it has been in existence, the Federal Reserve System has been exceptional only in its complete and utter failure in performing its stated function. In the 98 years that the Fed has been in charge of this nation's monetary policy, the real buying power of the U.S. dollar has *decreased* nearly 94 percent![22]

How is this possible? Look at the track record. In 1970, the SEC turned a blind eye while the directors of the Penn Central Railroad were able to unload 1.8 million shares of pumped up stock two weeks before revealing that the company was defaulting on $100 million in bank loans. The Fed stepped in with $125 million in loans guaranteed by the Congress in the Emergency Rail Services Act of 1970. The following year, the federal government nationalized the gutted Penn Central Railroad with the National Railroad Passenger Corporation, and AMTRAK was born.[23] Over the next decade, using taxpayer guaranteed money that it created out of thin air, the Fed arranged bailouts for Lockheed, Chrysler, New York City, the Commonwealth Bank of Detroit, Continental Illinois Bank, and the First Pennsylvania Bank—the original Bank of North America started by Robert Morris, Alexander Hamilton's mentor.

This brings us back to Alexander Hamilton.

What relevance does the nation's first Treasury secretary have today? He has become the patron saint of those who worship at the altar of Big Government and eternal deficit spending. Robert Rubin, the former Goldman Sachs co-chairman and U.S. Treasury secretary during the Clinton administration, has started a forum to honor Hamilton and to further his philosophy of government and economics. "The Hamilton Project" is under the auspices of the Brookings Institution, a liberal think tank based in Washington, D.C. The stated philosophy of this new venture is "long-term prosperity is best achieved by fostering economic growth and *broad participation in that growth*, by enhancing individual economic security, and by embracing a role for effective government in making needed public investments."

It is a fitting tribute to Hamilton, the man who created the system that made it all possible. Unfortunately, the phrase "broad participation" doesn't mean that there should be a sharing of the economic growth by a greater number of Americans. You must remember, this is "banker-speak." The correct interpretation is finding a wider assortment of ways for the greedy bankers and the compromised federal bureaucrats to appropriate the fruits of that economic growth for their personal aggrandizement.

Rust never sleeps and corruption never ceases on its own accord. The Progressive agenda has repeatedly been shown to be nothing more than the same old failed socialist policies in new party hats. Yet, they continue to promote, cajole, and sneak their ideology into our lives. They will never stop unless we completely expose, refute, and eradicate them once and for all.

Notes

1. Forrester McDonald, *Alexander Hamilton: A Biography* (New York: W.W. Norton & Company, 1979), 4.
2. Ibid., 19.
3. James Madison, *Notes of Debates in the Federal Convention of 1787* (New York: W. W, Norton & Company, by arrangement with Ohio University Press, 1840), 129.
4. Ron Chernow, *Alexander Hamilton* (New York: Penguin Press, 2004), 237.
5. Thomas J. DiLorenzo, *Hamilton's Curse: How Jefferson's Archenemy Betrayed the American Revolution—and What It Means for Americans Today* (New York: Three Rivers Press, 2008), 45.
6. *Alexander Hamilton: First Report on the Public Credit* (Chicago: Encyclopedia Britannica, 1982), "Annals of America," Vol. 3, 407–415.
7. DiLorenzo, *Hamilton's Curse*, 41.
8. McDonald, *Alexander Hamilton*, 123.
9. Herman E. Kroos, ed. *Documentary History of Banking and Currency in the United States* (New York: Chelsea House, 1983), Vol. III, 147–148.
10. Chernow, *Alexander Hamilton*, 354.
11. John Steele Gordon, *Hamilton's Blessing: The Extraordinary Life and Times of Our National Debt* (New York: Penguin, 1997), 29.
12. Murray N. Rothbard, *A History of Money and Banking in the United States: The Colonial Era to World War II* (Auburn, AL: Ludwig von Mises Institute, 2002), 69.
13. Walter Lowrie and Matthew Clarke, eds., *American State Papers, Documents, Legislative and Executive, of the Congress of the United States, etc. etc.*, (Washington DC: Gales & Seaton, 1832), Volume V, 123–144.
14. DiLorenzo, *Hamilton's Curse*, (New York: Three Rivers Press), 103.

15. Ibid., 26.
16. Chernow, *Alexander Hamilton*, 355.
17. Thomas P. Kane, *The Romance and Tragedy of Banking* (Boston: Bankers Publishing, 1922), 6.
18. Ibid., 47.
19. Burton W. Folsom Jr., *The Myth of the Robber Barons* (Herndon, VA: Young America's Foundation, 2010), 18–19.
20. Gabriel Kolko, *The Triumph of Conservatism* (New York: Free Press of Glencoe, a division of the Macmillan Co., 1963), 140.
21. Murray N. Rothbard, *The Case against the Fed* (Auburn, AL: Ludwig von Mises Institute, 1994), 108–129.
22. The AIER Chart Book, *Economic Bulletin,* Vol. L, No. 7, July 2010 (Great Barrington, MA: American Institute of Economic Research, 2010), 3.
23. G. Edward Griffin, *The Creature from Jekyll Island: A Second Look at the Federal Reserve* (Westlake Village, CA: American Media, 1995), 41–56.

Chapter 4

The Face of the Enemy

History is littered with monetary managers who believed they were in total control—until the disaster hit. It is hubris of the first order to believe oneself the master of the universe, but hubris is endemic in Washington.

—Llewellyn H. Rockwell, Jr., founder and chairman of the Mises Institute

From January 2009 until January 2011, the 111th Congress of the United States behaved in a manner that can only be described as arrogantly frenzied.

The Democratic Party had garnered filibuster-proof majorities in the House and Senate on the coattails of the junior senator from Illinois. Harry Reid, the senior senator from Nevada, became the Senate majority leader. The Speaker of the House at the time was Nancy Pelosi, whose 8th Congressional district covers most of the city of San Francisco. Together, they orchestrated a legislative carpet bombing of America that saw 33 new bills enacted, including the S-CHIP program, the $787 billion American Recovery and

Reinvestment Act of 2009 (ARRA), the Homeless Emergency Assistance and Rapid Transition to Housing (HEARTH) Act, the Credit Card Accountability Responsibility and Disclosure (Credit CARD) Act of 2009, and the Hiring Incentives to Restore Employment (HIRE) Act of 2010.

The most famous legislation was the Patient Protection and Affordable Care Act, also known as Obamacare, and the Dodd-Frank Wall Street Reform Act, both of which consisted of hundreds and hundreds of pages cobbled together from a multitude of somewhat related legislative proposals, mostly written by lobbyists, which had been lingering around Congress for years looking for a home.

My personal favorite was the Securing the Protection of our Enduring and Established Constitutional Heritage (SPEECH) Act. Now Mahmoud Ahmadinejad can't enforce the defamation judgment against me, awarded to him by the Islamic Revolutionary Court for my calling him a heretical lunatic.

When the Speaker of the House, Nancy Pelosi, was addressing the 2010 Legislative Conference of the National Association of Counties, she felt comfortable enough to joke that Democrats consider devising a good acronym to be an integral part of the legislative process; however, the speech is not remembered for that insight into our representatives, but for yet another of the Speaker's famous "wide-eyed innocent" remarks. She was praising the imminent passage of the then 2,000-plus page Patient Protection and Affordable Care Act, the nationalization of the health care industry that became known as Obamacare.

"But we have to pass the bill," she said, "so that you can find out what is in it."

In this one statement, Speaker Pelosi made the news cycles for days. The blogosphere erupted with calls from the Left for her to "revise and extend her comments" to questions from the Right regarding the Speaker's competence; everyone agreed on the need for further clarification, if not outright explanation. The conservative talk shows blasted the apparent insolent ambivalence of the Countess of the Left Coast, likening it to being close in tone to "Let them eat cake!"

Lost in the dustup was the rest of the speech, in which she revealed the real agenda behind the frenetic push of the 111th Congress. It was the realization, she said, of the 100-year old dream of Theodore Roosevelt. The 26th president was a Republican, the Speaker made sure to point out. He is generally regarded as one of the first people to champion the late-nineteenth-century ideology of Progressivism, even leaving the GOP to form the Progressive Party in 1912, the campaign in which Roosevelt first mentioned a proposal for the protection of home life against illness, poverty, and old age.

What Roosevelt had proposed was fulfilled between the passage of Social Security under FDR and the passage of Medicare under LBJ. This subtle shading of the facts illustrates the core principle of what has become known as the Progressive ideology today; truth is useful only to the point where it can be altered to reinforce the desired outcome, because the desired outcome is more important than a concept called truth.

So why was Speaker Pelosi invoking a Republican endorsement of a massive nationalization of the health care industry?

"We have to do this in partnership," she said, then proceeded to run off a laundry list of social ills the new legislation would solve—legislation, I remind you, that she had just claimed had to be passed before its details could be known. She also admitted that the current health care system, including Medicaid and Medicare, was unsustainable. That was true, but it was only to set up her big finish. This new and improved health care reform was about job creation. Obamacare would eventually create 4 million jobs!

"We have this responsibility," she said with righteous fervor in her voice, "to ensure that health care in America is a right, not a privilege."[1]

The desired outcome of this bill was to take a service for which people traditionally paid and make it free for everyone, whether the person receiving medical care contributed to the cost in any way or not. It sounds good and noble, but it is, in reality, taking a person's investment of the required dedication, education, and the commitment of years of one's life, not to mention thousands of dollars spent, just to get to the point of being licensed to practice professional medical care and telling him or her that the federal government will now determine what their training, their expertise, their talent, and their livelihood are worth. The federal government will now determine which specialty they will study, based on which specialty the federal government determines needs more practitioners. The federal government will tell them where their services are needed. They will see the patients that the federal government tells them they can see. It is not an enlightened approach to ending pain and suffering. It is an inhuman and repressive restriction of freedom and liberty. It is, in fact, theft and the installation of the foundations of a national servitude more reminiscent of 1917 Soviet Russia than 1912 Roosevelt.

Who Are the Progressives

The Progressive movement started and developed between 1890 and 1920 with a flurry of social activism and reform aimed at purifying government of corruption and the influence of political bosses. It was also a push-back against the large gulf that had developed between the fantastically rich and everyone else during the Gilded Age. Never mind the repeated instances in which someone born into poverty had studied and worked hard to attain the American Dream and become one of the wealthy. The fundamental tenet of the Progressive theology was "Fairness." If a wealthy lifestyle could not be easily attained and enjoyed by all, then something needed to be corrected in the society to level the playing field.

Progressives believed that science, technology, and modern management techniques were the solution to society's weaknesses. They believed that human beings could be taught, like obedient children or pets, to develop their full potential as productive and caring members of society and that this potential could be harnessed and best utilized within the framework of a scientifically managed economy under the wise control of a benevolent and Progressive federal government.

Progressives believed in mankind's ability to improve the environment and conditions of life by concerted effort, communal cooperation, and abandonment of traditional, old-fashioned beliefs, heritage, religion, or philosophy promoting personal responsibility, morality, or individual sovereignty. In order to enforce compliance to that mandate, Progressives believed that society had an obligation to accept and encourage the judicious use of governmental authority to intervene in economic and social affairs. As long as you lived your life as a model modern citizen and happily allowed the government to appropriate a fair share of your profits, society would prosper and peace would prevail.

Many of the early Progressives were honest, sincere, and altruistic reformers. They were true believers. Some were blinded by science, some were blinded by religion, and some hoped to reconcile the two. Some just wanted to give back, like Andrew Carnegie's giving back the one thing he knew was truly valuable—the knowledge contained in one of the 1,689 libraries built in the United States between 1889 and 1929 with funding from the Carnegie Foundation. Some wanted to remake the nation in their own image. A number of early Progressive leaders appeared to acknowledge if not openly embrace socialism, communism, or other anti-American doctrines.

Reform in education was a main focus as teaching became a profession and social studies in areas like history, economics, and political organization became social sciences. The Progressives worked hard to reform and modernize the schools at the local level. The era was notable for a dramatic expansion in the number of schools and students served, especially in the fast-growing metropolitan cities. The result was the rapid growth of the educated middle class, who typically were the grassroots supporters of progressive measures because of how and what they were taught. Academic tenure was based on scholarly research and publication in the new scholarly journals and presses, the unintended consequence being the tenured professor's subjective and often political influence on the curriculum, its tone, and its substance. This produced teachers who were left leaning and sympathetic to the utopian dream of a Progressive society.

After almost 100 years of the enlightened influence of Progressives in the American education system, we now have public high schools graduating students who can neither read nor balance a checkbook; we have universities handing out degrees for which there are no legitimate career paths and graduate schools turning out amoral, hedonistic manipulators who view finance, law, and politics as games in which quick riches determine winners and the losers are only the ones who get caught.

Modern Progressives are not derivative of Theodore Roosevelt in any way, shape, or form. If anything, they are antithetical to the Bull Moose Party platform in motive, methods, and morality. Modern Progressive ideology is based on pragmatism: there is no fundamental difference between practical and theoretical reason or between facts and values. In other words, if a proposed solution seems like the right thing to do, then the cost or the social disruption doesn't matter. The end justifies the means. Starting from the world as it is, not as I would like it to be. Never waste a crisis.

What it has evolved into today is a humanistic, narcissistic, amoral belief system that relies on the twisting of truth, stirring of passions, demonizing of opponents, and the use of blatant propaganda. It is a simplistic ideology of black-and-white extremes marked by a religious worship of its leaders and a blind hatred of its opponents.[2]

Modern Progressives preach that we must be inclusive and accepting of each other, but will not countenance anyone who challenges the logic and validity of their thesis. Whether or not this confiscation and redistribution of wealth is equitable or even reasonable is inconsequential; the desired outcome is more important than a concept called reason. Modern Progressives call for universal love and understanding, but will try to destroy anyone who threatens to expose their fiscal Ponzi scheme. They take great pride and often boast openly about their ability to intimidate and denigrate anyone honest enough to question them, their motives, or their own agendas. They shame the innate honor and nobility of the diverse races and lifestyles of those they pretend to champion, all the while ensuring that these very same constituents are led into the hidden slavery of the Progressive Plantation.

The Democratic Party and the moderate wing of the Republican Party have been, in one way or another, compromised by the Progressives, and we are now reaping the fruit of their ignorant and ill-conceived policies. The 2008 economic collapse wasn't caused by free-market capitalism run amok. It was born out of the completely absurd notion that everyone has the right to own a home, whether they can afford one or not. It was Progressive politicians, not Wall Street, who enacted legislation that forced banks to compromise mortgage lending practices that had evolved over 200 years in order to comply with social engineering experiments like the Community Reinvestment Act. In the process of pursuing their utopian pipe dream, they nearly destroyed the wealth preservation vehicle that made this nation the unique Promised Land for people from all parts of the globe. It was Progressives like Barney Frank and Chris Dodd who purposely covered up the warning signs that the mortgage market was overheating from the Fed's easy credit policies. It was arrogant, greedy bankers like Blankfein and Paulson who appeared to throw professional risk management and ethics out the window to wring more profit from the market and protect the interests of their cronies.

Hubris by Any Other Name

The truth is that the Progressive theology is based on hubris and cannot succeed. The *American Heritage Dictionary* defines *hubris* as overbearing pride or arrogance. The Hudson Institute is a nonpartisan policy research organization dedicated to innovative research and analysis that promotes global security, prosperity, and freedom. In 2002, Herbert I. London, the president emeritus of the Hudson Institute, published an essay in *American Outlook* magazine entitled "The Dangers of Hubris." He warned about the historical evidence showing that pride is indeed a prescient indicator of implosion, collapse, complete and utter failure, and defeat. He wrote:

It should also be noted that the administration of Lyndon Johnson was built on the hubristic notion that, given sufficient political support and adequate resources, the government possessed the know-how to eradicate perennial social problems. Remember the War on Poverty? After the expenditure of trillions of dollars beginning in the 1960s, the problems persist today—as does, nonetheless, many people's exaggerated confidence in the manipulative power of experts who in many instances have failed to digest the lessons of history. Good government requires recognition of the limits of public policy, which in turn allows recognition of the corrosive effects of hubris.

It is important, of course, not to confuse hubris with confidence. Faith in one's proven ability is perfectly reasonable, healthy, and often rewarding; it is arrogance and pride that do in successful people, institutions, and nations.[3]

Detroit, Michigan, was one of the Model Cities in LBJ's utopian Great Society. Michigan congressmen John Dingell and John Conyers were around when that comprehensive government makeover was shoved through Congress by veto-proof majorities in the 89th Congress. The program was a noble reinforcing action in the War on Poverty and a colossal failure by any objective standard. This Progressive scheme was not just going to rebuild the minority-dominated neighborhoods of the inner city, it was going to rehabilitate the residents, deliver a smorgasbord of social services, and organize the community into citizen participation groups. The proof that Progressivism is a cultlike religion is in the fact that these are the two longest continuously seated representatives in the House. The people of the Michigan 14th and 15th congressional districts just keep sending these two old bagmen back to D.C., and they keep sending federal dollars back to Detroit for more programs and community organizations. Even in the face of the blighted despair all around them, constituents of these two lifetime politicians still appear on local television news reports proclaiming their absolute conviction that it's all going to be all right because Mr. Obama is going to send them some of his money. I suppose, of course, that is what their community organizers told them.

The current resident of the Oval Office was once one of those community organizers, albeit in Chicago. He is still a true believer in the omnipotence and benevolent potential of a central command-and-control government as preached by Saul Alinsky. In his campaign to get elected president, Barack Obama promised a transparent and responsive government, one that would change the way business was done in the nation's capital. He offered a government in which the people could put their hope, their energy, and their ideas.

Once in power, he took off his mask and revealed his true identity. He installed other Alinsky disciples in his administration; they picked up and resumed the same tired, worn-out, and discredited statist policies and overreaching programs that have been force-fed to the American people, from Hamilton through Lincoln, and made over by Wilson and FDR. Obama called his leftist advisers "czars" and has endeavored to change the United States into a European-style bureaucratic Utopia where everyone is, in one way or another, a worker of the state. Like some alien sleeper cell that was given the signal to activate and pursue their nefarious agenda, the Progressives in the 111th Congress tried every way they could to turn this nation into a central command-and-control economy with the government involved in every aspect of public and private life. Their mantra seemed to be that famous line that Ronald Reagan described as the scariest phrase in America:

We're from the government and we're here to help you.

Adherents to the Progressive dogma are usually well educated; after all, the Progressive movement started out as a scientific, objective approach to social administration of government and education. It was a counter to the Victorian influences of the Gilded Age and sought to eliminate subjective influences like religion, morality, and tradition. Over time, the elimination of spiritual values has produced a humanistic ideology that is emotionally oriented, reactionary, and relentless. It doesn't matter that the Progressive dogma cannot stand up to any objective critical analysis; logic, reason, and critical thought are no longer undergraduate prerequisites at most of our universities. Progressives have become a corrosive, corrupting influence on our society's framework. They have thoroughly infiltrated our academic institutions, infecting our youth with disdain for concepts like individual sovereignty, capitalism, and moral imperatives. They have compromised our political processes, pushing their government-is-god agenda and weakening our republic, devoid of even the smallest amount of common sense or reason.

Let me make it very clear that I am in no way espousing that America should become a theocracy. History has made it very clear that a government built on religion eventually becomes tyrannical in its zealousness for strict adherence to the dogma for which it stands. At the same time, you cannot go to the extreme in the opposite direction, either. There is something metaphysical if not spiritual about man, and the most successful forms of human government have been the ones that acknowledged that fact.

I believe this nation's founding documents are replete with references to a higher power to which man should aspire. Progressivism, in substituting man as the highest and potentially purest prime mover, shows itself for the egomaniacal cult that it really is. The fundamental principles under which the American people have been subjugated for the past century have proven themselves irreparably flawed and unsustainable. The brightest and the best have become the dazed and confused, and the only global unity that the Progressive agenda can deliver is one of misery, suffering, and lowered expectations. They have become addicted to the power and the control, declaring war on our inalienable rights to life, liberty, and the pursuit of happiness.

This is a war that we must and shall win with better ideas and proven performance. The odds appear to be stacked against us, but that is just an illusion by the popular media, which now functions openly as the Progressive propaganda machine. Major television networks that used to pride themselves in getting the story behind the news and educating the American viewer about what their government was really doing now serve as perpetual spin doctors for the administration. Practically every nightly network news anchor reads almost verbatim from the same lead talking points. Do they think we are really that stupid? Yes. They do.

Frankly, it doesn't matter how many of the talking heads say the same thing; that doesn't make it true. It isn't true that you cannot succeed without government assistance. It isn't moral for you to be forced to share part of what you have produced and earned with those who choose less than freedom and liberty. Life is not fair. People are different. Everyone does have an opportunity. There are winners and there are losers.

The fact is that you do not have to allow them to manipulate you with fear. The fact that they control the bulk of the media outlets does not mean they have total control of the message. The advance of technology has made their standard operating procedure of plausible deniability inoperative. It is impossible now to say one thing, do another, and get away cleanly. It is almost impossible to plant rumor and innuendo to marginalize your opposition without somebody's blowing the whistle on the Internet. You can no longer pretend that you are benevolent and humanitarian when your policies undercut potential and entrap generations in financial serfdom. That's why they are trotting out legislative proposals like the "Fairness Doctrine" and the "Protecting Cyberspace as a National Asset Act." They want to shut you up.

For years, Progressives have convinced everyone that they were nicer, smarter, and cooler than anyone else. We have discovered that is not even close to the reality. You may be a well-read movie star, but if you are a high school dropout, there is no way your opinion on international finance and geopolitics is more valid than mine. I believe in a world where everyone has the same opportunity and the government serves and protects the people instead of punishing and abusing them.

They are the Progressives, and they are the enemy. They can be left or right, red or blue, east or west, rich or poor, Democrat or Republican; it is their ideology that has become a threat to our existence. You may claim through organizations like MoveOn.org that more people really do believe in the validity of socialist principles and that free-market capitalism is dead, but we know it just isn't true.

And there are more of us than you.

The Bankers

If you listen to the news, read financial blogs, or talk to your friends at the local watering hole, you would think that everyone on Wall Street got rich at the expense of the American taxpayer, unless your watering hole was The Irish Punt or Moran's in lower Manhattan. Some of the familiar faces are not around anymore. A lot of people, some friends of mine, have lost their jobs in the financial industry and watched their fortunes dissipate. All of this carnage was due to the deliberate actions of just a small group of who believed themselves a cut above the rest, who thought of themselves as smarter, wiser, craftier than the competition, full of so much hubris that they believed themselves to be too large, too rich, and too connected to ever face more than a slap on the wrist or, at most, a fine.

Too much power has been concentrated in the hands of too few people for too long. When Sydney Weinberg organized the best executives from the best companies to come to Washington and serve on the War Production Board during World War II, he was doing his public service. When Lloyd Blankfein threw a hissy fit on the weekend of September 13–14, 2008, and demanded that Goldman Sachs be paid the money it was due as one of AIG's biggest creditors,[4] that was corruption. Blankfein had played the Big Short. It is now public knowledge that he knew Goldman had bet both ends against the middle, selling garbage investments in AAA-rated wrapping paper out of one side of the store while purchasing a credit default swap out of the other side, in case the purchaser started wondering what the awful smell was. Blankfein had the gall to tell a London newspaper that he was "doing God's work." If Mario Puzo had written a novel about Blankfein, it would probably be more aptly called "doing the Godfather's work."

Goldman acted with apparent impunity because they were, in fact, running the show. Treasury Secretary Henry Paulson was their boy, and he was clearly using the auspices of his office to make sure that Goldman's bad bets were covered. If Henry Paulson was playing on the up and up, why did he not demand the resignation of Lloyd Blankfein before arranging for Goldman Sachs to get their swaps covered by AIG? Hadn't he done as much with Jon Corzine? Wouldn't that have been the responsible, prudent thing to do? After all, that was the reason Goldman Sachs was in trouble in the first place. And it happened on Blankfein's watch.

The revolving door between Goldman Sachs and the U.S. Treasury Department needs to be shut down once and for all. It has become apparent that, under recent leadership, Goldman Sachs has become a bad actor whose name keeps coming up whenever there is a financial crisis. I think it is interesting to note the Blankfein lived in Winthrop House while at Harvard. Other notable Winthrop alumni included United States Senator Edward Kennedy (D-MA), Federal Reserve chairman Ben Bernanke, Clinton administration Treasury Secretary Robert Rubin, and United States Representative Barney Frank (D-MA). What's the old adage about "Where there's smoke, there's fire?" In Goldman's case, the smoke has the distinctive scent of brimstone. One cannot help but speculate about a single, handwritten file somewhere in the bowels of Goldman's storage facility labeled "Clarksdale Crossing agreement." How else can you explain an organization that seems to be present at most of the largest financial crises in the last 80 years and yet manages to remain unscathed? Some would say they've even prospered. You would think they would lay low for a while until the heat blows over.

Not Goldman Sachs. They've hired a team of uber-lobbyists to work both sides of the political aisle and meet with top officials in the White House and at the regulatory agencies. Blankfein himself went and met with SEC chairman Mary Shapiro. It seems the Volcker Rule contained in the new Dodd-Frank Wall Street Reform and Consumer Protection Act is not going to be fair to them. It could cost them an estimated $3.7 billion dollars in annual income and billions more in future business.[5] Well, isn't that a shame?

What happens if Goldman Sachs does not get its way this time? What if the American people choose to return to the rule of law and revoke the "Get Out of Jail Free" card under which these bankers have been operating? Blankfein has gotten pretty good at figuring out ways to hedge the firm's bets. He recently trotted out staff economist Andrew Tilton to give everyone a rosy forecast of the economy for the next six quarters. It's like a scene from the *Wizard of Oz* where the giant head tells everyone to pay no attention to the balding, beady-eyed little man behind the curtain. Meanwhile, a conversation is overheard at one of the Wall Street watering holes by a bartender who misses one of his old customers. It seems that Gollum is planning to move U.S. operations to Singapore. Why should this be a surprise to anyone?

The Progressives in Congress and the White House think they can just cozy up to Wall Street, take nearly a million dollars in campaign contributions from Goldman alone, and then bully and manipulate them the way they do their academic and business cohorts. They are overlooking an underlying financial principle, one that was defined most succinctly by former general and Secretary of State Colin Powell in a speech to the American Chamber of Commerce in South Africa in 2002.

> Capital is a coward. It flees from corruption and bad policies, conflict, and unpredictability. It shuns ignorance, disease, and illiteracy. Capital goes where it is welcomed and where investors can be confident of a return on the resources they have put at risk. It goes to countries where women can work, children can read, and entrepreneurs can dream.[6]

The Progressives may dream of a day when the world may be as one and everyone sits around holding hands and singing "Kumbaya," but nobody is going to finance that plan voluntarily. There is no return on investment. Progressives don't care. They not only believe in using other people's money, they view it as their administrative commission.

Politics as Usual

Speaking of Barney Frank, when Henry Paulson dictated his "perfect memory" account of the economic meltdown, he had Frank write the foreword. He claimed it was because they trusted each other. Paulson was directly involved in pouring funding fuel on the economic wildfire, and Frank failed to control the fiscal arsonists at Fannie and Freddie. I guess they should trust each other. They had been involved in starting the fire and were damned lucky to get it as much under control as they did.

Frank is a fiscally conservative, socially progressive Democrat who teamed up with former Connecticut senator Christopher Dodd to pass legislation designed to "promote the financial stability of the United States by improving accountability and transparency in the financial system, to end 'too big to fail,' to protect the American taxpayer by ending bailouts, to protect consumers from abusive financial services practices, and for other purposes."

It is that phrase ". . . and for other purposes . . ." that should cause most Americans heartburn over their economic future. Like nearly every piece of legislation that the federal government introduces to close the barn door after the horse has taken off, this law doesn't do very much to reduce systemic risk; it does, however, greatly expand the central government bureaucratic control over the financial industry. The short title was the Dodd-Frank Wall Street Reform and Consumer Protection Act. It should have been called the Wesley Mouch Wall Street Reform and Moocher Protection Act because it reads like it was written by the incompetent and treacherous lobbyist from Ayn Rand's 1957 novel *Atlas Shrugged*.

Title I of this massive overhaul of the financial sector establishes the Financial Stability Oversight Council. This esteemed group is chaired by the secretary of the Treasury, who effectively has veto power over the rest of the Council. Other members are the chairman of the Board of Governors of the Federal Reserve System, the comptroller of the currency, the chairman of the Securities and Exchange Commission (SEC), the chairperson of the Federal Deposit Insurance Corporation (FDIC), the chairperson of the Commodity Futures Trading Commission (CFTC), the Director of the Federal Housing Finance Agency, the Chairman of the National Credit Union Administration Board (NCUA), and an independent member appointed by the president, by and with the advice and consent of the Senate, having insurance expertise. It also includes the director of the newly established Bureau of Consumer Financial Protection (BCFP). True to form, the Democrats' answer to any problem is the creation of more government bureaucracy with more power to regulate and control.

So we're going to take the same people who did not protect us from systemic risk and put them together in a new economic star chamber, where they will magically transform into a financial Justice League? Not to worry, we are also going to create the Office of Financial Research (OFR) to do all of the Council's heavy lifting. The OFR will collect data from member agencies and market participants to help the Council determine which companies are "systemically important." Some lower-level bureaucrat sitting in an office in Washington, D.C., will now determine which companies are winners and which ones are losers.

Who will determine whether the failure of your company will pose a systemic risk? Well, ultimately the Treasury secretary, but only after the recommendation has been made and approved by a super-majority of the boards of the Federal Reserve and the FDIC. Once that happens, the new Orderly Liquidation Authority mechanism can kick in, permitting the FDIC to seize control of your company and proceed to liquidate it. It doesn't matter if your situation may be seasonal or due to some temporary situation that you can work through, if your company has assets that "are, or are likely to be, less than its obligations to creditors and others," the Liquidation Authority can be exercised against you.

This new legislation makes the Federal Reserve the new financial supercop with heightened authority and enforcement powers, but doesn't address who regulates the Fed. This is where the banks have to dance with the one who brought them to the ball. In addition to the Volcker Rule, which prohibits proprietary trading and bans hedge fund and private equity activity at banks, there is page after page after page of detailed rules for banks and other insured depositories. That's why Goldman Sachs wants an extension; they became a bank after the Troubled Asset Relief Program (TARP) bailout.

The law makes a decent attempt at restoring integrity to the securitization, credit rating processes, and derivatives, but bungles some definitions. It creates five new regulatory entities and establishes a loan-loss reserve fund. In memory of the tragic death of Long-Term Capital Management, the law lumps all private equity investors with the hedge fund managers and eliminates the private adviser exemption. Everyone must register with the SEC—except, of course, those who have exemptions and, just like Obamacare, there are numerous exemptions. It is a patchwork quilt that seems to have something for just about everybody.

The authority of the SEC is broadened with respect to issues of corporate governance and executive compensation. The Bureau of Consumer Financial Protection has been created with extensive authority to regulate and enforce substantive standards for any person who engages in the offer or sale of a financial product or service to any consumer. Only in Washington, D.C., is an agency named for consumer protection when its purpose is to control who buys and who sells, but you know those Progressives. They love to throw a banzai wave of legislation at a problem; if somebody questions the legality of some of their proposals and throws them out, they will still have made inroads.

An example of this is one of the most disturbing parts of the Dodd-Frank Wall Street Reform Act. Section 750 establishes an inter-agency working group of department chieftains, this one chaired by the chairman of the CFTC. Group members include the secretary of agriculture, the secretary of the Treasury, the chairman of the SEC, the administrator of the Environmental Protection Agency, the chair-man of the Federal Energy Regulatory Commission, the commissioner of the Federal Trade Commission, and the administrator of the Energy Information Administration.

Part B of Section 750 provides the interagency group with "such administrative support services as are necessary to enable the inter-agency group to carry out the functions of the interagency group under this section."

What are the functions of this esteemed group?

They are to consult with "representatives of exchanges, clearing-houses, self-regulatory bodies, major carbon market participants, consumers, and the general public, as the interagency group deter-mines to be appropriate" and then report the results in a study of "the oversight of existing and prospective carbon markets to ensure an efficient, secure, and transparent carbon market, including oversight of spot markets and derivative markets."

I'm not sure the interagency group would determine this to be appropriate, but, as a member of the general public, I have a question.

Why?

Why is Washington, D.C., ignoring the fact that the entire man-made global warming threat has been exposed as nothing less than a global power grabbing financial scam? Why are we writing a blank check to create yet another administrative support services office with a broad and vaguely defined mandate? Why are we giving these important political appointees more staff to do their bidding and more meetings to attend? Why are legitimate and accredited climate scien-tists and meteorological researchers not being consulted about the feasibility of creating a fantasy market in which to trade leniencies for nonexistent man-made global warming? How is this expenditure going to correct what is wrong with our economy? Why hasn't the Environmental Protection Agency issued a public statement disavowing Al Gore and the UN-sponsored climate-change agenda? Who is paying for this? More importantly, who is getting paid for this?

Outside Influences

Who is responsible for the flood of legislation that was passed by the 111th Congress? Bills having more than a thousand pages of detailed rules and regulations seemed to appear overnight. The Democrats found themselves in the indefensible position of voting for laws that they themselves hadn't even read. The answer, of course, is that they were taking their cues from the minions of K Street, the legions of lawyers and former government staffers who make up the lobbyist contingent in Washington, D.C.

Lobbyists are generally organized based on their interest or patrons. There are trade and professional organizations like the American Bankers Association or the Association of Trial Lawyers of America, corporations, labor unions, citizen's groups like the American Association of Retired Persons (AARP) or the National Rifle Association (NRA), intergovernmental associations like the U.S. Conference of Mayors or the National Governors' Association, and, finally, charitable and religious groups like the Family Research Council or the Girl Scouts of America.

The lobbyist is ostensibly a resource for the legislator, providing background research, statistics, and polling results on topics being considered. They attempt to influence legislators' votes on certain issues in order to gain a favorable tax status or business climate for their clients. In the cases of Obamacare and Dodd-Frank, for example, it is obvious that the lobbyists are also writing the legislation, too. In John R. Wright's 2003 political science classic, *Interest Groups and Congress*, his central thesis is that interest groups achieve influence through the acquisition and strategic transmission of information that legislators need to make good policy and get reelected.[7] According to the Center for Responsive Politics, there were 12,998 registered lobbyists in the nation's capital who spent a combined $3.5 billion trying to influence legislation on behalf of their clients.[8] How does a constituent from the district compete with that?

It is fairly obvious that this is an activity that has gotten totally out of control despite efforts on the part of politicians to rein it in. On his first day in office, January 21, 2009, President Obama issued Executive Order 13490, Ethics Commitments by Executive Branch Personnel. In it he laid out rules for how his administration was going to conduct itself and to curb the undue influence over the Oval Office by lobbyists. He also froze the salaries of White House staffers making more than $100,000 per year.

"Families are tightening their belts, and so should Washington," Obama said.[9]

It is historically important to note how quickly that message changed from one of transparency and accountability to late night votes and runaway spending.

Money and power make a heady cocktail. Both must be handled responsibly individually, even more so when combined. It is our constitutional right to petition the government for a redress of grievances, and people have assembled themselves into interest groups to make sure that their interests are promoted, protected, or provided for in legislation. People have the right to support this lobbying activity in whatever way they wish. I don't believe in prohibition or censorship. Ideas should be free to stand or fall on their own merit. My concern is when the motives behind the idea are misrepresented or the true identities of the group's supporters are hidden. Free speech is only free insofar as it is responsible and honest.

It becomes especially dubious when the influence peddlers are being funded by organizations or individuals with ulterior motives. Nongovernmental agencies and privately funded organizations exist on both sides of the political spectrum. The Koch Brothers, David and Charles, established the Charles G. Koch Charitable Foundation with the mission of advancing social progress and well-being through the development, application, and dissemination of "the Science of Liberty." The Koch brothers' various foundations have provided millions of dollars to a variety of organizations, usually libertarian or conservative organizations such as Americans for Prosperity Foundation, the Cato Institute, the Mercatus Center, the Institute for Humane Studies, Citizens for a Sound Economy, the Institute for Justice, the Alexis de Tocqueville Institution, the Institute for Energy Research, the Foundation for Research on Economics and the Environment, Heritage Foundation, the Manhattan Institute, the George C. Marshall Institute, the Reason Foundation, and the American Enterprise Institute.

On the other side of the political divide stands the Black Knight himself. Schwartz György is his Hungarian birth name, which literally translates to Black landowner or knight. His father changed the family name to Soros because Georgie Schwarz sounded just too Jewish for the late 1930s in Budapest. At 13, his first job was advising fellow Jews that they were going to be deported. He's been very good at seizing opportunity—and squeezing profit—out of human shortcomings and crises. In fact, the guiding philosophy of his life is reflexivity, a school of thought based on the precept that all human constructs are flawed. George Soros has made his fortune on bringing down human constructs. Forbes consistently lists him as one of the 50 richest people in the world. While the Koch Brothers spread their fortunes widely, seeking to protect and restore classical liberalism and free enterprise, Soros is very precise with his expenditures, boring down into the foundation of American society, judiciously undermining the concept of a traditional American society with a Progressive call for open society and economic justice.

An example is a Soros organization called the Open Society Foundation, which has a fund called the Democracy and Power Fund. The fund invests in projects aimed at advocacy of issues and building organizations aimed at inspiring and activating people of color, young people, immigrants, and low-income communities. The fund aims to expand access to democracy for all and build power for lasting social justice and systemic change. One example is a $100,000 grant in 2008, which was given to support the New Organizing Institute's (NOI) efforts to provide technology training to nonprofit organizations, which would help ensure that their work makes the most effective and efficient use of Web-based and other technologies. NOI is an umbrella organization with expertise in developing the practice of engagement organizing and leaders who are great at it.

At its core, America is built on one transcendent principle: democracy. Ask any schoolchild, any senior, any immigrant, any conservative or progressive or anyone in between, and they will tell you that we are a nation "of the people, by the people, for the people." For over 200 years, America has risen to the top of the world because of this principle. Because democracy works. On the whole, "the people" make better choices for themselves than any *dictator, aristocracy or CEO.*[10]

The italics are mine; so much for inclusion, love, and understanding. This group is using technology to unite and solidify a Progressive army, under the banner of democracy, to replace the federal republican form of government and a capitalistic economy with a socialistic central statist government, swept into power by mob rule based on class envy, naïveté, and hubris. It is the coming revolution. The Black Knight bides his time and waits for America to collapse in a super bubble.[11]

Good people everywhere feel frightened and overwhelmed by the Progressive onslaught, but now is not the time to cower. Now is the time to rise up and launch the counteroffensive. There are primary campaigns to wage, state and local races to contest, ballot referendums to decide, and local school boards to man. Our special forces are an informed and energized electorate and our ammunition is our ballots and our resources. Whether it is money or time, everyone can participate in this peaceful and patriotic civil uprising. You must learn to recognize the rhetoric, dissect the disinformation, and know the face of the Enemy. When you step into the voting booth, from school board to county commissioner to state representative to presidential election, you must visualize that face. And when you see the whites of their eyes, pull the lever and cast your vote.

Notes

1. Transcript of speech by Speaker of the House, Nancy Pelosi, Office of the Speaker of the House, March 23, 2009. Retrieved from www.prnewswire .com/news-releases/pelosi-remarks-at-the-2010-legislative-conference-for -national-association-of-counties-87131117.html.

2. Ann Coulter, *Demonic: How the Liberal Mob Is Endangering America* (New York: Crown Forum, 2011), 4–6.

3. Herbert I. London, "The Dangers of Hubris," *American Outlook*, April 7, 2002. Retrieved from www.herblondon.org/1384/the-dangers-of-hubris.

4. Matt Taibbi, *Griftopia* (New York: Spiegel & Grau, Random House, 2010), 155–119.

5. Lauren LaCapra, "Goldman Lobbying Hard to Weaken Volcker Rule," Reuters News Wire, New York. Retrieved from www.reuters.com/article/2011/05/04/us-goldman-volcker-idUSTRE7434PZ20110504.

6. Colin Powell, Speech at the American Chamber of Commerce, Johannesburg, South Africa, September 18, 2002. Retrieved from http://pretoria.usembassy.gov/wwwhambhume020918.html.

7. John R. Wright, *Interest Groups and Congress: Lobbying, Contributions, and Influence* (New York: Longman Classics, 2003), 2.

8. The Center for Responsive Politics, Lobbying Database. OpenSecrets.org web site. Retrieved from www.opensecrets.org/lobby/.

9. *NBC News and News Services Report*, "Obama's First Day: Pay Freeze, Lobbying Rules. MSNBC.com web site, www.msnbc.msn.com/cleanprint/CleanPrintProxy.aspx?unique=1309481092864.

10. From the web site of the New Organizing Institute (2011). Retrieved from http://neworganizing.com/about/what-we-do/.

11. George Soros, *The New Paradigm for Financial Markets: The Credit Crisis of 2008 and What It Means* (New York: Perseus Books Group, 2009), 93–94.

Chapter 5

Warfare, Not Terrorism

Concern for man and his fate must always form the chief interest of all technical endeavors. Never forget this in the midst of your diagrams and equations.

—Albert Einstein (1879–1955), physicist

I am not a big believer in conspiracy theories. It has always seemed to me to be a far too convenient way to either assign or deflect blame for something that is beyond our ability to either understand or control. While I find the revolving door between Wall Street and Washington troubling and personally feel no small animus toward the recent management decisions of Goldman Sachs, I don't buy into the theory of some talk show hosts and commentators that Lloyd Blankfein has the number "666" tattooed on the back of his head. Of course, I've never had the opportunity to examine Mr. Blankfein's head that closely. I can testify with a great deal of certainty that there isn't anything on the top of his head.

That being the case, as a nation we have been conditioned to be dangerously naïve to the darker forces that operate beyond the spotlight of the mainstream media. We have been blinded to what has been developing throughout the world. An analysis of our current crisis that focuses only on the past few years of economic activity fails to reveal the history and context that are vital to reaching an understanding of the root cause. What we have been experiencing is not the result of an unforeseen economic crash that appeared out of the blue with the collapse of the housing market. It was not caused by people who bought homes they couldn't afford. To even blame it on a small group of greedy bankers, while essentially accurate, also misses the most vital point.

This crisis is the direct result of a perfect storm of conditions that permitted a finite number of highly placed people to game the system and effectively stage a strategic economic attack on the existence of the American middle class and democracy worldwide. The stock market and economy have been manipulated by an imperial, international banking cartel known as the Bank for International Settlements (BIS) in Basel, Switzerland, which has dictated rules on accounting for value, reserve ratios, tax shelters, and international money movement. Our own engines of prosperity have been made into weapons of mass oppression to impose order and exploit the masses. This crisis boldly manifests the evolution of the fascist One World theology reasserting itself as the dominant global ideology.

Any fairytale notions of the United States being a democratic republic built on the rule of law have been utterly dispelled. People just don't want to believe it. To do so would admit our complicity in our own demise, but it doesn't change the facts illustrated in the evidence. By any measure you want to consult, our society is suffering decay on every front. We are physically one of the unhealthiest, most obese and cancer-ridden societies on earth. Intellectually, our literacy test scores are falling, and American innovation is becoming the exception instead of the rule. We lead the world in violent crime and drug use; privately operated prisons have become a growth industry. Our political leaders seem to be incapable of providing any new solutions, and the answers they do offer only seem to exacerbate the problem they are supposed to address.

On March 18, 2010, President Obama signed into law a $17.5 billion jobs bill called the Hiring Incentives to Restore Employment

Act of 2010 (HIRE). The president said this bill would jump-start hiring and help small business owners. The hiring incentives of the bill included $17.5 billion in tax cuts, business credits, and subsidies for state and local construction bonds, and moved $20 billion into the highway trust fund for spending on highway and transit programs. This translated into union road construction companies throwing up orange barrels and repaving hundreds of miles of the federal interstate highway system, much of which was in need of little, if any, repair. State and local highways and bridges that were literally crumbling benefitted very little under this make-work charade. Very few new jobs were created at all. On June 13, 2011, President Obama's Council on Jobs and Competitiveness met in Durham, North Carolina. When it was pointed out to him that the federal government's permitting requirements, specifically those of the EPA, often delay construction and infrastructure projects for months and sometimes years, Obama smiled and glibly interjected, "Shovel-ready was not as . . . uh . . . shovel-ready as we expected."

Not to be dissuaded by the reality of his failed policies, Mr. Obama called a joint session of Congress on Thursday, September 8, 2011, and laid out a new jobs plan that he claimed was a patchwork of programs that had already gained bipartisan support and was "fully funded." He demanded, 17 different times during the speech, that Congress immediately "pass this bill," despite the fact that no one in the legislature had seen it, much less read it. No wonder Representative Pelosi was so quick to stand and applaud at every opportunity. The nationally televised prime time speech was characterized across the political spectrum as tired, unoriginal, evasive in detail, misleading in cost, arrogant, and presumptuous. When legislators got to look into the details of the president's proposal the next day, it was revealed once and for all that the Emperor has no ideas. The program was paid for by more taxes and heavily biased toward union construction jobs.The help for small-business owners in the HIRE Act was just as anemic. The bill exempted businesses that hired unemployed workers from paying the payroll security tax through December 2010. Critics of the bill said that it would have little impact on employment, estimating that it would possibly add 250,000 jobs by the end of 2010. The Associated Press even pointed out that this was an insignificant figure against the 8.4

million jobs that had been lost since the recession began and the bill was panned as just another in a seemingly endless stream of acts destined to expand the government payroll to infinity. Nobody cared about it and, apparently, nobody read it, either.

Hidden in the 48 pages of this seemingly innocuous piece of legislation was something that should have been trumpeted on every news program and newspaper headline across the nation. It was called "Offset Provisions—Subtitle A—Foreign Account Tax Compliance." It read like something lifted from an old Soviet Union Economic Planning Handbook. It required foreign banks to withhold 30 percent of all outgoing capital flows and disclose the full details of nonexempt account holders to the IRS or close the account. Nonparticipation would, no doubt, be dealt with through the BIS, so global compliance was expected. If you didn't like having your secret Swiss bank account suddenly opened to the IRS, you were labeled a Recalcitrant Account Holder. That meant you failed to comply with "reasonable requests" for the information. I'm sure such a label would have a negative impact on your credit score.

Fortunately, the 112th Congress repealed some of the more onerous passages in this blatant attempt to grab more and more of the wealth earned by citizens of this country; but don't relax, it hasn't stopped them from hatching yet another wealth redistribution program. Already, President Obama's administration is talking about federalizing 401(k) retirement programs. This is just political doubletalk for stealing the money you have now and replacing it with government-backed IOUs that will repay you, somehow, sometime in the future—paid with, in all probability, inflation-diminished worthless paper currency.

They say this measure is necessary to pay off the debt while at the same time they are spending more money every day. Nobody in Washington, D.C., seems to grasp the simple concept that you cannot spend your way out of debt. They seem to be totally clueless that it is federal spending that is pushing our economy closer and closer to the precipice. They may come on the television news program and say that they understand the need to make some cuts, but then they go back into the committee rooms and defend their pet projects or attach riders that drain even more of our tax dollars for the enrichment of their campaign contributors. How is such reckless and grossly immature behavior given credence? What kind of deranged mind conceives legislation that games the financial system in such a way as to make it impossible for the average American to invest in anything but Treasuries?

When Reverend Jeremiah Wright proclaimed that America's chickens had come home to roost, he was more right than the talking heads on Fox News or CNN dared to admit. The founders of this nation never conceived of a professional political class. They would have found it unthinkable that an entire industry of facilitators and parasitic lobbyists would spring up to manipulate and feed the power lust of the politicos with campaign contributions, resort vacations, sex, drugs, fame, or whatever other fuel their egos crave.

For nearly a century after the bankers got control of the nation's money supply, the engine of American industry provided enough profit to meet everyone's needs. As long as there was a conflict somewhere in the world, there were investment opportunities. As long as there were investment opportunities, there were jobs created, goods produced, commodities consumed, and a quality of life enjoyed. The engine hummed right along, and whenever it sputtered, Wall Street would concoct a new recipe, which K Street would feed to the Fat Cats on the Hill. A subsidy here, a tariff there, a tax loophole for this company, a little tweak of the foreign policy and—voila!—the engine started purring again.

Hamilton wanted the rich to be the underwriters of the government's spending. He was an intelligent and creative man who was able to convince millions of people that meanings existed beyond the words that had been written. Yet even he could never have imagined the rise of a cult so brazen, so demonically avaricious that common sense and the principles of risk and reward were swept away in a mad scramble to come up with the perfect, foolproof quantitative formula for squeezing gold out of thin air. Devising new securitization schemes became the quest for the perfect score. Bonus checks and stock options became the codpieces and powdered wigs of the New Aristocracy. Everyone lost sight of the basic fundamentals that separate us from the primates—that we live to build a community that protects the weak, honors the responsible, and rewards the righteous.

The economic imperialism that has blown back on the United States and Europe has been brewing and bubbling for decades and can be directly traced back to the end of World War II to the birth of the Central Intelligence Agency (CIA), the International Monetary Fund (IMF), and the World Bank. Those of us who have been paying attention to economic imperial operations that have been carried out against countries throughout the world find this scenario all too familiar. The IMF and global bankers have conquered the second and third world, and they have now moved on to countries within the first world. Western European and American working classes are in their crosshairs now. Economic and societal indicators, along with recent G-20 policy decisions, clearly demonstrate that they are carrying out and escalating systemic economic attacks throughout Europe and the United States.

To state it plainly, I believe the United States government is being systematically taken over by a revolutionary network. They call themselves Progressives, but we know they are really leftist radicals, dedicated to the demise of the free-market capitalist system. They have co-opted and bought off leaders of both the Republican and Democratic parties, established a dominant role in all three branches of government and thoroughly co-opted the mainstream media.

We are engaged in a war. It is an economic war over our sovereignty as human beings with inalienable rights to life, liberty, and the pursuit of happiness. The "pursuit of happiness" means the right to create wealth through our labor and to enjoy the fruits thereof. The battle now is over who has the moral, the ethical, and the legal right to the fruits of our labor. Are we to be free, or are we to be slaves? Just whose money is it anyway?

In just the past three years we have lost an unprecedented amount of national wealth. Trillions upon trillions of our tax dollars have been looted or lost by Wall Street, used to finance the endless wars and fund enormous subsidies for the most profitable global corporations. Never before in the history of civilization has a nation been so thoroughly and systematically fleeced. This is all the result of a coordinated economic attack by a global banking cartel against 99 percent of the U.S. population. The unintended consequence of this assault is that the fallout has sickened the global economy, as well.

Until we can become politically intelligent enough to see this as the reality and root cause of our current crisis, we will not be able to overcome it. Our living standards will continue to decline, and we will all be sentenced to a slow death in a neofeudal system built on debt slavery. It is a fact that the average American is horribly naïve to just how depraved, corrupt, and addicted to power this politico-banking cartel is. Through their control and domination of the mass media, they have kept their crimes against humanity out of public consciousness. We have been shielded from the global devastation and death toll that they have already wrought. The result is an unsuspecting population having their future ripped out from under them, right before their eyes, without any organized defense or resistance.

Let me illustrate just how entrenched the Money Changers have become. The BIS was established in Basel, Switzerland, in 1930 to administer reparations payments imposed on Germany by the Treaty of Versailles following the First World War. The mission of the BIS has evolved to that of arbiter of monetary policy administered by its member central banks in their respective nations. In other words, a bank in Switzerland ostensibly determines how the United States and every other member country will manage its own money supply, interest rates, currency restrictions, valuations, and various other aspects of its internal economy. In the bank's founding charter, the Swiss government grants it sovereign immunity: the "buildings or parts of buildings and surrounding land which, whoever may be the owner thereof, are used for the purposes of the Bank shall be inviolable."[1]

This is not a governmental agency or even a diplomatic embassy! The BIS is a private financial entity owned by a cartel of 57 other central banks, which has been elevated to international sovereign status. It is *the* central bank of the world's central banks, a commercial enterprise. There are many in the financial community who will object to calling the BIS a private bank, but that is purely semantics. It is owned by private banking cartels. That makes it private. How does this affect you? The BIS dictates the rules by which the vast majority of the global financial system will operate, including mandating the rules that determine generally accepted accounting principles (GAAP) that we use in our daily business activities. It executes these mandates in this country through the Federal Reserve System. The BIS is not accountable to any government in the world.

The Fed, itself a private banking cartel, has shown a complete disregard and contempt for the members of Congress who are supposed to be monitoring its activities. It has consistently resisted calls for transparency in its policy formation and its execution of monetary control. The chairman of the Federal Reserve may take a call from the president, but the president cannot tell the Fed what it will and will not do. The president may appoint the chairman of the Federal Reserve System and its Board of Governors, but he does so from a predetermined list of candidates given to him by the Fed itself. Frankenstein's monster is not only alive but very much in control!

The Return of Civil Disobedience

As the global banking cartel continues to control domestic political policy, I believe the next phase of this crisis is appearing in a return of 1960s-era protests and demonstrations that will continue to grow and, when inevitably downplayed or ignored by Washington, will potentially escalate into mass violence. The Army War College has stated publicly that the Pentagon is, in fact, currently discussing possible responses for "violent, strategic dislocation inside the United States" and "widespread civil violence" due to natural disaster or *economic collapse*.[2] These professional strategists have seen the signs of what is to come. Rioting and violence as a result of economic turmoil have already been experienced in many countries throughout the world. The fact that it hasn't yet happened within the United States does not mean it cannot or will not.

There are many theories as to why there has been so little resistance from the U.S. population toward an increasingly hostile and antithetical expansion of governmental power thus far, and several factors play into it. Part of it is the intentional dumbing down of the American people by a highly politicized and ideologically corrupt education system. The façade of political neutrality among academia at all levels of the public education system has been thoroughly exposed for the sham that it is. Educators in America are

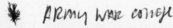

ARMY WAR COLLEGE

overwhelmingly liberal, if not outright vengeful Progressives, in their personal political philosophies and over the past 30 years have been increasingly disposed to indoctrinating students with their statist, anti-capitalist bias. This leftist brainwashing is further ingrained in the overwhelming majority of our colleges and universities. The result is at least two generations of voters who have been taught that it is only natural to expect the rich to engage in greedy, selfish, and antisocial behavior. This anticapitalist mantra is reinforced by the mesmerizing omnipresence of the media, which is almost exclusively populated by zealous proselytizers of a leftist, politically correct dogma. Journalism today seems to be more interested in stirring controversy and steering public opinion than in revealing truth and relating cause and effect.

The most significant factor is the numbing effect of government-sponsored social safety net programs. As pointed out earlier, these programs were largely instituted under Lyndon Johnson's Great Society experiment. We now have three generations of people who have grown up or grown old subsisting on government largesse. These programs have expanded to provide a wide range of subsidies, training, and other forms of relief that have been vital in preventing people from resorting to extreme measures. Currently, more than 52 million Americans are receiving life-sustaining assistance from government antipoverty programs, such as food stamps, unemployment benefits, Medicaid, and Medicare. This has put a terrible strain on a social safety net system that was designed to be temporary and to handle signifi-cantly fewer people. This system has now been drained of all reserve resources over the past two years, and is obviously not sustainable under current economic and political conditions.

As social safety net programs have been drained of reserves, many U.S. citizens have also been burning through their personal savings. Over the past few years, the percentage of Americans living paycheck to paycheck has dramatically increased. In 2007, 43 percent of Ameri-cans were living on the edge, paycheck-to-paycheck. In 2008, the percentage increased to 49 percent. In 2009, the number skyrocketed up to 61 percent. As of June 2010, a Harris poll conducted on behalf of CareerBuilder revealed that number has exploded to a shocking 77 percent![3] This means in our nation of 310 million citizens, 239 million

Americans are one setback away from economic ruin and millions more are in danger of having to rely on government assistance for survival.

As this prolonged economic crisis continues, the safety nets, already overwhelmed, will inevitably break down. The average American is caught in the crossfire of an economic firefight as the governments of once prosperous industrialized states, like Wisconsin, Indiana, Ohio, and Michigan, have had to implement budget cuts to both state welfare programs and public employee benefit plans.

The 52 million Americans currently surviving on antipoverty programs are gradually going to have their government assistance reduced. The 239 million people now living paycheck to paycheck are beginning to realize that things are not going to be getting any better. This is the new normal, and things are not going to return to the way they were. Stress and pressure are already beginning to build. Social unrest and outbursts of violence will begin to bubble up to the surface. The ruling elite will no longer be able to maintain power by simply deceiving the masses via mainstream media propaganda.

Organized labor and government-supported community organizations are playing a role in the disintegration of our society as well. They have formed a public pact to fight for their own survival, even if it means bringing down the nation's economy. At a fund-raiser held in May 2011 for U.S. Senator Debbie Stabenow, a Democrat career politician from Michigan, the president of the United Auto Workers, Bob King, gave a speech heavily laden with biblical references. He referred to Republicans as "antidemocratic" and "anti-Christian" as he called for workers to take their destiny into their own hands and bring about a "new social justice movement in America."[4] Stabenow, the junior senator from the state hardest hit by the failing fortunes of the auto industry, has long been known as a puppet for organized labor and has one of the most liberal voting records in the Senate, according to the ratings published by the American Conservative Union and Project Vote Smart. That much of the economic devastation in Michigan occurred on her watch and can be directly attributed to some of her votes isn't discussed among the union loyalists who have funneled millions into her campaign coffers.

This renewal of the unholy marriage vows between labor unions, community organizations, and the Democratic Party only serves to underscore the desperation of the status quo elitists. People are beginning to wake up to the realization of two very important facts.

The first is that the majority of labor unions no longer represent the working man and are, in fact, nothing more than the political arms of organized criminal enterprises, using members' dues to buy influence, corrupt the political process, and extort money from the business sector.

The second fact is that an entire industry has been created in this country and built upon maintaining the generally accepted, but wholly false, notion that citizens who are members of racial or ethnic minorities are victims, do not have equal access to opportunity, and are therefore justified in partaking in criminal acts to achieve parity.

For years, so-called community organizers have been promoting the race-based fallacy that the deck has been stacked against minority Americans by the selfish majority and the only way they will ever get any kind of fair shot at equal opportunity is through a government-sponsored program or a government-mandated advantage. These organizations have spread misinformation, bigotry, and fear in order to cement their place in the community hierarchy and to exercise control over an entire segment of our society. In the process, they have enriched themselves from the millions and million of tax dollars spent on redundant and wholly ineffective programs aimed at fighting ignorance and poverty.

Men who publicly and frequently profess to represent the poor and disadvantaged have become millionaires by using extortive threats and outright disinformation to extract payoffs from business and political leaders. They are, in fact, racist provocateurs who have persuaded an entire segment of our population to willingly exchange the physical cotton plantation for the mental and spiritual federal plantation. They have promoted living in the shadows on the fringes of society as preferable to partaking in responsible citizenship. They are keeping the very people they claim to represent locked out of the American promise through largely unfounded racial provocation and envy-based manipulation.

Given my constant dealings over the past two decades with many very wealthy self-made people, I can name dozens of men and women, from all races and ethnic backgrounds, who have risen to affluence and influence based solely upon their merit and hard work despite the fact that they are considered members of a minority demographic. That class envy and race baiting still prevail as their weapons of choice just illustrates the intellectual vapidity of the liberals. They have been allowed to construct an entire subculture in this country dedicated to nothing more than grabbing power and redistributing wealth from those who have created it to those who will sell their support in exchange for a subsistence lifestyle free of honest labor and personal responsibility.

Just how desperate is this leftist coalition to hang on to the power they have enjoyed for the past 50 or 60 years? Stephen Lerner, formerly of Service Employees International Union (SEIU), one of the country's most powerful unions, was recently caught on tape at a seminar at Pace University discussing his plan for destabilizing the economy. The plan is to push JPMorgan into insolvency, crash the stock market, and weaken Wall Street's grip on power, thus creating the conditions necessary for a redistribution of wealth and a change in government. Utilizing a mass, coordinated people's strike on mortgage, student loan, and local government debt payments, he believes the unions and community organizations can bring the banks to the edge of insolvency and force them to renegotiate the terms of their loans. This destabilization and turmoil, Lerner hopes, will cause a crash in the stock market, isolating the banking class and allowing for a transfer of power. Lerner stated:

> For example, 10 percent of homeowners are "underwater." They are paying more for (their home) than it is worth. 10 percent of those people are in strategic default, meaning they are refusing to pay but they are staying in their home. That's totally spontaneous! They have figured out it takes a year (for the banks) to kick them out of their home because foreclosures are so backed up. If you could double that number, you would put banks at the edge of insolvency again.

He continued:

We have an entire economy that is built on debt and banks; so the question would be what would happen if we organized homeowners en masse to do a mortgage strike? If we get half a million people to agree to stop paying their mortgages, it would literally cause a new financial crisis for the banks. Not for us! We would be doing quite well. We wouldn't be paying anything.[5]

Such basic ignorance of economic theory is a serious threat to our national security and should be treated as what it is: the seditious ranting of a madman. These are the people with whom Barack Obama, Debbie Stabenow, and every other Democratic politician in this country have aligned themselves. Is it any wonder their poll numbers continue to drop?

When an overwhelming majority of the population directly feels the increasingly negative effects on their own living standards, the propaganda system that has been propping up this incompetent administration will collapse. I believe the illusion will come crashing down and people will finally start to get wise to the horrific scam that has been played on them. When they wake from their media-induced dream state and realize that they are now living in a totally un-American nightmare, people will actually stop voting against their own interests. The apathetic majority who haven't bothered to vote in the past will become active in the interests of self-preservation as their survival instincts kick in.

The handwriting is on the wall. The ruling class is beginning to realize, as the 2012 elections approach, that there are going to be wholesale changes in Congress and their corrupt puppet politicians are going to be voted out of office. There may be efforts at rigging the election or voter intimidation by unions and special interest groups, but this will only guarantee a violent backlash. The general population has become better informed thanks to the Internet and the New Media. They are not happy.

Looking at this from a purely technocratic sociological viewpoint, avoiding mass riots and violence while this many desperate people lose life-sustaining programs appears to be an impossible task. Given our current economic and political environment, this social break-down seems inevitable. What's going to happen in this society when these people are without jobs, when their families hurt, when they lose their homes in massive numbers, entire neighborhoods at a time?

The scenarios are grim. Former U.S. Director of National Intel-ligence Dennis Blair recently testified before the Senate Intelligence Committee stating that the greatest threat facing the United States is not terrorism, it's the continuing economic crisis.

> The primary near-term security concern of the United States is the global economic crisis and its geopolitical implications. The crisis has been ongoing for over a year, and economists are divided over whether and when we could hit bottom. Some even fear that the recession could further deepen and reach the level of the Great Depression. Of course, all of us recall the dramatic political consequences wrought by the economic turmoil of the 1920s and 1930s in Europe, the instability, and high levels of violent extremism.[6]

This propaganda effort is only a temporary measure and will not suffice over the long term. As the economy continues to collapse, the banking elite risk being overthrown as a result of their own greed. So they will then turn to physical violence to suppress populations that can no longer be controlled through propaganda and economic coer-cion. The classic strategy of an endangered oligarchy is to divert discontent among the population into nationalistic militarism. It is time, once again, for them to bang the drums of war and whip the citizenry into a patriotic fervor. An increased external threat will lead to an increased internal crackdown, which creates the pretext and conditions for a police state. As we have already seen in the first phase of the crackdown on civil liberties since the War on Terror began, when rioting and outbursts of armed insurrection begin within the United States, external threats, real or imagined, will again be pre-sented to justify extreme measures to suppress American citizens, and to further repress internal dissent. Without an external enemy to rally the population against, the population will rally against the preexisting internal powers.

To put a slight twist on what my father once told me back in 1988: The banking-political coalition "constructs its own inconceivable foe: terrorism. Its wish is to be judged by its enemies rather than by its results. The story of terrorism is written by the state and it is therefore highly instructive. But they must always know enough to convince the people that compared with terrorism, everything else must be acceptable, or in any case, more rational and democratic."

In this case, the "terrorism" is domestic and economically driven. It is based on the specious—and communist—notion that collective bargaining is a worker's right. It would not surprise me in the least if some enterprising guerilla journalist were to uncover the fact that people like Stephen Lerner were actually on the payroll of one or more of the Wall Street bankers. The art of misdirection is not just confined to the world of politics. The average American is dreadfully unaware of just how depraved these people are. The little regard they have for human life is beyond common comprehension.

Is history repeating itself? Not to oversimplify an extremely complex situation, but this is all too similar to the origins of World War II. The looting of the masses by unaccountable Wall Street elites led to the Great Depression and set the conditions for WWII. Desperate and impoverished populations increasingly supported more and more extreme leaders. The conditions are now so ripe for world war that even the leading leftist intellectual, Noam Chomsky, was quoted in the April 2010 edition of *The Progressive* comparing modern-day America to Weimar Germany prior to the outbreak of WWII. Research the history of prewar societies and you will see how our current political environment fits historical precedent like a glove.

After analyzing our current crisis and studying well-established historical precedents, I must conclude that the global bankers have only three possible cards left to play.

The first is admitting culpability and working to restore the American economic engine to its free-market potential. History has taught us that the ruling class rarely admits error and never concedes power.

The second is to foment so much civil unrest and fear that the general population will be clamoring for a global dictator who will provide them food, shelter, and security in exchange for their individual freedom and sovereignty. I see the emerging militancy of the labor union movement playing right into this scenario.

The final play is global conflict where they can try and control the outcome by means of funding both sides.

Of course, the one-tenth of 1 percent of the global population hoarding our wealth could give back a significant amount of the $275 billion that still hasn't been repaid from the Troubled Asset Relief Program (TARP). That would certainly go a long way to fixing the crisis they have caused, but that's another thing the ruling class never does. They never give any money back, no matter how excessive and ill-gotten their gains.

Is Free-Market Capitalism Dead?

Is free-market capitalism, as historically practiced in the United States, still alive, or is it now just a footnote in our economic history? Americans have traditionally believed that the invisible hand of the market means that capitalism will benefit all of us without requiring any oversight. However, Adam Smith never said nor did he believe in a magically benevolent market that operated for the benefit of all without any checks and balances. He railed against monopolies and the political influence that accompanies economic power, worrying about the encroachment of government on economic activity; but his concerns were directed at least as much toward parish councils, church wardens, big corporations, guilds, and religious institutions as to the national government, since these institutions were part and parcel of eighteenth-century government. Smith was sometimes tolerant of government intervention, especially when the object is to reduce poverty.

"When the regulation, therefore, is in support of the workman," Smith passionately argued, "it is always just and equitable; but it is sometimes otherwise when in favor of the masters."[7]

He saw a tacit conspiracy on the part of employers "always and everywhere" to keep wages as low as possible. While Adam Smith may have been the father of free-market economics, he argued that bank regulation was as necessary as fire codes on urban buildings and called for a ban on high-risk, high-interest lending—the eighteenth-century version of the subprime loan.

Rama Cont, one of the leaders of the new science of financial modeling, recently asserted his belief that Adam Smith was wrong about the "Invisible Hand."[8] Specifically, investors in financial markets rationally pursuing individual profit can produce outcomes that are bad for almost everyone. Simple forecasts can also be mistaken, argues Cont, if they fail to account for the actions of market participants themselves. Investor strategies can influence prices, which in turn influence future strategies in a feedback loop that can cause considerable instability.

Cont recalls the severe stock market crash of October 1987, which seemed to strike out of the blue, since nothing significant was happening in the real economy. Subsequent research, though, blamed the crash in part on a new investment strategy, "portfolio insurance," which a large number of fund managers had simultaneously adopted.

Based on the famous Black-Scholes options-pricing model, a quantitative mathematical formula that is used to price stock options, this strategy recommended that fund managers reduce their risks by automatically selling shares whenever their values fell. But the approach didn't take into account what would happen if many investors followed it simultaneously; a massive sell-off that could send the market plummeting. The 1987 crash was thus not provoked by events in the real economy but by a supposedly smart risk-management strategy—and the current downturn, of course, also derives at least partly from a global craze for a seemingly foolproof financial innovation.

Investors in financial markets rationally pursuing individual profit, then, can produce outcomes that are globally negative. Doesn't that contradict classical economic theory?

"Both theory and empirical facts do tend to show that," says Cont. "On the financial markets, the 'Invisible Hand' does not always lead to welfare-improving general outcomes."

Free-market capitalism is not dead, but, by the same token, I'm not sure that there is any better alternative. I strongly believe that capitalism has to grow up and become less naïve, relying less on a blind faith in the invisible hand and more on an understanding of

human nature, including insights from the field of behavioral economics. It must include sophisticated checks and balances to make sure
that the system is not gamed, instead of childish ideas about the inherent stability of the market. And it must make sure that the poker game
doesn't suddenly end when one of the players gets all of the chips.

In 2009, Barack Obama compared American Exceptionalism to
"British exceptionalism, and the Greeks in Greek exceptionalism."[9]
There is just one problem with that statement. It is wrong. The British
built an empire that ruled the world based on the might of their navy.
The Greeks built a civilization based on the power of their intellect.
They were both unique, even great; but they were not exceptional.
Exceptional is a nation that can rise in less than 200 years to become
the strongest, most dynamic economy in history; a nation born not
of ancient tribes but of the brightest, the best, and the hardest working
the rest of the world's nations had to offer. That is what makes
America "exceptional." There is no other nation like this nation on
Planet Earth. There never has been and there probably never will be
again.

It is not too late to restore the global standing of America and
stop the systematic pilfering of the American people. We have the
resources and the capital to restart the engines of our economy and
put Americans back to work. All we need is the resolve and the
courage.

The time has come for a regime change in America. If we are
going to save ourselves, we must reclaim and overhaul our government. We must have a second American Revolution—a revolution
using ballots, not bullets. We must reclaim our economic liberty.

The best way to protect yourself and your family in this time of
uncertainty is to create wealth for yourself. Don't believe the media
doomsayers or financial pundits who tell you that it cannot be done
today. It can. America still provides many opportunities for an individual to create real, significant wealth. Despite the best efforts of the
anticapitalists who have taken over the national debate, you can still
get rich in America. The question is for how much longer you will
be able to do that and how much of your earnings you will be allowed
to keep. I am not interested in teaching you how to create wealth. I
am interested in you developing the mind-set to maintain and grow

that wealth once you have attained it. I am interested in your becoming Machiavellian in your quest for economic safety and security for you and your family, turning the tables on those who have stolen from you, utilizing their secret strategies and tactics for effectively engaging in economic warfare and securing your opportunities for creating wealth. It takes a lot of effort and some time, but you can create your own safety net. You *can* join the ranks of the rich.

Notes

1. Agreement between the Swiss Federal Council and the Bank for International Settlements to determine the Bank's legal status in Switzerland (of 10 February 1987; text as amended . . .), Section I, Article 3, para 1.
2. Nathan Freier, *Known Unknowns: Unconventional "Strategic Shocks" in Defense Strategy Development* (Carlisle, PA: Strategic Studies Institute, U.S. Army War College, 2008), 31–33.
3. Jennifer Grasz, "One-in-Five Workers Have Trouble Making Ends Meet as More Indicate They Live Paycheck to Paycheck, Reveals New CareerBuilder Survey," Press release. CareerBuilder.com, Gannett Co., Chicago, September 1, 2010.
4. Barrie Barber, "Rise Up for Social Justice, UAW Leader Urges," *Flint Journal*, p. A14.
5. Henry Blodget, , ed., "Caught on Tape: Former SEIU Official Reveals Secret Plan to Destroy JPMorgan, Crash the Stock Market and Redistribute Wealth in America, *Business Insider,* March 22, 2011. Retrieved from www .businessinsider.com/seiu-union-plan-to-destroy-jpmorgan#ixzz1HLixtwxB.
6. "Annual Threat Assessment of the Intelligence Community for the Senate Select Committee on Intelligence," February 12, 2009. Dennis C. Blair, Director of National Intelligence, p. 2.
7. Adam Smith, *An Inquiry into the Nature and Causes of the Wealth of Nations.* R. H. Campbell and A. S. Skinner, eds. (Glasgow Edition of the Works and Correspondence of Adam Smith—2 vols., Oxford University Press, 1976), Book I, Chapter X, Part II, 168.
8. Guy Sorman, "Wild Randomness," Forbes.com. Retrieved from www .forbes.com/2009/08/03/rama-cont-benoit-mandelbrot-columbia-economics -opinions-contributors-guy-sorman.html.
9. Arthur C. Brooks, *The Battle: How the Fight between Free Enterprise and Big Government Will Shape America's Future* (New York: Basic Books, 2010), 15.

Chapter 6

Battle Plans

I always tried to turn every disaster into an opportunity.
—John D. Rockefeller (1839–1937), American industrialist
and philanthropist, founder of the Standard Oil Company

There is a new and unique development in human history taking place around the world today. It is unprecedented in reach and volume, and it is also the greatest threat to all global power structures: the *global political awakening*. The term was coined in a New York Times opinion-editorial published December 16, 2008. The writer was Zbigniew Brzezinski, President Jimmy Carter's national security adviser, who is now serving as a trustee and counselor at the Center for Strategic and International Studies (CSIS).

For the first time in history almost all of humanity is politically activated, politically conscious and politically interactive. Global activism is generating a surge in the quest for cultural respect and economic opportunity in a world scarred by memories of colonial or imperial domination.[1]

There are indeed only a few pockets of humanity left in the remotest corners of the world that are not politically alert and engaged with the political turmoil and stirrings that are so widespread today around the world. The resulting global political activism is generating a surge in the quest for personal dignity, cultural respect, and economic opportunity. I believe that the central challenge of our time will be posed not by global terrorism, but rather by the intensifying turbulence caused by the phenomenon of global political awakening. That awakening is socially massive and politically radicalizing.

It is no overstatement that today the population of much of the developing world is politically stirring and in many places seething with unrest. It is a population acutely conscious of social injustice to an unprecedented degree and often resentful of its perceived lack of political dignity. The nearly universal access to radio, television, and the Internet is creating a community of shared perceptions. This global media presence is enlightening and educating, but it is also fostering envy that can be galvanized and channeled by demagogic political or religious passions. These energies transcend sovereign borders and pose a challenge to existing states as well as to the existing global hierarchy, on top of which America still perches.

The youth of the third world are particularly restless and resentful. The demographic revolution they embody is a political time bomb. With the exception of Europe, Japan, and America, the rapidly expanding demographic bulge in the 25-year-old-and-under age bracket is creating a huge mass of impatient young people. Their minds have been stirred by sounds and images that emanate from afar and intensify their disaffection with what is at hand.

Their potential revolutionary spearhead is likely to emerge from among the scores of millions of students concentrated in the often intellectually dubious tertiary-level educational institutions of developing countries. Depending on the definition of the tertiary educational level, there are currently worldwide between 80 and 130 million college students. Typically originating from the socially insecure lower middle class and inflamed by a globally pervasive sense of entitlement, these millions of students are revolutionaries-in-waiting. They are already semimobilized in virtual communities, connected by the Internet and programmed for displays of social and political outrage aimed predominantly at the West and specifically at the United States. Large-scale uprisings are occurring all around the world as this youthful energy and emotion waits to be triggered by a social cause, a fanatical faith, or an irrational hatred.

What Should America's Global Role Be?

Politically awakened mankind craves political dignity, which democracy can enhance, but political dignity also encompasses ethnic or national self-determination, religious self-definition, and human and social rights in a world now acutely aware of economic, racial, and ethnic inequities. The quest for political dignity, especially through national self-determination and social transformation, is part of the pulse of self-assertion by the underprivileged.

It is a fact that today's global elites are actually terrified of the mass political awakening that is occurring worldwide. They sense that their worldwide con game has been discovered and that people have realized that their power is only an illusion, a misdirection devoid of any legal, ethical, or moral sanction. The misdiagnosis of our foreign policy pertains to a relatively vague, excessively abstract, highly emotional, semitheological definition of the chief menace that we face today in the world. It has been kept purposely vague in order to invoke the greatest amount of fear and apprehension and, consequently, to allow the greatest opportunity for manipulation and coercion.

These spontaneous uprisings are not the work of fundamentalist terrorists interested in global jihad. They are young people who have awakened to the possibilities of a better life than the one their parents lived. That they are being systematically manipulated by their own power brokers is obvious when one realizes that the source for their expanded awareness, the lifestyle and material goods they desire, and the target for their anger are one and the same. Unfortunately, youthful zeal and emotional frustration are usually bereft of logic and reason.

America needs to face squarely a centrally important new global reality: the world's population is experiencing a political awakening unprecedented in scope and intensity, with the result that the politics of populism are transforming the politics of power. We need to respond to the historic challenge that this global phenomenon poses to our uniquely sovereign nation.

If we wake up fast enough, we can reclaim our power and dignity. If we awaken, we can shake off those who would steal everything we have, including our money, opportunity, and freedom. If we rise to the challenge, we can restore America to its rightful place as a beacon of freedom and liberty, the shining city set on the hill. We can meet the uprising with opportunity and example. We can resume our place as leaders in innovation and teachers of entrepreneurship. We can once again be viewed by the rest of the world as that *exceptional* nation. The nineteenth-century poet Ralph Waldo Emerson wrote, "America is another name for Opportunity." I believe that is still true today.

My General Philosophy for Creating "Wealth"

One of the rules of the rich is that if you wish to stay wealthy, you need to either buy or create assets that produce value. In other words, you start a company that provides a good or service that people believe they need and are willing to purchase from you because they feel that the value of your product, service, information, or whatever is equal to or exceeds the price paid. This is generation of income. If the amount of income generated by your assets exceeds the amount of your costs, then you have made a profit. An entrepreneur is someone who solves people's problems on a profit margin.

The key is to select attractive assets that can produce income or appreciate. An asset can either produce current income, appreciate (and depreciate), or both. The choice of which is a decision that is personal in nature, but a good way to establish a baseline is to ask yourself if you were to stop working, would your assets continue to put food on the table and pay your monthly obligations? Having your investments not only sustain you but produce more than you need is one way in which wealth was created for hundreds of years before

Wall Street got so sophisticated and abstract that financial games came into the picture.

If you want to make real money, then the first thing I suggest is that you get educated. Making money is an intrinsic activity of all of humanity, and mankind has developed countless ways to do it. There is nothing inherently evil in the process of making money, and the notion is illogical, but that is one of the underlying tenets in our present education system. We are taught from an early age that making money is hard and that those who make lots of money are morally suspect. American culture studies programs at some of the nation's leading universities have even gone so far as to teach the absurd and illogical notion that the rich became rich because they enjoy privilege earned on the backs of African slaves. Minority millionaires like entrepreneur Herman Cain, Earl Graves, Sr., and Reginald F. Lewis prove the utter nonsense of this notion, yet this is the illogical Progressive philosophy that has permeated our education system.

The truth is that it is not difficult to make money once you understand that money is a tool and that it can be used, through various processes known collectively as *finance* to create real, tangible wealth. The most difficult thing about our relationship with money is giving up the idea of what that income is or should be and where it will come from. For example, most people would argue that they are on a fixed income and there is only so much money they receive each month. Others say their monthly paycheck is XYZ dollars and they don't want to get a second job.

In the first example above, the person has defined the boundaries of his income and he does not allow the space for other income to flow. In the second example, the person has defined a limited channel of how and where the money is to appear.

I believe that to create real wealth one must be willing to abandon one's limited thinking, remove the boundaries around our abundance, and stop outlining how it is to appear in our lives. Remember *not* to create boundaries and remember *not* to define the outcome. Most importantly, stop letting people who are motivated by jealousy and envy dictate what your limitations are. Maybe they think that wealth is evil and that rich people are heartless, but they never can answer the one basic fundamental question: if you, Miss Liberal, take away the money from those who make it to give it to those who only choose to take from society, how are you going to force the wealth creators to continue creating what you so freely take? When the wealth creators go away, Mr. Progressive, who is going to pay your bills? After you've created a level playing field and enforced economic equality and social justice on everyone, Comrade Communist, how are you going to provide basic goods, like food, and basic services, like electricity and clean water? If everyone is equal and everyone is entitled, what is the incentive for anyone to initiate any activity? The ultimate answer for your utopian dream is slavery and dictatorial tyranny. History has shown time and time again that there is no such thing as all things being equal. That is why Jefferson wrote that our inalienable rights were life, liberty, and the *pursuit* of happiness. Nothing is guaranteed in life, especially happiness.

The Specifics of the Wealth Creation Process

People often ask what I think is likely to happen in the financial world in the coming months and years. I have no crystal ball, but I can assure you that the dangers are more numerous and larger than ever before in my lifetime. I strongly believe that if we do not make some serious and educated choices about the future direction of this nation, it may be years before we, as a nation, experience anything remotely defined as the level of prosperity we enjoyed during the late 1980s and into the 1990s. If we individually choose wisely and in our true self-interest as sovereign individuals, we can, as a nation, enjoy even greater prosperity. It is possible to make money in any economic environment if one is educated and uses his head.

We cannot survive four more years of Woodrow Wilson Light and his merry band of regulatory czars; liberal Ivy League academics who live in an abstract, theoretical world; and sarcastic leftist pundits who are only good at obfuscating facts in order to manipulate their ignorant constituency. This administration has winked at the wrongdoing on Wall Street in order to maintain its hold on political power. Both are blinded to the fact that they are in a death spiral and taking the entire nation down with them.

In the past 100 years, wealth protection could be obtained by keeping your net worth in cash or government bonds. Mortgages and other forms of debts are over tenfold greater now than before 1970, which can cause manifold increases in bankruptcy auctions. A tenfold increase in people hopelessly indebted will lead to multiplying rates of personal bankruptcy. This will result in an economic tsunami as many businesses that extend credit without collateral are forced to absorb losses. The transfer of mortgage-backed debts from Fannie Mae and Freddie Mac to the Federal Reserve is going to emerge as a serious liquidity issue, which could spell the death knell for the central bank. An electoral war is brewing as the once silent majority of voters is beginning to grow increasingly hostile toward government-backed bailouts and lifestyle subsidies. When the Fed is forced to demand legislation that overtly protects its interests while financially oppressing the general populace and throttling economic growth, the swift and violent political backlash will force legislators to finally face up to their constitutional obligations.

Obsolescence is likely to have a devastating effect in a wide variety of human activities, especially in those where advancement is hindered by labor unions or other bureaucracies or by government regulations. Increasing freedom of competition is likely to cause most established institutions to disappear within the next 50 years. Accelerating competition is likely to cause profit margins to continue to decrease and even become negative in various industries. Surplus capacity, which leads to intense competition, has already shown devastating effects on airline companies and is now beginning to show up in companies like shipping, trucking, and other economic "floor joist" activities. The present surpluses of cash and liquid assets have pushed yields on bonds and mortgages almost to zero when adjusted for higher cost of living. Clearly, major corrections are likely in the next few years.

For the business sector of higher education, there are revolutionary changes on the horizon. The business model based on on-campus student residency is becoming hopelessly obsolete. Failure of these institutions to embrace technological change and adapt their delivery methods will result in the disappearance of at least half of the universities in the world over the next two decades, many of them considered ivy-covered academic stalwarts.

The chickens are indeed coming home to roost as the global banking cartel's crimes are being exposed left and right. To start with, on September 2, 2011, the Federal Housing Finance Agency (FHFA), filed a $196 billion lawsuit against 17 financial institutions, certain of their officers and various unaffiliated lead underwriters. The suits allege violations of federal securities laws and common law in the sale of residential private-label, mortgage-backed securities (PLS) to the enterprises. Bank of America is severely exposed on this lawsuit. As the parent company of Countrywide and Merrill Lynch, they are on the hook for $57.4 billion. JPMorgan is next in the line of fire with $33 billion. And many death-spiraling European banks are facing billions in losses as well.

These complaints were filed in federal or state court in New York or the federal court in Connecticut. The complaints seek damages and civil penalties under the Securities Act of 1933, similar in content to the complaint FHFA filed against UBS Americas, Inc. on July 27, 2011. In addition, each complaint seeks compensatory damages for negligent misrepresentation. Certain complaints also allege state securities law violations or common-law fraud.

U.S. securities regulators have also taken the unprecedented step of asking high-frequency trading firms to hand over the details of their trading strategies, and in some cases, their secret computer codes. The requests for proprietary code and algorithm parameters by the Financial Industry Regulatory Authority (FINRA), a Wall Street brokerage regulator, are part of investigations into suspicious market activity.

A former senior analyst at Moody's has gone public with his story of how one of the country's most important rating agencies is corrupted to the core. The analyst, William J. Harrington, worked for Moody's for 11 years, from 1999 until his resignation in 2010. From 2006 to 2010, Harrington was a senior vice president in the derivative products group, which was responsible for producing many of the disastrous ratings Moody's issued during the housing bubble. Harrington has made his story public in the form of a 78-page "comment" to the SEC's proposed rules about rating agency reform. Some of the key points in his comments reveal that Moody's ratings often did not reflect its analysts' private conclusions. Instead, rating committees privately concluded that certain securities deserve certain ratings, but then voted with management to give the securities the higher ratings that issuer clients want. Moody's management and "compliance" officers did everything possible to make issuer clients happy and viewed analysts who do not do the same as "troublesome." Management employed a variety of tactics to transform these troublesome analysts into "pliant corporate citizens" who had Moody's best interests at heart; keeping clients happy and growing Moody's business.

What about the SEC? An explosive report brought by political reporter Matt Taibbi from *Rolling Stone* magazine recently exposed how the SEC destroyed records of thousands of investigations, whitewashing the files of some of the nation's largest banks and hedge funds, including AIG, Wells Fargo, Lehman Brothers, Goldman Sachs, Bank of America, and top Wall Street broker Bernard Madoff. Republican Senator Chuck Grassley of Iowa revealed that an agency whistleblower had sent him a letter detailing the unlawful destruction of records detailing more than 9,000 information investigations.

So with the entire gloomy picture out there, how on earth do you keep creating wealth in those real difficult times we're all facing today?

Now, with over 200 independent nations on earth and rapid advancements in communication, the top 1 percent of people is likely to progress more rapidly than the others. The mainstream media machine would have you believe that this top 1 percent is comprised solely of the super-rich, but that is not the case at all. There is going to be a premium put on intellectual wealth in the future due to the massive failure of the past century of Progressive education. Intellectual abilities, innovation, and just plain common sense are going to be valuable commodities in the foreseeable future. The end result of the federalization of the education system is grade-school students who are well versed on homosexuality as an alternative lifestyle, high-school graduates who cannot read or balance a checkbook, college students who know more about cheat codes in Halo than the basic thoughts of Plato, and graduate students who see no connection between personal excellence and professional success. If you are an educated person with a modicum of common sense, you are going to be a highly sought after commodity in the very near future. Someone will have to be able to run things like an adult.

Studies have shown that prosperity flows toward those nations having the most freedom of innovation and competition. I strongly believe there are always other people who are as smart, if not smarter, than I am. I go to great lengths to find those rare individuals, listen to them, and back them up in any way I can. Simultaneously, on the political front, I involve myself with like-minded groups to lobby and empower smart people who know what they are doing and have real-world experience in creating wealth, managing organizations, and building value.

The future is challenging, but there are many opportunities. For instance, technical innovations in shale gas production have created huge changes in the dynamics of a market that was not considered economically viable as recently as three years ago. The geopolitical implications are already emerging. Despite the debacle of "light rail" and the ongoing debate over "high-speed rail," the transportation sector is poised for enormous growth. Other than control and switching schemes, rail technology is basically the same as it was 150 years ago—a ripe plum for innovation and technological advances. The potential upheaval resulting from fusion-based energy, which is getting ever closer to commercial realization, will create massive opportunities. Imagine being able to mine a landfill, producing energy from carbon-based solid waste material. The need for increased food production is also generating innovation and the increasing use of renewable resources in the area of fertilizers, soil conditioners, and non–genetically modified seeds.

There is no real magic formula for creating wealth, but there are a few ways and means that have always worked for my clients and me.

It all boils down to the people of this nation making the right choices and knowing how to pick up the right people, put the obliterating "firepower" of adequate resources behind them, and execute on our common business and political agendas. I see no better method to prosper during the ongoing global financial chaos, which is likely to last many years, than to back the leanest and meanest global operators who are running companies that have proven to have the widest profit margins and the most rapidly increasing profits. Add proven business operations experience to intelligent innovation and seasoned market analysis, then you tell me how much wealth you want to create.

A paradigm shift is required in terms of attitudes toward investing in and supporting technical research and development and the small businesses that come from it. A good example of this is to take a once prosperous manufacturing city in the Midwest that, despite its current blighted condition, has a quality university that is geared toward teaching scientific research, technical innovation, and solid business principles. Coupling growth-oriented governmental policies with visionary entrepreneurial spirit and long-term investment capital could foster the development of a research-and-development campus and business incubator adjacent to and connected with the university. The fortunes of that community could be reversed in short order if the fiscally retarding forces of unionization, entitlement exploitation, and bureaucratic overregulation were held at bay. Leadership is about assembling and leading a powerful group toward the common vision of changing that which must and can be changed. As noted anthropologist Margaret Mead said, "Never doubt that a small group of thoughtful and committed people can change the world. Indeed, it is the only thing that ever has."

Risks, Rewards, and Opportunities

People often ask me how my partners and I manage relationships, trigger rewards, and create opportunities with all of the inherent risks running our operation entails.

The answer is frankly very simple: At its most fundamental level, I believe that risk management is a corporate culture issue. To manage risks effectively over time, employees must put the welfare and preservation of important client relationships ahead of everything else.

Risk is risk, and you can't be perfect at managing it. In a nutshell, I can tell you that the bulk of our risks do not result from proprietary trading, but rather from facilitating client objectives. Being an effective adviser, for example, means giving advice that is actionable, which frequently requires the advisory firm to support the client through capital and other balance sheet commitments. And this "clients first" approach has derived from our long Wall Street experience.

It is sad to see that the current Wall Street credit bloodbath clearly emanated from a widespread cultural breakdown—a loss of focus on client relationships and client-centered values. When a firm tries to explain away its losses by saying, "Our risk management broke down," the explanation won't wash. Give an experienced trader a new rule-book on risk, and he will figure out how to game the new rules in minutes. Far from being over, the impact of the financial mess we are still witnessing, globally as well as domestically, is just beginning to be felt.

Ultimately, I believe it will affect not only rules and regulations, but Wall Street leadership as well. On the heels of Wall Street's stock-touting scandals of 2000, many firms ousted their leaders whose backgrounds were in investment banking or retail brokerage, turning instead to their fixed-income departments for a new generation of leadership. The Street's fixed-income business quickly tripled in size as equity businesses receded. Fixed income tends to be a win-lose business, because a bond is a commodity with little value creation. Every time you trade a government bond, someone wins and someone else loses; but Wall Street should be a win-win proposition, one that creates value for issuer and investor alike.

In the past, U.S. financial institutions have proven resilient in the aftermath of crises—nimble in their ability to take their medicine and move on. At the moment, however, with the U.S. economy still seeking the new equilibrium, it's questionable when the industry will regain sufficient strength to resume its fundamental job: reallocating capital to the right places.

Whatever the situation is, I remain fundamentally optimistic about Wall Street as a marketplace and as a vehicle for wealth creation. Its future will rightly depend on several variables, chief among them being human choices; whether they be rationally, emotionally, sub-jectively or objectively made. Financial engineering taught us that if it could be quantified, it could be qualified. We learned about how to use leverage and have abused that knowledge for a myriad of reasons. We became practitioners of the transaction-based model, but forgot that long before the abacus there was trust and integrity, anchors of relationship-based models common with Middle East and Asian markets. It goes back to a handshake, the first and enduring example of mutual consensus.

Wealth creation is not a mathematical formula, as the truth-seeking quant geeks still want everyone to believe. In the end, their lack of real-world experience and pride corrupted their mathematical genius and destroyed them. You may be able to digitize a daVinci, but that does not make it daVinci. Creating wealth is personal. It is creating assets, creating value, or whatever act of self-perpetuation that drives us to create a legacy.

Basic Tenets of My Investment and Wealth Creation Philosophy

What are the basic tenets of my investment and wealth creation philosophy in a world that is increasingly dangerous, regulated, and volatile?

First, I do not believe in diversification. Take a close look at some of the greatest entrepreneurs in U.S. history. Henry Ford never diversified; Bill Gates didn't diversify. I strongly believe that the best way to create real wealth is to put one's eggs in one basket and watch that basket (the right one) very carefully. In fact, one can go broke diversifying. Ask anyone who's diversified in the past three years. They've lost money. Nonprofessionals are always running around reading this column or that book or attending a seminar by the latest expert. They think that spreading their investments across a diversified portfolio will mitigate their risk and maximize their return. If they have a big success in one venture, they think they can go out and do it again in another deal. Quick success often leads to pride and, too late, the realization sets in that investing does not follow a template or a surefire recipe. The only sure thing is to invest in what you know and what you understand. Warren Buffett, one of the most astute investors of the late twentieth century, wrote about his opposition to diversification of the portfolio in a 1965 letter to his partners:

I am willing to give up quite a bit in terms of leveling of year-to-year results (remember when I talk of "results," I am talking of performance relative to the Dow) in order to achieve better overall long-term performance. Simply stated, this means I am willing to concentrate quite heavily in what I believe to be the best investment opportunities recognizing very well that this may cause an occasional very sour year—one somewhat more sour, probably, than if I had diversified more. While this means our results will bounce around more, I think it also means that our long-term margin of superiority should be greater.

Second, I do not believe in supporting bailouts without strong ramifications. It is a fool's fantasy to think we can live in a globally connected economy and never have a situation arise where the government prudently steps in to prevent a failure that might lead to catastrophic ramifications. In most cases, I believe it would be much better to let bailed-out companies fail when they have mismanaged themselves, rather than waste taxpayer money propping up greedy idiots who are trying to salvage their own bonuses; however, there are exceptions to almost every rule. The wiser course would be to penalize the CEO or board of directors who drove the company to the brink of failure. The most obvious punishment would be the elimination of any "golden parachutes" or bonuses for the executive and seizure of all company-derived assets, including any attempts to hide company assets in the spouse's name. When C-level executives come to the realization that managing a company is not a game and that there are serious consequences for their actions, we will see fewer instances of requests for bailouts.

The system can recover from bankruptcies, as it has done throughout history. After Lehman went down, the stock market didn't really collapse right away. It happened a month later, but people started blaming it on Lehman in hindsight. Would the world really have come to an end had AIG gone into bankruptcy or Goldman Sachs been forced to liquidate and close its doors? I seriously doubt it.

Bankruptcy cleans out the system. What's wrong with that? South Korea went through this in the late 1990s. They didn't have anyone to bail them out, and they had to go through the pain. Sweden did it in the early 1990s. Mexico did it. Russia did it. The list goes on and on. Competent people take over the assets from incompetent people and rebuild from a solid base. Business has always been survival of the fittest and Darwinism at its best. After all, this is what capitalism is all about.

Third, I do not believe in the power of brand names or in emulating any of the brand name investors out there. It is a fact that all—if not at least most—of the biggest names in American finance and industry out there today have proven after the 2008 crisis to be some of the most incompetent people there are. Starting with the untouchable Goldman Sachs, who was bailed out by over $5 billion from Warren Buffett, to AIG and Citibank, who were bailed out by the hundreds of billions of dollars from the Troubled Asset Relief Program (TARP), having a name and a history does not make you the brightest and the best. All it takes is one nincompoop with a huge ego or a board of directors who think they are smarter than everyone else to destroy what has taken generations to build. Just ask the former employees of Bear Stearns, Lehman Brothers, Merrill Lynch, and the like, who literally closed shop. So when people tell you that this venerable firm or private investor invested X millions of dollars in that entity and that it is a good investment, be skeptical and stay open to the option of running as far as you can in the opposite direction. We have all seen the biggest names on Wall Street along with the largest sovereign wealth funds on the planet make the dumbest investments ever made. Do your due diligence; ask the right questions, and most important, check out the character of the people involved unless you want to end up being prey to another master of the universe à la Bernie Madoff.

The Future of Commodities

I believe that the best way to make money this decade will be in commodities. The up cycle for commodities is only on the rise; and if history is any guide, we have further to go. The only sector of the world economy where the fundamentals are getting better is, in fact, commodities. Farmers can't get loans for fertilizers, which is constraining crop supply. It takes 10 years to open a new mine. Stocks peaked in October 2007 and commodities kept going up until July 2008. If the world economy is going to revive, I believe commodities are going to lead it back up. If the world economy is not going to revive, commodities are still the place to be—especially with governments printing so much money. Look at the 1970s. The world economy was in the tank, but commodities did very well. There are some supply constraints that must be taken into consideration. Oil production, for instance, is declining.

Frankly, given the political prospects for a number of strategic countries across the region, the possibility of long-term uncertainties, and the threat to oil supplies, I'm surprised gold has not performed better, especially in light of its own bullish market fundamentals.

Most important, gold will also benefit from unfettered Asian buying and central bank reserve accumulation. Both are sustainable long-term trends that not only bid up current prices but also put gold in strong hands that will hold it for years, if not generations.

In an age of diminished expectations, I strongly believe in the fact that there's still plenty of money and plenty of private equity capital available around the globe. What are in short supply are great entrepreneurs and great teams. A trading opportunity or a company's biggest challenge is and has always been the team behind it. There's enormous change under way in every facet of the world. Some is technology driven, some is market driven. All that change creates unprecedented opportunity, but to take full advantage of such opportunities I mostly focus on the team. The right teams and right people behind those opportunities always win. There is no secret sauce. Trading and investing has, in my experience, boiled down to building relationships and exchanging value. It consists of striking the right balance between backing and interacting with the right teams with the right business model at the right time and with the right amount of money.

Last but not least, I strongly believe that the best economic policy for any administration is the one that seeks to produce more entrepreneurs, not just more minimally educated college graduates with nowhere to go. Nothing against recent college graduates, but many of today's best universities are no longer providing the basics of a classical liberal education. I have a friend whose son recently graduated with a sociology degree from one of the nation's top universities without ever having taken a single class in logic, critical thought, or anything more than an overview of economics and Western philosophy. That's like giving someone a license to be a carpenter without giving them a claw hammer or teaching them how to read a tape measure and use a level. Let's also remember that some of the most successful entrepreneurs in modern America, including Bill Gates and Paul Allen of Microsoft, Apple's Steve Jobs, Mark Zuckerberg of Facebook, Enterprise Rent-a-Car's Jack Taylor, Oracle's Larry Ellison, Dell Computer's Michael Dell, movie and music producer David Geffen, and Sheldon Adelson, the CEO of the Sands Hotel and Casino in Las Vegas, never graduated from college.

That is why the single most important economic issue of our time—and one that impacts the poor and middle class alike—will be how we treat the entrepreneurs and wealth creators among us, from both the government and the private-sector viewpoints.

How to Best Protect Your Assets in the Turbulent Times Ahead

I believe the best strategies for protecting your assets in these turbulent times ahead include getting out of stocks, bonds, and speculative real estate markets and reducing your debts as much as possible.

- Convert your U.S.-backed assets such as cash into Swiss francs, kroners, or a couple of other strong currencies.
- Deposit your cash into offshore banks in Hong Kong, Panama, or other nations that have so far resisted the U.S. government's assertion that citizenship means that everything you own is, by inference, the property of the federal government and that the IRS is the sole arbiter of how much of your assets you should be allowed to keep.
- Be smart about this and seek counsel from an expert in international private banking. It is legal to do if you do it correctly, but it can (and probably will) be made to look like something very illegal if you don't do it in the proper manner.

If you are going to form a company in today's business environment, maximize your asset and identity protection by using a corporation organization formed in the state of Oklahoma, New Mexico, Indiana, Missouri, or Delaware. Form a revocable family living trust for estate purposes.

- If you invest, buy hard assets such as gold bullion, silver, diamonds, and a number of other commodities.
- Buy short-term government instruments and money market funds.
- Buy exchange-traded funds and stocks representing commodity businesses that will move up with the price of gold, silver, oil, and other commodities.
- Buy quality stocks that have paid dividends for many years and focus on companies that are in the food, water, and health businesses along with the ones that are in technologies that enable those types of companies. If you need to purchase real estate for the next few years, buy only residential and commercial real estate owned properties directly from the Federal Deposit Insurance Corporation (FDIC) or from lending institutions that presently own real estate in default.

To make a long story short, set your goals and missions to meet the new global financial order.

I have a friend who had a very successful career in the army and seemed to enjoy every single minute of it. I've heard others relate stories of how hard it was to endure their single two-year stint in the army. When I asked my first friend why his experience was so different from others', he told me the secret was that he thoroughly learned the rules. He found that if he knew the rules in intimate detail, he invariably found it was easier to function smoothly and effectively within the bureaucratic system. Remember, almost all financial and regulatory systems are bureaucracies.

When I compare the corporate culture of Drexel to Blackhawk, and think about what made me found Blackhawk, I see that two of the most important lessons I have learned in finance came from the Drexel experience. I am sure that I will remember them for the rest of my life.

The first lesson is that the sky is indeed the limit, if you associate yourself with people with a similar Drexel-type DNA. The sheer volume of deals, the market share you could have, your ability to add value to clients, how you could drive your competition nuts, and how much wealth you could create are all possible if you work with the right people. It was an institution where hard work and good ideas were rewarded, hierarchies were absent, talent abounded, and the potential to be very, very rich was palatable.

Second, there's a difference between being very competitive and can-do, and winning at all costs. At Drexel, we recognized that the "at all costs" modifier is indeed costly, and there were definitely lines that none of us would cross for the sake of our personal as well as the company's reputation; but if there was a deal to be made, we went after it with everything we had. No matter what people at large thought of Drexel Burnham, my former colleagues and I seem to agree on this much: there may never be another firm quite like it. Drexel had a certain chutzpah that hasn't been seen since. People seem to forget, though, that it was the only major financial firm to be shut down by regulators, sending a strong message that chutzpah shouldn't continue. And by most accounts, it hasn't.

So how does this translate into Blackhawk? My business is, indeed, first and foremost, a people's business, not a dollar-and-cents business. No matter how profitable the transaction under consideration may be, I will not entertain any size deal if the people behind it have not been very carefully vetted and have not been proven to be of the highest integrity. Too many people today on Wall Street go for the quick buck at the expense of their reputation and client satisfaction, the rationale being "let's make the money while we can and retire early in the sun." For me, this is not a sprint but a marathon, besides the fact that, in my definition, overnight success is 15 years. Anyone who does not understand the basic tenets of this philosophy is not someone I can or will do business with. You cannot imagine the number of times we were introduced to some shady Arab princes, Russian oligarchs, Chinese titans, or American entrepreneurs seeking the quick buck at all costs, which I gracefully declined despite all the money they would have showered on me. It's just not worth it.

While I am open to opportunities wherever they can be found, I tend to focus on sectors in which I have access to intelligence second to none and a management team that totally defies the norm. In a world awash with information, insight is often in short supply. Our edge at Blackhawk is our ability to leverage the local insight of our partners, closely collaborating from deal sourcing and due diligence through portfolio company development and building long-term trading relationships.

The result is a much broader view of potential investment and trading opportunities and deeper level of expertise, creating value that translates into superior returns.

Invest in Yourself

Last but not least, do everything you can to stay in good health. Drink plenty of good, clean water. Eat moderate amounts of healthy food. Make it a habit to walk a mile or two every day. Get an adequate amount of quality sleep every day. Read a wide variety of genres, and read everything you can get your hands on. Challenge your beliefs and educate yourself so that you can defend your personal dogma with logic and reason. Understand why you believe in what you believe; avoid the herd mentality. Learn a new language. Get a second degree. Travel to a foreign country. Develop a new hobby. Try something different every year.

Why do I tell you all of this?

Because only the strong, the smart, and the supple are going to survive; you need to do everything to minimize the effects of stress on your body, your mind, and your spirit if you are going to be a successful economic warrior.

Man is a threefold being with a body, a soul, and a spirit.

The body is the most obvious sign of a healthy person. It requires good fuel, plenty of exercise, and physical challenge to stay in peak performing condition.

The soul of man—his mind, intellect, thoughts, motivations—is not as obvious as the person's physical appearance, but the condition of the soul bears the most telling fruit as to the overall health of the individual.

Finally, there is the spirit of the human being. I believe this is what the Bible is referring to when it says that we are made in "the image of God." Our spirit is part of the universal, eternal life force. It is pure energy. When we are operating in perfect alignment, with the spirit directing the soul and the soul controlling the body, we are capable of achieving anything! Misalignment in any way leads to resistance, friction, and usually to failure.

I am not promoting any particular religion; all I'm saying is that you ultimately have to be motivated and guided by something larger than yourself if you are ever to truly experience a wealthy life, a life worth living. When you're doing what you're supposed to be doing, it rests softly inside your being with no fear, no judgment, and no imbalance. You just *know!*

Note

1. "The Global Political Awakening," Editorial, *New York Times*, December 16, 2008, online. Retrieved from www.nytimes.com/2008/12/16/opinion/16iht -YEbrzezinski.1.18730411.html?pagewanted=all.

Chapter 7

Strategic Goals

Never forget: the secret of creating riches for oneself is to create them for others.

—Sir John Templeton (1883–1970)
American-born businessman and investor

As I have shown, we are all in a global economic war. Whether your particular battlefront involves deciding to become an entrepreneur, making a midlife career change, revisiting your retirement plans, charting your company's research-and-development strategies, or advising your clients on where to invest for the next few years, the financial decisions that we all make and the strategies that we choose to use have far greater importance now than they did even a few years ago. We are engaged in a battle for the continuation of our capitalist, free-market economic model; our way of life; and our liberty.

The enemy is anticapitalist, believes in big government, embraces collectivist ideologies, and has, over the past century, infiltrated every level of our government and most of the banking industry. They don't care about patriotism, although they may sport the red, white, and blue and the stars and stripes on their bumper stickers. They don't care about personal responsibility or civic duty. They don't share your sense of honor. All they care about is power and control over your money and every aspect of your life.

The vehicle that I use to engage in this battle is private equity investing. More specifically, my investment vehicle is a private family office. I have developed very specific strategies for investing, and I am confident in the array of weapons at my disposal. I know how to use them to create the maximum amount of return on investment for my clients. This may or may not be the method that you should use to create wealth, but I feel it is important to give you some working knowledge about this particular option. As the economic battle shifts, knowledge becomes vital to our success. Consider this one more wealth creation vehicle that you may utilize in the future. Having options is always a good thing.

About the Private Equity Business Today

The private equity business is the biggest wealth creation money machine created by venture financiers in the past 30 years; however, it is under tremendous pressure today. In fact, recent research has shown that most private equity firms expect the fund-raising environment to remain very difficult and still experience significant downward pressure on fees. While a great number of the managing partners at the private equity funds are looking to raise capital, the great majority of them expect the process to be increasingly challenging, and this includes a number of existing $1 billion-plus funds, not just the new funds in formation.

This is where the private family office comes in.

What is a private family office? It is basically a private company that advises and manages investments and trusts on behalf of a single or multiple wealthy family investors. Traditional family offices provide personal services such as managing household staff and making travel arrangements. Other services typically handled by the traditional family office include property management, day-to-day accounting and payroll activities, and management of legal affairs. Family offices often provide family management services, which includes family governance, financial and investment education, philanthropy coordination, and succession planning. Some family offices accept non–family members. More recently, the term *family office* or *multifamily office* is used to refer primarily to financial services for a group of relatively wealthy families.

Single-family offices are an exceptional source of funds for many private equity firms as well as entrepreneurs. In general, single-family offices have significant money to invest in private companies. Single-family offices tend to have long-term investment horizons and are comfortable with the dynamics of investing in these companies, as that's how their own fortunes were often made. Well over half of the single-family offices are investing today in private equity, primarily through funds. However, there's a growing trend for these family offices as well as ultra-affluent investors to invest directly in companies, often alongside their peers.

Family offices interested in aligned investment opportunities are likely to commit substantial monies to private equity deals or funds they understand well. Such investments tend to represent a substantial portion, if not the majority, of their investable assets. They find this approach much more appealing than a diversified portfolio.

While the wealthy have always coinvested in private equity deals, I am seeing a strong surge in this approach with which entrepreneurs should seriously consider partnering. In fact, single-family offices and individual ultra-affluent investors are increasingly teaming up to invest in everything from start-ups to providing mezzanine financing and even select smaller management buyouts. As a result, many single-family offices as well as an increasing number of ultra-affluent investors are forming highly selective private equity investment clubs. When one of them comes across an interesting deal, the members of their club, and occasionally friends of members, each get a chance to kick the tires and see if they believe the firm in question would be a good investment. While private equity funds are still in demand by single-family offices and ultra-affluent investors, the opportunity to invest directly alongside others who are putting their own money on the line is especially appealing. In this scenario, it's very clear how committed each investor is to the deal. This is the model that I personally follow.

One of the more insightful research results that recently surfaced was that nearly 40 percent of the single-family offices investing in private equity are seeking deals that are well aligned with the way they created their fortunes. This means they're inclined to invest in funds that are similar to the businesses that produced their wealth. These are business ventures they understand well. Therefore, if a single-family office made its money in banking and has a high level of alignment between its source of wealth and its philosophy, the single-family office tends to be predisposed to invest in banks or funds that invest in banks. The fact that the fee structure is more appealing compared to a typical fund is also proving attractive to the super-rich and entrepreneurs seeking capital alike. By and large, the management fees and carried interest of a fund are somewhat minimized and, in some cases, even nonexistent. When the parties co-invest, they're keenly focused on the success of their investments, since that is how they're going to profit. Another consideration is being able to work with people who have an in-depth knowledge of a specific field such as health care, Internet technology, or manufacturing.

The single-family office or ultra-affluent investor sourcing deals usually has a deep understanding and a very well established network in a particular field. For example, one family office I know of in the Far East has done lots of business with investments extensively in biotech firms. The founding family made its fortune by creating a biotech company that it eventually sold to a major pharmaceutical firm. This is an area it knows exceptionally well, and it also knows all the key players. Today, it is part of a small number of family offices that shares deals with my associates and me on a global basis.

A significant consideration for those single-family offices and wealthy individuals investing directly in private equity opportunities is their ability to evaluate the deals. They need to be able to conduct their own due diligence and analysis of each company seeking money that crosses their radar. Such expertise is in-house for some single-family offices and wealthy investors. For other super-rich private equity investors, the use of boutique private investment banks is the solution. Either way, what I am seeing is an expanding interest in individual deals that's likely to lead to more and more single-family offices as well as ultra-affluent investors investing directly in promising private companies.

My recommendation for all entrepreneurs out there with good ideas and strong execution capabilities is to seriously start considering this path rather than looking to raise their own fund or going through the excruciating path and layers of bureaucracy when dealing with your "classic" private equity funds. As deal sizes have grown and valuations have escalated, so-called club deals involving consortia of financial and sometimes a combination of financial and strategic investors are becoming the norm.

This phenomenon of single-family office investing and club deals, and its complexities, has been widely reported. Commentators have provided sound advice as to how to avoid the more common pitfalls of club deals to make them work more efficiently. In this context, the trade press has also reported on the increasing frequency with which private equity firms rely on coinvestors to complete large transactions, and the challenges of involving coinvestors directly in the deal-making process. Less frequently discussed, however, is the growing use of so-called side-car or overallocation funds to meet the need for additional equity capital to complete larger acquisitions, and this is exactly where private family offices can also come in handy for the private equity funds as well.

Side-car funds bring with them several technical complications and are not a panacea for the challenges of today's mega-deal marketplace. They can, however, provide an attractive alternative to fund sponsors and private equity funds alike seeking to reduce their participation in club deals, and especially for those who do not believe they have a mix of limited partners (LPs) who are ready, willing, and able to provide the necessary magnitude of coinvestment capital within critical time constraints. Side cars work best for midsized funds looking to top up their availability of unfunded capital. Under all circumstances, the decision to proceed with a side-car fund-raise should be made in consultation with experienced counsel. With a little luck, elegant solutions can be found that maximize the flexibility available to the fund sponsor, while ensuring a healthy alignment of interests with private family offices whose loyalties have been well earned.

The Five Myths of Private Equity

I meet face to face with an average of 500 entrepreneurs a year, and I keep hearing the same question: why is every private equity fund with which we meet trying to take advantage of us? I will be the first to admit there are some real predators out there looking for an opportunity to take advantage of someone in need of financial backing; however, I don't believe there are as many sharks as the hysteria-prone financial press would have you believe. If there were, the investment sector would soon be shut down. As venture capital and private equity continue to make news headlines, some entrepreneurs may find it challenging to distinguish fact from fiction. I always counter these challenges with three simple questions:

1. Do investors always win at the expense of entrepreneurs?
2. Are investors always out to wrest control from management?
3. Finally, is an investor's sole focus on the final liquidity event?

Misperceptions can prevent an entrepreneur from making rational, fact-based decisions. During my 25 years as an investor and financier, I have come to identify what I call "The Five Myths of Private Equity."

The first is that private equity is a win-lose game. In this scenario, investors win and entrepreneurs lose. This is the favorite myth of people who are looking for someone to blame for their bad choices. They didn't read the contract they signed, they were too lazy to do their due diligence, or some other negative outcome occurred that caused them to lose control of their enterprise. They're understandably angry, hurt, and looking to place the blame on someone other than themselves. According to this myth, private investors somehow make off with the value of your company, perhaps buying at a low price and cutting you out of the eventual rewards that you'd earn from going public or selling to another company. The important fact to remember is that private equity investors make money only if the value of your company appreciates. It is also a fact that, in most cases, the entrepreneur retains a substantial interest in the business. After all, it's in the investor's best interest to help you grow your company and increase its value. So, by default, if the investor wins, the entrepreneur wins.

The second myth is that valuations are the only consideration when you're shopping the deal. Valuation is certainly an important consideration. You want to get a fair price when you sell your company; however, it's equally important to partner with an investor who shares your goals and who will work with you to achieve them. When you focus exclusively on valuation, you risk ending up with a partner who doesn't understand your company, your growth strategies, or your industry. For example, let's say you sell your company to an investor whose expectations for your business are unrealistically high. You may obtain a good price for your company, but that relationship is likely to sour as the business fails to meet the investor's expectations. However, an investor with a more nuanced understanding of your company would work with you to increase its value in a realistic and sustainable way.

The third myth is that private equity investors don't add value because they haven't been in an operating role. This may be true in some cases but should be avoided as a generalization. Most financiers and professional investors I know have ample experience with operating issues. Also, though they don't usually try to micromanage portfolio companies, they can look at the operation from an objective perspective and add value by challenging management to think outside the box. Investors who have backed many different companies at rapid growth stages can recognize patterns that may not be obvious to the management team. They may have a network of relationships that can also assist companies in recruiting talent at the board and management level. They can often help companies explore strategic partnerships with other firms.

The fourth most common myth is that the taking of venture capital or private equity money means you lose control of your company. This often refers to the sharks and other predators looking for quick kill and smelling desperation. It can also stem from a person who is so determined to get their idea to market that they will accept any terms offered. As an entrepreneur, you cannot abdicate your responsibility for the sake of expedience. Nobody is forcing you to take a deal and surrender control. I have found that the people who recount horror stories of how they had to take a backseat to an investor almost always did one of three things. They either did not contact more than a few investors or took the first deal that was offered to them, or they sold more of their interest in order to gain access to some quick money.

The first instance is just plain laziness. The second is desperation. The third, more often than not, is due to the fact that the entrepreneur has exhausted all of his available resources and needs to cover the demands of his creditors.

The reality is that if you take on a minority investment, you can continue to control your company, make all operating decisions, and have the ultimate say over strategic issues. It is my experience that the majority of investors do not want to run your company. They are busy running their own. Selling less than half of your company leaves you in charge, while providing liquidity to you and other early shareholders.

The last myth—namely, that private equity investors are interested only in your exit strategy—is one that ignores some basic realities about investing. When a private equity firm invests in your company, they do expect to exit their investment within the next five to seven years. Since the firm has limited partners who expect liquidity at some point, they can't hold their investment forever. However, this doesn't mean that you will have to sell your company or take it public. Alternatives might include recapping the company with bank debt, swapping out one investor with a new private equity investor, or raising capital from a strategic partner. In any event, your private equity partner has a vested interest in growing your company over the next several years up to the exit event. Their goal during this period is the same as yours: to increase the value of your company by expanding the business.

Whether or not to take on private equity financing is a complex decision, requiring in-depth analysis of your personal and business goals, the market environment, and the financing options available. Focusing on these important considerations and avoiding the more common misperceptions will help you make the right decision. It's time to put the myths to rest.

My Personal View on the Biggest Challenges in the Private Equity Industry Today

It is a fact that the private equity industry today faces an ever complicated and difficult environment as credit markets are trying to absorb maturing debt from large leveraged buyouts and as a number of the most credible financial sponsors out there are still scrambling to prepare for the rounds of refinancing that will start coming into the marketplace in 2012.

If you take a close look at the ratio of credit to gross domestic product over the past 100 years, the figure over most of that time ranged from 140 percent to 160 percent, but it spiked to 265 percent before the Great Depression. It rose to the highest levels ever, more than 300 percent, approaching the current downturn. Returning to more natural levels will require high savings rates, inflation, or a massive markdown of bad debt.

In the boom years from 2005 to 2007, private equity deals were completed with as little as 15 percent equity, leaving leveraged portions at a higher rate than in the 1980s and 1990s. Since the economic meltdown that began in late 2007, 35 percent to 40 percent equity has been required. For smaller buyouts, the equity requirement is 50 percent to 75 percent.

During the last big wave of private equity financing, hedge funds were flush and found it easy to leverage syndicated products. In 2006, financial sector market capitalizations had doubled from just a few years earlier. Looking forward three or four years, it is clear that the industry will have decreased dramatically, with hedge funds no longer leveraging deals with 90 percent debt levels. All these companies will have to refinance into a much smaller market. So we're going to see a general perception of more distress than ever before.

It is a fact that there is today a wave of private equity bank financing that is coming to maturity in 2012 and 2013. Because of this, private equity firms must and are aggressively increasing cash margins. In order to conserve cash, some private equity firm managers are closing plants and trying to sell assets; however, asset sales are difficult in this current environment, and we are frankly questioning whether some traditional business models and assumptions are viable even after significant cost cuts. It is also a fact that companies are paring down and taking a strategic look at their business models. If a portfolio company's model requires cash early on to meet the promise of opportunity later, you have to get rid of it. Operational team meetings are being set to devise 100-day plans focusing on issues such as supply-chain management and sales programs. Basically, management teams are being told to batten down the hatches and take more severe actions.

I personally believe that private equity firms around the world, especially in the United States, will experience a much slower period over the next three to four years in which firms can restructure, buy back portfolio company debt, or take other operational steps to be all set to have handsome returns when the refinancing hits. Some companies are approaching private equity firms about partnerships. When the dust settles, there will be more private equity going into corporate partnerships than corporate money going into private equity firms.

I am also afraid that relationships mean much less in today's environment. In the past few years, as the economy boomed, banks were eager to lend. If a borrower had a problem, the bank would fall back on relationships and cooperate with management as it worked through the difficulty. Now, relationships have to give way to concerns about the bottom line. In today's market, reason and understanding have disappeared on the part of fund managers, who are watching the red ink rise, and lenders are instructed to push as hard as possible to extract as much value as they can.

It is clear that the emphasis today is on operations. Quite frankly, I believe this is a refreshing change in emphasis. We at Blackhawk look at each company under consideration and question the business model, the cash flows, the management experience and expertise, the marketing strategy, and every other aspect that would impact the company's ability to compete in today's marketplace. We even discuss taking advantage of potential consolidation or investments with strategic buyers or investors, because we expect economic conditions to remain murky for the near term. We would rather do something today and shore up the capital structure than wait until later when there are fewer options. From a family office standpoint, these potential partners are looking for us to be thoughtful and creative. Returns are going to matter a great deal in the near future, because when it is time to raise money again, our family offices will want to see how well we managed our companies during the recession. Possible solutions could be capital injections and also being very operationally involved in the businesses. Although all is not doom and gloom, most buyers in the private equity markets would like to see higher prices to help complete exit transactions, while at the same time prices are sharply lower for those interested in strategic acquisitions.

Regarding the risk-return ratio, I believe the debt market represents one of the best investment options. Think about this market as two different buckets. One is the debt of healthy companies returning 15 percent to 25 percent. The other is the debt of distressed companies that could be purchased to gain control of the business or drive it into a restructuring. Such an approach has become increasingly popular and will be even more so as time goes by. A lack of covenants and other mechanisms that would trigger default sooner are delaying inevitable restructurings. Given the maturities, this is going to continue for four or five years at a minimum. We're in the top of the first inning in terms of restructuring and distressed-debt opportunities.

Forced divestitures will also provide opportunity. Major companies under pressure will need to unload desirable businesses. It will take a while for the expectations of both buyer and seller to line up. However, the companies that become available to us will be at valuations that are more attractive.

Which Industries Are Particularly Interesting for "Distressed Investing"?

I believe the retail sector is a particularly interesting one in this regard. There are no straightforward leveraged buyouts to be done in there, but there are ways we can come in to shore up the capital structure or help buy a competitor and achieve synergy. It's an area where having a good understanding of the space will matter. Longer term, I believe both retail and health care will provide opportunities for creative, smart strategies because they are undergoing dramatic change and because, in past recessions, the price to acquire competitors has declined.

A second opportunity will come in remaking the financial sector itself. Restructuring the industry will create opportunities for new business models that people have not thought of yet and that put private equity capital behind new financial businesses.

What Sectors of the Private Equity Markets Are We Focusing on Today?

With all the current challenges facing the private equity markets, it's no secret that noncyclical sectors are the best ones to invest in today.

In this regard, I see three industry sectors that are heating up in today's environment and that are worth focusing on. These are energy, health care, and technology.

Energy

Energy consumption in the United States is projected to rise by 31 percent by 2030, according to U.S. Energy Department projections. We are undoubtedly ready to take advantage of the growth opportunities in the sector. Since the beginning of 2008, $15 billion has been poured into the sector, with $10 billion in private equity funds raised for investment. There are about 100,000 energy companies globally, with more than $8 trillion in assets under management. All types of energy deals are seeing activity these days, but alternative energy is certainly garnering most of the attention. I believe alternative energy will grow from about 20 percent of the deals we now do per year to as much as 40 percent, depending on market conditions.

The growth in alternative energy is being driven by new regulatory requirements and higher commodity prices. State-by-state renewable portfolio standard requirements in the electricity space, ethanol blending targets in the biofuel space, and technologies that were completely nascent or didn't exist 10 years ago are starting to approach commercialization; however, while transactions in alternative energy can vary widely, sector fragmentation is the single attribute that remains constant. There are a lot of highly fragmented services in the energy sector, especially in oilfield services. This industry has been depressed for the past 15 years, and many entrepreneurs are considering exiting or retiring. In addition, we have seen a significant trend in children who don't want to take over family businesses anymore, so these businesses will likely be sold. This creates an incredible opportunity to roll these companies up, and that is what we do best.

Another factor driving energy deals is the price of oil. As the price of a barrel of oil continues to remain high, spending the money to find an alternative makes economic sense. At $110 a barrel, alternative energy becomes feasible and many traditional energy companies look attractive.

A coming investment opportunity will be in regards to infrastructure, especially the electrical distribution network downstream from the transmission grid. A friend of mine in the electrical engineering business recently participated in a seasonal preparedness survey for a large utility in a major metropolitan area. At one electrical substation he inspected, he found an aging oil-filled distribution transformer was leaking so badly that the station technicians had rigged up a plastic children's wading pool to collect the oil and a small pump to recycle it back into the tank. The backup transformer was offline and had been waiting for replacement parts for three months. This leaking, worn-out transformer happened to be providing electrical power for the city's downtown financial center and a major university! This was not, my friend insisted, an isolated case.

While the current administration touts its investment in infrastructure by funding visible projects such as repaving roads and rebuilding bridges, the network that provides for our basic security and quality of life is worn out and teetering on the brink of nationwide failure. I see utilities making very strong investments in modernization of distribution and control networks in the near future. Much of the nation's public and private electrical distribution equipment is at or past the end of its rated service life. This could make electrical engineering, construction, and electrical equipment manufacturing very strong investment areas in the near term. Upgrades will happen, hopefully, before the rolling blackouts start turning out the lights across the country.

Health Care

The health care industry has become an especially popular destination for us to allocate capital these days. The industry is generally viewed as a recession-resistant safe haven when times are bad. In good times, it's as appealing as any other growth sector. But with the Baby Boomers coming of age, the need for health care companies continues to grow every day.

We are seeing the aging population accelerate faster and faster. So there will be plenty of different opportunities in this space for the next 10 to 15 years. There will be more and more people to be served. A disconnect currently exists between the number of services available and the projected population growth. We are working hard to fill that gap. Overall, merger-and-acquisition deal volume is still increasing, and a lot of our partners are interested in the health care space. It's considered recession-proof. And unlike many industries where you can have a short product cycle, health care companies have a longer life span. Most important, the pace of change is not excessively rapid.

We strongly believe that people are always going to need health care and services, and we are in a great position to take advantage of the growing demands. However, there are a number of risks. The major one is a decrease in the reimbursement rate, which will most likely be seen if the current administration's massive national health care bill survives court challenges to its constitutionality and gets put into place. A change in reimbursement rates will adjust any company's earnings, in most cases not for the better. Such drastic changes to government regulation always have to be considered as part of risk management; however, the coming technological advances that are transforming the health care industry certainly make it an attractive place to look for strong investment opportunities.

Technology

The recent credit crunch has paralyzed almost every industry; however, we are still active in the technology sector, which today is bustling as if there is no tomorrow. The thing about tech is that you always have to be thinking about the future, the next thing. Even a boring tech company needs to be looking ahead. And just like in the early 2000s, now is a good time to be working on the next thing so companies are ready.

The second factor that makes tech strong is that competition for deals has eased, due in part to the departure of generalist firms that have been scared off by the lack of credit. However, for firms that play in the tech space, the lack of leverage is common. Market conditions aren't so far off from what they were prior to the past few years, and these companies use less leverage than your normal buyout.

In the technology sector, I have always had to look at all the ways to get a deal done, and sometimes it's with less leverage. I have also noticed that corporate orphans are easier to buy these days because companies are looking to shed noncore assets. Furthermore, the industry has matured, making it easier for investors to understand the business propositions. Additionally, because of their maturity, these firms now have an operating history, making them easier to evaluate and more attractive than ever to opportunistic private equity investors.

I hope this sets the record straight regarding my views on these three key industry sectors and how I plan on capitalizing on the opportunities ahead. Now, let me give you some inside information about what I look for in a presentation and what you should never, ever bring to me if you are looking to have me finance your enterprise.

Private Equity Deal Killers

Here are some of the classic "deal killers" that I encounter when reviewing the more than 2,000 business plans that come across my desk every year. By "deal killers" I really mean the generic statements for you to avoid when submitting your pitch. I hope that by sharing this information, you will be better prepared to fine-tune your unique sales proposition (USP) when approaching me or anyone else, for that matter, for funding.

These are the fairly common faux pas that my peers and I see on a daily basis. Under normal economic conditions, I might be tempted to overlook some of these blunders in the hopes that I might stumble upon a diamond in the rough. That is not the case in the current economic environment. There are too many people vying for a limited amount of resources and I am not willing to take the unnecessary risk of dealing with someone who is not professional or astute enough to avoid these obvious pitfalls. From my conversations with my peers and all of the articles I've read, I am not alone in that reservation. So, if you are serious about getting me or someone like me to fund your next big thing, pay attention.

No Competition

The number one way to ensure that your proposal is going to rain down from my office window onto the passersby below like confetti on New Year's Eve is to make the statement that your business idea has no competition. While it may be true that no other company sells a product substantially similar to yours, this does not imply a lack of competition. Any substitute product, process, or service that satisfies the same need is a competitive solution. Stating that no competition exists reveals either a lack of market research or imagination on your part. While you may intend such a statement to imply that your new product, process, or service is so unique, proprietary, or innovative that it will corner the market overnight, I have to err on the side of caution and interpret the lack of competition as evidence that there is no perceived need for your product, process, or service. If there is a perceived need, then the market is either so risky, undesirable, or miniscule as to be unprofitable. Such a statement is an instant deal killer for me.

Inept Competitors

A close cousin to "there is no competition" is the statement that the existing competition is too lazy, stupid, or any other adjective you might use to denigrate your competition. This will detract from your business plan more than it adds. The statement offers me no insight into why your company will succeed against an entrenched company; however, it will tell me much about your emotional maturity and indicate a great deal about how you will react under pressure when things do not go as planned—which, by the way, is almost always the case. If the competition has failed to seize the initiative due to its organizational structure, speak to the lack of incentives implied by this type of organization and contrast how your organizational structure remedies that shortcoming. Identify weaknesses in the competition that are difficult to change, as opposed to poor leadership, which is relatively easy to change. Offer me information that shows me you have a thorough understanding of the competitive landscape rather than hurl invectives against the existing companies. All that is going to accomplish is having me hurl invectives against you.

Sweat Equity

The next misstep is telling me that the founders of your enterprise have invested X number of hours of their time in the company, thus having X amount of sweat equity. I do like to see that the founders of an entrepreneurial company seeking funding believe in their business enough to make investment and personal sacrifice to sustain its survival, but please do not confuse the two. While forgone salary represents an economic cost of the venture to an entrepreneur, it is not an investment into the business. Investment translates to "cash" spent for costs related to starting and developing the business. If you have spent a significant amount to do this, please make sure to include the figure somewhere in the financial section of your business plan. If you haven't put your own money into the venture, don't expect me to.

Start-up Investment Model

The fourth deal killer is particular to me and my investment model. I know this is disappointing to some, but I make no apologies for it because my track record speaks for itself. I don't do start-ups.

Why not?

Well, it basically boils down to how one interprets the historical statistics. According to PricewaterhouseCoopers's MoneyTree report, the definitive source of information on emerging companies that receive financing and the venture capital firms that provide it, only 5 percent of companies will hit $50 million in sales at the 5-year mark. Of those that will reach that milestone, only 5 percent will hit the $1 billion sales level within their first 10 years of operation. And these are the companies that generate the new jobs in the economy.

This means, as an investor on this side of the deal looking at the same statistics, that 95 percent of start-ups will *not* hit $50 million in sales in five years, and 95 percent of the 5 percent that do reach that milestone will *never* reach the $1 billion in sales mark. There will still be many good new jobs created, but only a very few companies will provide a substantive return on my investment. Remember, my prime objective is creating wealth, not creating jobs.

On that same note, any statement similar in content to "Our projections are very conservative and we will break even or be profitable in X years from today" will get you immediately bounced from consideration. If you haven't already generated profits and haven't attracted enough clients to show me that you're actually running a business as opposed to just tinkering with an idea, you and I are most probably not a fit. I'm interested in operators, and "track record" is a key variable in how I size up the attractiveness of a potential investment. Don't confuse this preference with an aversion to risk. I have been known to go out on a limb and back an entrepreneur who made it big time and lost it all. I would rather do that than fund someone who never generated profits or had to make a payroll and is still conceptualizing his or her thoughts. Ideas are a dime a dozen. Execution is everything.

Exaggeration

Don't use hyperbole in estimating your market or how much market share you project you will capture. I just shake my head whenever I see statements like "We will sell into the $X trillion global market. . . ." Incorrectly sizing the market tells me one of two things: management lacks either the knowledge to assess who would buy the product or the integrity to delimit this statistic accurately. If it is the first, I will think you are either too lazy or too stupid to succeed. If it is the latter, I don't want to be in business with you. Either way, I'm not going to back your plan. I operate on the basic premise that business is "war" and the only way to win is to be armed with better intelligence. Let me give you a little insight. No matter what numbers you put in your plan, I am going to have my analysts and my intelligence network confirm them. If there is a variation of more than a few percentage points, I'm going to think you are not smart enough to know how to take my investment and build it into a healthy return. Pay attention to details and be honest. You are not going to impress me with your fantastic claims and wishful notions.

Use of Funds

This leads to deal killer number 6, the absence of information regarding how funding will be used. Knowing *why* you are raising the capital is as important to me as knowing for *what* you are raising capital. I have some experience in determining operating expenses and like to think I have a pretty good idea of what is required for certain businesses to succeed. Also, if I am going to fund your business, we are partners in a very real sense. I believe that gives me the right and, more important, the obligation as part of my duty and service to you to know what you are or will be doing with the money. I am not interested in funding lifestyle entrepreneurs who have somehow convinced themselves that in order to be taken seriously in their business, they have to have a penthouse overlooking South Beach, a chauffeured limousine, and a private jet. I'm looking to fund a performance entrepreneur who leases a space in an office park, drives an appropriate vehicle, and, if it is a requirement, has a membership with a service providing fractional ownership of a corporate jet. I am not opposed to utilizing all of the tools necessary to drive or even force your venture into success. Just show me that you understand concepts like opportunity cost, risk and return and deferred reward. The trappings of success come to those who have earned them, not to those who are living on someone else's dime.

The bottom line is that I use the old fruit stand analogy when evaluating a business plan: "Lemons ripen early, plums ripen late." If the deal looks like a lemon early, it probably is a lemon.

How Do You Turn Billion-Dollar Ideas into Billion-Dollar Businesses?

According to David Thomson, who has been leading business growth for 20 years in general management and executive sales and marketing roles at Nortel Networks and Hewlett-Packard and also served as an associate principal during his five years at McKinsey & Company, the seven essentials for turning a billion-dollar idea into a billion-dollar business begins with creating and sustaining what he calls a breakthrough value proposition. This means distilling the authentic vision of the company into a statement that differentiates your product or service from the competition in such an effective way that it becomes your identifying theme. It must instantly transmit the value you bring to the marketplace to your existing and potential clients. It defines your brand's unique differentiator and potential.

The second essential element is being able to exploit a high-growth market segment. It doesn't do you much good if you have an idea for the greatest corset cinching machine ever conceived. There is simply no market for the product.

Third, it helps if you have "star" customers who are going to contribute to revenue generation. This is due to the fact that either they are trendsetters and will have many followers or they are centers of influence and will serve as word-of-mouth evangelists for your product or service. Remember Joe Girard's Rule of 250: people tell 250 other people about a product or service that they have purchased, whether it is a good experience or a bad one.

Fourth is to leverage "big brother" alliances for breaking into new markets. If someone you know and have some affinity with has already blazed the trail into a market that you have targeted, make them an affiliate or do a joint venture with them. There is nothing wrong about piggybacking off of someone else's hard work and success as long as you make it a win–win proposition for all involved.

Fifth, become the master of exponential returns. If your costs are $1 and you can easily sell your product for $4, see if you can market it as a perceived value at $10 or $15. It is often *how* you market a product that determines sales volume more than the actual merits of the product itself.

The sixth element to turning your billion-dollar idea into a billion-dollar business is to back an "inside-outside leadership" management team. This means that the people who run the company not only have the education and experience to be effective managers, but they also possess the integrity, character, and values to be inspiring leaders. It is not easy to get to the top of the mountain, and you can't do it by pulling or pushing your team. They have to be willing to follow you.

Finally, put together a board comprised of real experts who have wisdom gained through experience and networks that can lead you to sources you never knew existed. Surround yourself with people who inspire, challenge, and motivate you to reach farther and try harder than you thought possible. These are the counselors who will guide you to the most satisfying success.

These are the ideas that have become pretty much the driving force in building our portfolio of clients. They are the framework that I try to instill in every person or group I back.

Chapter 8

Tactical Maneuvers

If an ordinary person is silent, it may be a tactical maneuver. If a writer is silent, he is lying.
—Jaroslav Seifert (1901–1986) Nobel Prize–winning
Czech writer, poet, and journalist

Once again, this is not a how-to book. You are not going to truly understand the techniques for how to create wealth unless you completely understand how the wealth creation system in this country has been structured, how the wealth creators in this country really operate, and how you can prosper, despite the best efforts of the Progressive anticapitalists.

I still believe it is possible to create wealth in the United States of America. I am also convinced that we are at a crossroads in our history as a nation. Whether we choose to correct our present course and reclaim our prosperity or whether we shuffle into the gray mediocrity of socialistic servitude will be determined by how engaged the American electorate is in the next election.

This book is a profile of my economic and political philosophies. In future books, I plan to walk through the detailed processes for

141

investing in various transactions and show the insider secrets for leveraging your investments with different vehicles. In this book, I am only
sharing what has worked for my partners and me over the past two
decades and allowed my clients and me to build real value while many
around me watched their fortunes disappear like sand blowing in the
desert.

Real Estate

Before the collapse of 2008, real estate was considered to be a sure
route to prosperity. While the market value of property was known
to rise and fall, there was the general perception that real estate was
a solid long-term investment. It was, for the most part, a finite
resource. The concept that an individual had the right to own his
property made America unique, and a major part of the American
Dream was being able to buy your own home; but the two concepts
are not synonymous. With the right to own private property comes
the responsibility to be able to afford and maintain your investment.
That's what made the subprime mortgage collapse so demoralizing.
An overwhelming majority of people in the United States and other
free-market countries considered their home to be an investment that
would provide them security in their retirement years. That dream
was wiped out for millions of people by the recklessness and greed of
a surprisingly few strategically placed individuals. So far, none of them
have been prosecuted for what was clearly behavior that violated every
professional standard of care and ethic under which they were supposedly operating.

Former *Wall Street Journal* reporter and columnist Roger Lowenstein published an article in the May 16, 2011, issue of *Bloomberg
Businessweek* in which he made the preposterous claim that "people
who contribute to a financial collapse aren't guilty of a crime absent
specific violations that make them so."[1] This semantically whitewashed
piece of fanciful hand-wringing could be taken for satire of the highest
form if not for the fact that Lowenstein is absolutely serious. In
framing his argument, he conveniently omits the one principle that
makes the subprime mortgage mess distinctive from a holdup of the

corner convenience store: a fiduciary duty is the highest standard of care at either equity or law. In other words, when a person serves in a capacity involving trust, confidence, and reliance on professional expertise, a fiduciary relationship exists. The client is depending on the fiduciary to exercise his discretion or expertise on the client's behalf. The law forbids the fiduciary from acting in any manner adverse or contrary to the interests of the client, or from acting for his own benefit in relation to the subject matter.

The fact is that a person acting in a fiduciary capacity who turns a blind eye to fraudulent mortgage application practices is a criminal. A person who convinces regulators to bend the rules so they can squeeze more profits out of the system before it crashes is a criminal. A person who sells garbage investments on one hand while betting against them on the other is a criminal. And a person who uses the power of their political office to cover the losses of their cronies while refusing to throw the same lifeline to their drowning competitors is a criminal. It is a sad commentary on the relativistic state of our collective morality that men like Paulson, Blankfein, Bernanke, Geithner, Mozilo, and Fuld aren't wearing orange cotton jumpsuits instead of custom-tailored wool suits and silk ties.

I have not invested in real estate for some time. I am not convinced we have seen the bottom of the real estate market yet, despite the recent media reports to the contrary. There is a glut of inventory in residential and commercial real estate that still needs to be processed. In 25 of the top real estate markets, 10 have a backup of nearly two years or more that will keep prices depressed for some time.[2] Florida is leading the nation in the supply of homes that are classified as "distressed." The state has about two years of supply, with almost half of the residential mortgages being in a negative equity position. Other states in similar situations are New Jersey, Illinois, Maine, Georgia, New York, Indiana, Minnesota, Maryland, and Michigan. Mississippi has a huge supply of distressed residential properties forecasted to last another five years or so, but most of that is still fallout from Hurricane Katrina.

According to the latest real estate market report from CoreLogic,[3] specific cities struggling with residential inventory include the Chicagoland area, where a quarter of homeowners are upside-down in their mortgages and there is a four year surplus of inventory. In the city of Detroit, there are residential properties that the city will reportedly sell you for $1. The suburbs of Detroit are a bit better value, but more than 40 percent of residential homeowners in southeastern Michigan are in a negative equity position. In Florida, metro areas like Tampa-St. Petersburg-Clearwater and Orlando-Kissimmee-Sanford are reporting about two years of inventory with nearly half of the mortgages in an upside-down position.[4]

The uncertainty regarding foreclosures must also be resolved. Sale of foreclosed properties now constitutes almost 24 percent of the market, according to Zillow Real Estate Research.[5] Banks seem to be exacerbating the problem instead of working toward a solution because they continue to try and squeeze every drop of profit out of the market possible. It would have been more beneficial to the national economy, in the long term, had the banks written off all of the bad mortgages and surrendered title to those whose mortgages could not be validated.

On the commercial real estate front, the news is equally troubling. Bill McBride reported in his finance and economics blog, Calculated Risk, that Moody's REAL All Property Type Aggregate Index declined 3.3 percent in February 2011.[6] According to Moody's, commercial real estate prices are down another 4.9 percent from a year ago and down about 44.7 percent from the peak in 2007. Prices are just above the post-bubble low last August. This puts them back at the same levels they were at in 2002.

Following the past three years of decline, I believe a full market recovery is highly unlikely until after the elections of 2012 at the earliest. Unless you are looking to buy and hold for a very long time, real estate is probably not an area that you want to invest in for the foreseeable future.

Alternative Investment Vehicles

The purpose of a hedge is to protect and shield. Thus, a hedge fund is a fund that protects and shields the investment and sometimes the investor. The most common type of hedge fund shields the investor from the market dips and takes advantage of market rallies. How they do it has been subject of many volumes more technical and scholarly than this one.

In a recent Reuters article, financial reporter Svea Herbst-Bayliss reported that assets of the hedge fund industry have reached a staggering $1.92 trillion, growing a record $149 billion just in the last quarter of 2010. Estimates of industry size vary widely today due to the absence of central statistics, the lack of an agreed definition of hedge funds, and the rapid growth of the industry. As a general indicator of scale, the industry may have managed around $2.5 trillion at its peak in the summer of 2008. The credit crunch has caused assets under management to fall sharply through a combination of trading losses and the withdrawal of assets from funds by investors.

Hedge funds are largely under the purview of a recently revamped Commodity Futures Trading Commission (CFTC). This agency has the far-reaching mandate to "assure the economic utility of the futures markets by encouraging their competitiveness and efficiency, ensuring their integrity, protecting market participants against manipulation, abusive trading practices, and fraud, and ensuring the financial integrity of the clearing process."[7]

Hedge funds are generally classified based on their particular method or sector of investing and trading. These include Global Macro, Statistical Arbitrage, Convertible Arbitrage, equities long and short, Commodity Trading Advisors (CTA), quant investing, fixed-income arbitrage, short-term trading, and multistrategy funds, to name just a few. Each one is distinctly different from the other, and the styles of managers, even when trading in the same subsector, can also be drastically different. The term *hedge fund* is a very loose term and makes it impossible to generalize when discussing this subject.

Financial journalist Alfred W. Jones is believed to be one of the first hedge fund managers, in 1949. Jones believed there was a correlation between performance of an asset and the performance of the overall market that influenced the price movements of the individual asset, usually in a negative manner. To counteract this market influence, he balanced his portfolio by buying assets whose price he expected to be stronger than the market and selling short assets he expected to be weaker than the market. He saw that price movements due to the overall market would be canceled out because, if the overall market rose, the loss on shorted assets would be canceled by the additional gain on longed assets and vice versa. Because the effect is to "hedge" that part of the risk due to overall market movements, this type of portfolio became known as a hedge fund.[8] This investment vehicle was further refined by two math professors from the University of California at Irvine, Ed Thorp and Sheen Kassouf, who found a way to mathematically predict volatility in stock warrants based on statistical rules that Thorp had developed to win at blackjack. Their 1967 book, *Beat the Market: A Scientific Stock Market System,* is considered the Rosetta stone of modern quantitative investing. This is a form of picking investments based on mathematical probabilities or discovering statistical patterns and anomalies. By 1968, there were over 140 hedge funds in operation, according to the Securities and Exchange Commission (SEC).[9] Today's quants use high-powered computers running sophisticated database tracking programs that look for asset movement correlations and price patterns.

The hedge fund market has indeed evolved from being just hedging vehicles to a class of investment in its own right. The origins of the modern hedge fund industry are actually in professional managed products that financial institutions used exclusively to manage their own risks and their own capital, and not offered to their customers. This also applies to derivatives that started out as tools to manage, hedge, and more efficiently trade certain markets. The advent of interest rate futures, for example, made it much easier for banks to hedge their interest rate exposures and lock in their funding spreads. Oil companies used oil futures to hedge against oil price fluctuations and so on. Over-the-counter derivatives played a key role in facilitating and reducing the cost of capital for many companies through financial innovations like interest rate swaps.

These systems are designed to trade across different markets. The markets must be liquid, such as foreign exchange with various currency pairing, commodities, interest rate futures, stock indices, and futures. They must cross various time horizons from short to medium term. They must offer diversification and simultaneous access to multiple markets. This is what distinguishes them and gives them the edge over traditional discretionary trading. It is also a fact that such funds continuously outperform the stock market as well as any traditional mutual fund. The power of diversification and objective risk analysis provides for a lowering of volatility and risk. They have managed to survive the tumultuous times very impressively.

Another crucial factor in the development of the hedge fund industry is in the marrying of mathematics and engineering principles to the financial industry. These types of traders are known as quants, and they are very different from the foreign exchange or stock markets traders or brokers. They are usually extremely gifted in the use of mathematical models for analysis and prediction of pricing trends. Traders relying just on gut feel couldn't manage such products, for example, nor identify all the risks associated with them. By combining super-fast computers and proprietary mathematical algorithms, quants figured out how to make fractions on nearly every tick of the share prices they were tracking. Even a tiny amount gained from millions of transactions begins to add up to serious money over time.

Many of the quants, who had started in the asset management groups of Wall Street investment bankers, eventually figured out that they would be doing a lot better for themselves if they went out and offered their services on their own. That's where the talent starting and managing today's hedge funds came from. The point here is that not every Tom, Dick, and Harry is qualified to manage a hedge fund, and even the brightest and the best can get caught up in the ever thinning air of a good run. Misuse of derivatives contributed greatly to our current economic crisis, and we may never fully comprehend the unfunded liabilities that were created by these math geeks and their proprietary algorithms. That's the downside and the poetic justice of hedge funds. When the hedge fund manager "hits midnight," he's not just playing with the house's money—he is the house.

It isn't just a case of investors taking a wild ride at the whim of the fund manager. There has to be full disclosure about the fund's philosophy and techniques, just never to the point where trade secrets are divulged. There is proven merit to trading across multiple markets to reduce volatility and risk. There's much more knowledge and skill used than may meet the eye. The managers who have had long careers and have made themselves and their partners a lot of money live, eat, and breathe the process. They design their own proprietary methodologies and systems to measure market volatility, momentum, volume, and other statistics and conduct relative strength index analyses and other tests designed to dilute risk and maximize returns.

It is a testament to the viability of the hedge fund industry that there are a large number of funds with long track records. They have outperformed the traditional investment industry, especially mutual funds. That is why they remain so attractive to so many investors. Investing in an alternative investment is not gambling or blind luck. It is not simply a matter of finding the right mathematical formula or designing the perfect system that will analyze and accurately predict movement in the market. The market is made up of people who invest for an infinite number of reasons and who react to an infinite number of motivating factors.

One of the best quant fund managers out there is Jim Simons, founder of investment management company, Renaissance Technologies. His success is most noteworthy in the fact that he uses his wealth for the advancement of science and math and unlocking autism. He has been successful for a long time and may be for a long time yet to come.

In November 2008, Simons was called to testify before Congress along with other notable hedge fund managers like John Paulson of Paulson & Co., Philip Falcone of the Harbinger Capital Partners Funds, Kenneth Griffin of the Chicago-based Citadel group of hedge funds, and George Soros from the Quantum Group of Funds. Simons would not acknowledge that the industry bore any significant responsibility for the economic crisis. In his opinion, the credit-rating agencies were the most culpable financial players in failing to adequately scrutinize mortgage-backed securities.

"They allowed sows' ears to be sold as silk purses," said Simons.[10]

What Part Did Hedge Funds Play in the Crash of 2008?

When Brooksley Born was interviewed on an episode of the PBS documentary series *Frontline* in October of 2009, it was the first time many viewers had ever heard of AIG's involvement with credit default swaps. It was definitely the first time the majority of the American people had ever heard anyone quantify the depth of the abyss upon the edge of which Wall Street was teetering.

"We had no regulation," testified the former chairman of the CFTC, who in 1998 had dared to cross swords with the great and powerful Greenspan.

No federal or state public official had any idea what was going on in those markets, so enormous leverage was permitted, enormous borrowing. There was also little or no capital being put up as collateral for the transactions. All the players in the marketplace were participants and counterparties to one another's contracts. This market had gotten to be over $680 trillion in notional value as of June 2008 when it topped up. I think that was the peak. And that is an enormous market. That's more than 10 times the gross national product of all the countries in the world.[11]

Not all derivatives are evil and destructive, but it is very crucial to understand the risks associated with these sophisticated products. This requires specialized high-tech knowledge by professionals who have the necessary insight and expertise to know what tool to use and when it is appropriate.

The vast majority of hedge funds did not suffer significant damage due to the meltdown, although all of them certainly felt the shock waves. The ones that were most exposed and most leveraged are no longer with us.

Why has this gone on so long with no end in sight? Because the media has created and perpetuated the general perception that only people with money to burn invest in hedge funds. It is generally believed that the SEC has the opinion that if these rich people are so dumb as to give their money to Wild West fly-by-night money slingers, then they deserve to lose it. If it were the regular public that were losing their life savings, they say, it would be different story.

This is typical bureaucratic perception of financial reality. The sad reality that everyone except the bureaucrats seems to have learned is that when all of the stupid rich people lose their money, the rest of the world economy suffers as well. This is why something real needs to be done about the more questionable hedge funds. I believe we need to have some regulation of the market, but it must be regulation that is well thought out and anticipates unintended consequences. I personally believe the SEC should require all hedge funds to operate in a true market-neutral mode or not be allowed to call themselves hedge funds. It would be true capitalist *caveat emptor* (let the buyer beware) at its best.

As people put more and more money into hedge funds, another 1998 Long-Term Capital Management (LTCM) debacle is just waiting around the corner to ignite another global financial crisis, requiring taxpayers to spend billions bailing out all of the firms that shouldn't have been investing in them in the first place. LTCM's issue was ironically very similar to the issues that plagued Citibank most recently. The problem was not in what the fund traded nor in the strategies they followed, but in the size of their books and the fact that they had no limits on the overall volume of their arbitrage trades. They effectively became the market and couldn't get out when things turned against them, and in the exposure of lenders to them, which no one was watching. It was therefore a question of unsupervised leverage, and that is where the problem is in that subsector of the hedge fund industry. It is where the largest regulatory loophole is located.

This is what happened to Citibank and others more recently when the overall size of all of these deals went unchecked. This is where the regulators must find a way to measure the systemic risk of any particular fund. It is also why former SEC Chairman William Donaldson, CFA, has said this is the most distressing period since 1929.

"As hedge funds struggle to achieve returns," he lamented, "I think there's a tendency to skate on thinner and thinner ice, and it's kind of an accident waiting to happen."[12]

Bottom Line on Hedge Funds

It is a fact that allocating a certain percentage of your investments to alternative investments does lower the volatility and risk of the traditional portfolio, but there is one very crucial difference between hedge funds and mutual funds.

Hedge funds are not infinitely scalable. Hedge fund managers cannot and do not accept unlimited amounts of capital. They all top out at some point and stop accepting additional investments as the capital available starts diluting their returns. Hedge fund managers rely instead on a small but steady inflow of investment capital that can be managed more easily.

In the last few years, there has been an average of 2,000 new hedge funds start per year, with about 1,500 closing within that time frame. This is not just due to losses. There are other factors, too; one of the main culprits is the inability to raise enough capital to sustain the operation. In general, allocators need at least two years of a successful track record before they may allocate money to a new fund. Many managers cannot survive the costs alone and join with other funds. This also includes managers retiring after a long run. The bottom line is that the net number of funds is increasing, not decreasing, as a direct function of demand and the limited capacity of existing funds.

This increased demand for additional hedge funds to handle the amount of capital coming into the market has led, in the past, to unqualified and incompetent people setting themselves up as hedge fund managers. This is a very powerful incentive for literally thousands of people to set up new fake hedge funds every year—and most have no experience running money whatsoever. The SEC has done a less-than-stellar job of supervising and registering hedge fund managers. Commodities traders and managers whose funds deal with investing in any type of futures market must be registered with and are regulated by the CFTC.

What's important is to close any regulatory loopholes that could cause a systemic problem due to the actions of one or more funds. The shenanigans of Bernie Madoff hurt not only his investors but also the hedge fund industry at large, although he was *not* running a hedge fund operation. It did not help that the media failed to serve their primary mandate to inform and educate. Instead, they overdramatized, sensationalized, and misrepresented the issues, exacerbating the damage caused to the honest and innocent managers by Madoff's actions.

The point is not to predict the future, but it is possible, for example, to identify trends. People need to understand the risks involved. There's no such thing as a "riskless" investment.

Private Equity Roll-ups

According to Nick Humphrey, partner and head of Private Equity at the Norton Rose Group in Sydney, Australia, a *roll-up* is most commonly described as a technique used by investors where multiple small companies in the same market are acquired and merged. The principal aim of a roll-up is to reduce costs through economies of scale. Roll-ups also have the effect of increasing the valuation multiples the business can command as it acquires greater scale. Roll-ups may also have the effect of rationalizing competition in crowded and fragmented markets, where there are often many small participants but room for only a few to succeed.

An investor faced with an opportunity to invest in two competing companies may reduce risk by simply investing in both and merging them. Roll-ups are often part of the shakeout and consolidation process during an economic downturn or as new market sectors begin to mature.

Roll-ups of complementary or unrelated companies may also be done to build a full-capability company, when it would be too costly or time consuming to develop the missing pieces through internal expansion. It may also be appropriate when the companies being blended have different financial metrics, helping to make the combined company easier to quantify and thus more attractive for investment, mergers and acquisitions, or an initial public offering.

The private equity roll-up is one of the plays on which I often focus. Although a number of more publicly known roll-ups have not had a stellar track record, I believe going this route can yield much better returns than acquiring an established business or funding a start-up. It is a fact that you can achieve an operational multiple and see an uptick in market multiples when going for a roll-up, while for an established business or a start-up you could have to do quite a bit just to get to a significant multiple.

Primedia is probably better remembered for the acquisitions that failed, such as About.com, than the deals that built the company. Its divestitures left more of a mark, as the company had to sell such titles as *Seventeen* and *New York Magazine,* when it ran into credit issues early last decade. For me, the roll-up isn't an option of last resort or a response to weakened credit markets. It rather goes back to the theory that strong management actually trumps the quality of assets when it comes to achieving returns. Would you rather invest in an "A" business with a "B" CEO, or an "A" CEO and a "B" business? I will take the latter scenario every time.

There are several key issues to look at when structuring industry roll-ups and to maximize the likelihood of our success.

One issue would be determining if the industry is suitable for consolidation. It is important to consider industry dynamics both pre and post consolidation. The implementation of your roll-up is likely to change the competitive landscape, sometimes dramatically. How will other competitors react to the aggregation? Will customers see the consolidation as beneficial? Hence, when determining whether an industry is suitable for consolidation, you should consider if the total size of the industry is big enough to generate economies of scale? For example, with local hardware stores, economies could be generated through centralized bulk purchasing of inventory and sharing of marketing costs under a national brand name. You should determine if consolidation will generate cost synergies. For instance, would standardized operating and pricing policies reduce customer uncertainty and increase service revenues if you were consolidating several area veterinarians under one brand name? If the customer interface represents a high percentage of the costs, the opportunity for economies of scale is limited. Some businesses benefit from being small, innovative, localized values that are not always enhanced by size and hence less suitable for consolidation.

Another issue would be determining the ease and cost of acquisitions. The professional costs of acquisition, including legal, accounting, tax, and strategic due diligence can be significant. On top of that, there are the possible hidden costs of your time spent in educating the business owner on the advantages of the merger and preparing them to participate in the acquisition process in the most beneficial manner for all parties involved. If you are seeking to buy businesses with a high risk of contingent liabilities, complex financial histories, or uncertain or unstable forecasts, then due diligence might be prohibitively expensive. It has to be a win–win proposition for all parties or it is not going to be beneficial in the long term.

Ask yourself if you have a strong platform. What I mean by that is does the platform you are working from include an experienced management team, a sound and proven business model for the resulting roll-up entity, and mature and scalable systems and infrastructure within which the roll-up can flourish. Trying to bring together a large number of equally small and unsophisticated companies is far less likely to succeed. If, however, you have a strong host business with a proven track record, it will not only serve as the "hub" of your operations, but also demonstrates to other targets what can be achieved with the right systems. It can also form a yardstick for assessing targets. In my opinion, a good candidate for a healthy "platform" will have earnings before interest, taxes, depreciation, and amortization (EBITDA) of at least $5 million over the past 12 months.

The next issue is determining how many companies you will need to acquire in order to achieve a successful roll-up. This is an important consideration, as it can tie up a significant amount of your resources. Growing too quickly restricts the ability of management to integrate into the existing acquisitions, both operationally and culturally. Not growing enough may not give you the scale you need to leverage the synergies gained through economy of scale. It is also easier to integrate a large number of small retail outlets or service businesses than to roll up larger, more complex businesses such as manufacturing facilities or large financial institutions.

Another consideration is your exit strategy. A successful exit through an initial public offering (IPO) usually requires a minimum market capitalization of $100 million in order to justify the costs of listing, shareholder spread and analyst coverage, legal and accounting fees, and other associated expenditures.

Another great benefit I find in roll-ups versus buying a stand-alone business or funding a start-up is basically the ability to arbitrage the difference in earnings multiples between private and public companies. Small private companies, as we all know, usually can be acquired for a lower earnings multiple than a publicly listed company. The sponsor can generally acquire a number of small companies for say 3.5 or 4 times EBITDA and then undertake a public offering at a multiple of 7 or 8 times EBITDA, if not much higher. The higher multiple is achievable from the improved liquidity and transparency gained due to audited accounts and the continuous disclosure requirements of public markets.

According to Investopedia.com, EBITDA is essentially net income with interest, taxes, depreciation, and amortization added back to it, and can be used to analyze and compare profitability between companies and industries because it eliminates the effects of financing and accounting decisions. It gives you a snapshot of a company's ability to service its debt or keep the operation going during seasonal or planned slowdowns. It is a supplement to analysis of the company's cash flow statement. It is also a means of demonstrating quite readily what the effect of a tax increase has on a business's ability to remain profitable. Higher taxes mean many companies start running in the red. No small-business czar is going to be able to force an owner to operate his company at a loss—at least not in a free and democratic society.

In addition to the earnings multiple arbitrage, some of the benefits that this type of consolidation may generate include cost synergies, resulting in lower insurance premiums and merchant fees and greater buying power for stock. You may also experience revenue synergies, including cross-selling of products or services and introducing large clients into other regions, leading to improved brand recognition. Cheaper access to capital is also an important ancillary benefit of not only the scale, but also the versatility of this type of consolidated group; it is much more attractive to private equity funding sources.

Rolling up a collection of smaller businesses allows you to leverage your fixed costs by being able to spread items like HQ administration or sales and marketing costs over a larger revenue base. Corporatization is also an easier process, allowing you to introduce company-wide improvements that serve to streamline the sales process, such as more sophisticated information technology and accounting systems. A key benefit of this is freeing up the time of the founders to get on with using their business expertise, rather than spending all their time doing administration, chasing bad debtors, or paying bills. This also allows for implementation of a secure and more efficient succession plan. Many small-business owners lack natural succession plans and the roll-up provides them with the security of a future retirement plan as the enterprise continues on after they leave.

On the downside, it is clear that consolidation usually brings enormous integration difficulties, clashes of culture/ego, and other risks. Challenges include integration risk; it will be difficult to integrate the different businesses acquired as they will all have different systems, infrastructure, management styles, and cultures. The more companies acquired, the greater the integration risk. Increased costs are another risk that must be considered. Sometimes the cost synergies don't outweigh the additional costs of a head office, additional staff, and the lease or mortgage expenses from additional facilities.

Once the founders have received a large cash payout as part of the roll-up, nonalignment of incentives can often become an issue. They lose focus and become distracted by their newfound wealth and spend more time contemplating which superfund to invest in and whether to buy a condo in Vail or a beach house in Bimini than they do driving their business forward. In some recent deals, there are numerous cases where the founder actually leaves the group to start a new competing business. When the founder is a compelling personality, there are often cultural issues resulting from their management style or lack thereof. Firms that find themselves the target of roll-ups often seem to be very informal with little or no corporate governance mechanisms in place and with limited finance/reporting systems. Under the new regime they will inevitably be forced to deal with a more formalized culture with far stricter reporting requirements and governance.

Execution risk should not be underestimated and applies at both the acquisition stage and eventual exit stage. The greater the number of counterparties with which to be negotiated means the greater the risk that the deal will not go ahead. It also increases the risk of "green mailing," where one stakeholder seeks to hold up the consolidation or the eventual exit by relying on some technical right (in other words, refusing to sign the relevant acquisition or sale documents) to get a special deal.

These risks can often be mitigated through the careful implementation of a few carefully chosen strategies. Where there is a potential
clash of personalities, utilize a governance model that is built around
the strengths of the founder. In these instances, the founder or founders retain a majority of the equity; the CEO is appointed by the
founder(s) and the majority of the board is appointed by the founder(s).
This will not only give a sense of continuity of operations but can
also alleviate any clash of culture issues.

Another mitigation strategy involves minimizing the number of
"cooks in the kitchen." If at all possible, use one legal team with a
single, mutually agreed upon leader. This makes for a standardized set
of legal documents and the same acquisition model for all parties.
Consider whether a decentralized model is appropriate rather than a
centralized structure. While it makes sense to integrate or centralize
certain aspects of the business, such as corporate governance, financial
controls/reporting, and management of future acquisitions, full integration is not always necessary.

Finally, align incentives for the participants to stay involved
with the business into the IPO phase and beyond. This will be
combination of "carrot and stick." The carrot could be options
over additional equity, warrants, or cash bonuses based on the performance of their original business entity prior to the amalgamation.
The stick might include such contractual features as extended non-
compete clauses, deferred compensation tied to earnings targets, shares
in escrow tied to performance benchmarks, and graduated buyout
structures.[13]

Skin in the Game

This is where I need to talk about one of my most important cardinal
rules: skin in the game.

I have had quite a few deals come across my desk over the past
couple of decades that have looked attractive, had good numbers,
smart operators, a timely product or service that filled a solid niche,
or some combination of all of these factors, but they had none of
their own money invested.

"But Ziad," they say, "we've got all of this sweat equity and our time in getting it to this point. We're looking for a money person to come in and finance our idea and we'll give you a nice piece of the pie for the pleasure."

I usually look at them as though I am looking at a three-eyed orangutan. While I am kicking them physically out of my office, I am saying something to them that is probably recognizable, but unprintable, in 14 different languages. Loosely translated, it goes something like this.

"Are you kidding me?"

Of course, being descended from Phoenician stock and growing up in Beirut, it is much more lively and colorful than that in its literal context, but the message is the same.

I find it utterly amazing that someone can be so singularly egocentric and oblivious that they can honestly believe that they deserve any control whatsoever over a business enterprise in which they have not invested a single penny. Granted, there are apparent exceptions, like the inventor who has spent his entire life savings developing an idea and getting it to the point of commercialization; but even then, he has "skin in the game." It has also been my experience that people who have gone through all of that personal sacrifice are usually so grateful for the opportunity to present their idea that they will take any deal offered just to see their dream come to fruition. In those cases, an angel investor must become a "guardian angel" and make sure the creator of the concept doesn't get scalped. But I'm talking about the cocky promoter who thinks he is going to put together such a thrilling presentation that people are going to throw bundles of cash at his feet. Give me a break.

Why do I require entrepreneurs to have skin in the game? Because I need to know they have something at risk. If they have nothing at risk, they have nothing to lose. They don't put forth their best effort, or they walk away when things don't go as smoothly as planned. Worse still, if there is a major problem that surfaces due to something's being missed during due diligence, all they do is shrug their shoulders and say, "Sorry."

Having cash of their own in the business will make them work much harder because the last thing they want is to have their own money wiped out. I am only going to put a small percentage of my resources into any deal, but I want you to put everything you've got into the deal. That's the only proof that I have that you don't just love me for my money. There is an old adage that says when it comes to a breakfast of ham and eggs, the chicken is associated but the pig is committed. I want you committed. I don't do business with chickens.

It is also a form of insurance for me. I have seen too many people go into deals that they thought were too good to pass up. Then something goes wrong and they are left holding the bag. I have seen situations where the investor not only lost their capital but found themselves facing civil or criminal liabilities, while the person truly responsible for the mess skipped town. If I know you have all of your chips on the table, you're not going to run when a challenge arises, but we're going to have each other's back and together come up with a solution.

The hard, cold truth is that if an entrepreneur cannot put money into a project because they either don't have it or they cannot borrow it, it usually means that person is not nor ever has been successful in business or ever made any money in his life. He is a bad business risk. Why should I let him try and grab the brass ring on my dime? Chances are he'll blow it even if he does manage to get the enterprise off the ground. It isn't a matter of whether he has tried and failed. In the real world, if you made $100 million and lost it all, you can always make it again. If you never made even a fraction of that, the statistical evidence suggests you probably never will. My advice to you who fit this category is to keep buying those lottery tickets. Maybe you'll get lucky.

If you have a great project and you are looking for a powerful partner, then we should talk. One of the first things I am going to get you to do is expand your horizons. As I said at the beginning of this chapter, I still believe it is possible to create wealth in the United States of America; however, there are other fronts on the economic battlefield that you should consider. Remember, we are fighting against those who want to control the world under a single governing bureaucracy with a tightly controlled central government. That makes this a global war.

Notes

1. Roger Lowenstein, "Not Guilty," *Bloomberg Businessweek*, May 16–22, 2011, 60–63.
2. Gregory White, "10 Cities Where Distressed Houses Will Be Flooding the Market for Years," BusinessInsider.com, May 20, 2011. Retrieved from www.businessinsider.com/distressed-home-supply-cities-2011-5?utm _source=twitterfeed&utm_medium=twitter&utm_campaign=Feed%3A+The MoneyGame+%28The+Money+Game%29#ixzz1N6017kvW.
3. Ibid.
4. Bill McBride, "Moody's: Commercial Real Estate Prices Declined 4.2% in March, Hit New Post-Bubble Low," Calculated Risk blog, May 24, 2011. Retrieved from www.calculatedriskblog.com/2011/05/moodys-commercial-real-estate-prices.html.
5. Stan Humphries, "No Respite from Housing Recession in First Quarter," Zillow Real Estate Research, May 8, 2011. Retrieved from www.zillow.com/blog/research/2011/05/08/no-respite-from-housing-recession-in-first-quarter/.
6. McBride, "Moody's."
7. Commodity Futures Trading Commission web site, 2011. Retrieved from http://en.wikipedia.org/wiki/Commodity_Futures_Trading_Commission.
8. François-Serge Lhabitant, *Handbook of Hedge Funds* (Hoboken, NJ: John Wiley & Sons, 2007), 10.
9. Scott Patterson, *The Quants: How a New Breed of Math Whizzes Conquered Wall Street and Nearly Destroyed It* (New York: Crown Business, 2010), 34.
10. Andrew Clark, "US Hedge Fund Bosses Threaten to Move to Britain," *The Guardian*, November 14, 2008, 32. Retrieved from www.guardian.co.uk/business/2008/nov/14/useconomy-investmentfunds.
11. Brooksley Born, Interview on *Frontline*, WGBH Educational Foundation, October 20, 2009. Retrieved from www.pbs.org/wgbh/pages/frontline/warning/interviews/born.html. Read more: www.pbs.org/wgbh/pages/frontline/warning/interviews/born.html#ixzz1PrXCELpb.
12. Mike Fulford, "Opinion on the Usage of Hedge Funds," Tools for Money web site. Retrieved from http://toolsformoney.com/hedge_funds.htm.
13. Nick Humphrey, "Key Structuring Issues in Industry Roll-ups." Presented on a panel as part of the Australian Private Equity & Venture Capital Association Limited (AVCAL) annual conference in September 2006. Retrieved from www.altassets.com/private-equity-knowledge-bank/learning-curve/article/nz14163.html.

Chapter 9

Global Fronts

Money is like a sixth sense—and you can't make use of the other five without it.
　　　　　—William Somerset Maugham (1874–1965), English writer

There are few problems in the world that cannot be solved by general economic prosperity. This seems so obvious, yet many do not see it, especially the politicians, bureaucrats, pundits, and academics that breathe the carbon-filled air of the nation's capital. A lot of speeches are being made while the media clamors for answers. A lot of legislation is being proposed and debated while the legislators' constituents clamor for their attention. The stock market indexes are up and it's business as usual, but it's not. The stock market drops and traders hold their breath, and then it rises again. Politicians seem to be in either campaign mode or offering a mea culpa. The speeches all seem to be excuses and empty apologies for failure and incompetence; for moral weakness, sexual deviancy, and perversion; for corrupt behavior, fraud, and deceit in the system.

The media feigns outrage, all the while simultaneously stirring the proverbial pot by probing and digging for more scandal and more dirt.

Lobbyists and special interests continuously poll the public like surfers looking for the perfect wave; waiting for an opportunity to introduce yet another tome of bureaucratic techno-babble that may or may not even be constitutional. Nobody knows for sure because nobody's read the complete bill. The legislation pretends to protect while it further chokes down economic control and strangles free enterprise. Meanwhile, the people who are bearing the full brunt and paying the tab are asking, "What on earth are you spending my tax dollars on, and why?"

The media expands the definition of Tea Party membership with sneering hints of subversive motives. The Keynesians cough out a call for more taxes, and everyone ignores the fact that the economic engine is leaving the station.

The Cato Institute issued a report during the winter holiday season of 2010 that was obviously overlooked by the ruling elite during their festive revelry. The report plainly stated the high corporate tax rate in the United States "scares away investment in new factories, makes it difficult for U.S. companies to compete in foreign markets, and provides strong incentives for corporations to avoid and evade taxes."[1]

There is an old financial adage that says "Capital is coward." It is true. Capital does not like to be inconvenienced, restricted, or threatened. Capital knows it has a choice and can leave for more accommodating environments. Making money is a sovereign human activity that is universally recognized as a natural right. History clearly shows that governments that have tried to contain, regulate, or otherwise usurp capital have failed. It is the same with brainpower; no one has a monopoly on brainpower. Controlling brainpower is like herding cats. Brainpower creates capital, and capital fuels brainpower. It is a fundamental dynamic principle. Great ideas, solutions, insights, or inventions will develop only where they are nurtured and properly rewarded. That is in a capitalist free market. That is America's true economic cornerstone, but that doesn't mean it is an exclusively American concept. Ignoring the United States is becoming an option for an increasing number of sovereign wealth funds and other major investors around the world. Ignoring this fact might be considered fiscally unwise, if not outright stupid.

At the World Economic Forum held in Switzerland in January 2010, Professor Xavier Sala-i-Martin, of Columbia University, issued his annual update of the Global Competitiveness Report 2010–2011.

The United States had fallen from second to fourth, behind Switzerland, Sweden, and Singapore as a place to do business on a global scale. The most significant reason for that slippage was a ranking of 32 in the foundational category of Basic Requirements. Out of 139 countries ranked in the Executive Survey, the United States ranked 40th in institutions, 15th in infrastructure, 42nd in the combined fields of health and primary education, and 87th in macroeconomic environment. We ranked first in market size and innovation, but scored terribly in specific competitiveness indicators such as government budget balance (118), national savings rate (130), inflation (15), interest rate spread (26), government debt (122), and the country's credit rating (11); all factors directly related to the policies of the federal government and the central bankers system over the past decade. Most important, the average citizen of the United States "does not demonstrate strong trust of politicians (54th), and the business community remains concerned about the government's ability to maintain arm's-length relationships with the private sector (55th) and considers that the government spends its resources relatively wastefully (68th).[2]

I am not making this stuff up.

The creation of wealth is not bound by artificial boundaries and borders. Nationalism is the underlying theme of the American blue collar philosophers who zealously espouse protectionist policies while denying fiscal reality. They readily sport bumper stickers that read "Buy American" alongside a sticker designating the labor local to which they belong. The absurdity of this reasoning is that being a nationalist has nothing to do with being a patriot or being a citizen. It is just another form of exclusionary distinction. History has shown us that nationalism can lead to tyranny, dictatorship, and inhumanity just as easily as socialism, communism, or any other form of fanaticism, even when it is rebranded and sold under the label of Progressivism, Liberalism, or Conservatism.

It is just those types of exclusive political and economic philosophies that have led us to this latest global economic crisis. That is why it is important to be able to separate the act of wealth creation from the illusion or hallucination of social engineering, social justice, wealth redistribution, or economic equality.

The only thing that is or should be equal in the creation of wealth is the opportunity to participate. Everything else is naturally and rightfully dependent on personal and often exclusively inherent advantages and disadvantages. The imagined outcomes and side benefits are impossible to guarantee. The shared human experience should have taught us, by any objective standard, that making a mirage your focus will undermine your chances of finding gold.

We now live in a global economy. We do not want nor do we need a global government entity trying to micromanage and control our existence, but the marketplace in which we all now trade is open around the clock every day of the year. There is every kind of deal you can imagine and probably even some you would never have dreamed possible. There are opportunities to do business almost anywhere on the face of the planet. Some regions of the globe are better places than others to invest; some may have been traditional safe havens, like the EU, that seem to be heading toward almost certain economic disaster due to promises that should never have been made and certainly cannot be kept. There are also areas where it may look attractive to invest, but everything is not as it seems. Discerning the reality is where the use of superior "intelligence gathering" and building global networks pays off. My partners and I are successful because we combine those elements with focus on our prime objective.

Remember, we are not in the market to create jobs, build an empire, or leave a legacy; those are the positive fallout of successful economic warfare.

Our prime objective is wealth creation.

Targets of Opportunity

So if you can invest anywhere in the world and beat the odds, how do you determine where?

In 2001, Jim O'Neill, the chairman of Goldman Sachs Asset Management, coined the acronym *BRIC* to describe countries that had recently emerged as economies with similarly advanced economic growth and industrial or technological development.[3] The acronym stood for Brazil, Russia, India, and China.

I don't think the term is a valid representation of emerging economies at this time. Valid emerging economies typically maintain high foreign reserves, have high current account surpluses, and are reducing their foreign debt levels. They typically have low levels of household debt and continue to experience real growth despite high inflation levels. They are also countries that have reduced their historical reliance on trading partners like the United States. China is a prime example of such economies. It has become a powerhouse that has recently focused inward and is beginning to sustain its own growth due to rapid industrialization and urbanization. She is relying less on traditional export growth as a result.

In a recent Hong Kong press briefing, O'Neill said the Chinese economy was "slowing down more than people realize," referring to it as a "happy landing."[4] New York University professor Nouriel Roubini sees it differently. Roubini, the economic guru who predicted the meltdown of 2008 two years before Lehman Brothers collapsed, believes the debt problem will "come to a head by 2013 at the latest," just when the world begins to realize the arrival of a convergence of risks brought on by rising commodity prices, rising interest rates in Asia, trade disruption in the aftermath of Japan's devastating earthquake, and continuing elevated unemployment rates in the United States. He now sees the fiscal woes in the United States, the debt crisis in the European Union, and the slowdown of the Chinese economy as another financial storm that may stunt economic growth in the near term.[5] I could not agree more.

More important, I believe that in order to win the economic war on the global front, you have to be focused in where you choose to strike in order to make the greatest impact in terms of creating wealth. Traditionally, that has been emerging economies, but the candidates seem to be changing rapidly as technology becomes more widespread.

Rules of Engagement

Before getting into details about particular areas of interest, let me lay out some basic ground rules that I follow before engaging in economic warfare on a global front.

First, my partners and I will not fund a company in any emerging market where the top brass are not Americans. The CEO doesn't necessarily have to be an American, but a majority of the board of directors and the senior management have to have some strong American capitalistic influence and education. Remember, the objective is to make as big a return on our investment as we can. We invest capital, we increase the profitability of the company or companies involved in the deal, and we exit in a prescribed manner with profit in hand. There has to be a basic understanding and appreciation of capitalist principles or, as any savvy global private equity investor knows, we will have difficulties down the road in execution of the plan. I don't mind, for example, funding an Indian enterprise because there is a historical exposure to business that is independent of government involvement. Even a Chinese native who has spent significant time in the West and studied at an American school, then worked for a period of time at an American firm, is an acceptable candidate for management leadership. What is important is that this person has developed an understanding and appreciation of the American entrepreneurial ethic.

Second, we do not fund a company in any emerging market if I don't know someone in the upper echelons of the government of the country into which I am investing. This is precisely why business and politics are so important and more intertwined than ever when investing in emerging markets. It is an immeasurable advantage to be able to make a phone call or send an e-mail that results in easing of the regulatory process and elimination of much of the bureaucratic red tape, simply because I have taken the time and initiative to build a global network. I also recognize that I have the good fortune to have friends from my youth who have risen to positions of influence and power in different countries.

Third, we do not fund a company in any emerging market without a local investment group co-investing in the deal. Not only does this give me someone directly involved who has "skin in the game," it gives me access to "real intel," which I could never have any other way. It also helps spread the risk.

Fourth, we do not fund a company in any emerging market if the participating company doesn't have at least three years' worth of consecutive audits by a Big Four international accounting firm. These are Deloitte, PricewaterhouseCoopers (PwC), Ernst & Young, and KPMG. It is unfortunate but often the case that a company that offers only locally audited books has usually "cooked the books." This is where a company creates the appearance of earnings that really didn't exist or attempts to hide liabilities that will impact the value of the company. Typically, a company will include incorrect information on its financial statements, such as manipulating expenses and earnings to improve their earnings per share of stock (EPS) or fail to record accurate equipment depreciation. I will fund only companies with at least $20 million in earnings before interest, taxes, depreciation, and amortization (EBITDA) when it comes to emerging markets, as opposed to the $5 million EBITDA benchmark for U.S.-based companies.

Last but not least, it is important to note that we would not fund any company in any of these countries without local American legal counsel totally familiar with contract enforcement in that jurisdiction. All of the big U.S. legal firms already have a strong presence in the countries on which I have focused. My typical exit strategy consists of listing these companies on U.S. stock exchanges and bringing them to the U.S. capital markets. Since many foreign companies use questionable accounting practices and have used backdoor methods to access the U.S. capital markets, I am extra diligent in making sure such companies have passed a most excruciating due diligence examination by my team of experts. This is the reason why we use only U.S. accounting, legal, and banking standards to facilitate the process and totally abide by Securities and Exchange Commission (SEC) rules and regulations.

One of the more serious issues that my partners and I have encountered, for example, are private foreign companies merging with U.S. shell public companies to raise capital. Many of these companies have been Chinese. In some cases they have used a procedure known as a reverse merger to bypass the due diligence of an initial public offering. Since January 2007, there have been over 600 backdoor registrations of this nature by foreign companies, 150 of which are based in China. This is something I am very aware of and take great precautions to avoid when I venture into such territory.

Now, let us examine some of these areas in more detail so that you understand why I choose whether or not to invest in a company in one of these countries. I want to start first with a look at the current status of the BRIC (Brazil, Russia, India, and China) opportunities and close with a look at the Middle East region at large.

Brazil

Although the value of investments in emerging markets has been hit hard by the financial crisis, we should keep in mind that the sources of the crisis were definitely not the emerging countries. These markets did not suffer any severe credit crises. Mortgages, which triggered the crisis, are not a cause for concern in this region. The Latin American economies were spared, in large part, because their mortgage systems are completely different from the U.S. system. Most Latin American mortgages are subsidized by the government. As a result, there was none of the speculation of housing prices and method of finance that we experienced here in the United States.

Some Latin American economies might, in fact, be better prepared to recover from the crisis than several of the more developed economies and are, in principle, in better economic shape as a number of them have generated stabilization funds to support their respective economies. A lot of those Western hemisphere countries are resource rich. They have enjoyed significant additional benefits from the economic development in China while the Chinese have used their recent economic muscle in an effort to corner the world's most strategic natural resources. This has contributed significantly to Latin America's rise.

I see the Latin American–Asian relationship strengthening further as China spends billions to gain access to Latin America's natural resources and create an infrastructure in the region that will not only enable resources to flow back to China, but provide a basis for further economic development and consequent political stability in South America.

Overall, I believe that the current supply-and-demand balance for natural resources is currently tilted excessively to the demand side and is likely to remain so for some time. In this respect, Latin America at large bodes well in this dynamic relative to the other emerging markets.

Why?

Because the demand for natural resources comes not only from the developed markets but also from the emerging markets, which are growing faster than the developed markets. This demand will continue unabated because the world simply needs these resources just to maintain their way of life (per-capita gross domestic product [GDP]), and it is likely that the supply for certain resources will peak and diminish. Finally, replacement of some of the resources will occur, but the time and engineering will take a long time as commercially viable renewables and alternatives come on line.

The winner in South America is definitely Brazil. The country's strong appeal arises from the size of its domestic market, the strength of the industrial sector, the country's demographics, and the expected high growth rates among several Brazilian industries. Much still needs to be done to improve Brazil's tax and legal systems, labor markets, infrastructure, and, above all, education. These bottlenecks still need to be addressed to lift productivity and returns on investment. Given the country's low savings rate, Brazil will inevitably also need to tap foreign savings to fund more investment in the short to medium term. But given the strong appetite that global investors at large have for Brazil, I don't think this should be a problem.

Brazil is rich in the commodities the world needs right now and has barely touched its full natural resources potential. As for the sectors to be watched closely, energy is and has always been high on my priority list, with specific focus on renewable energy. Big wind power projects have been announced by such international heavyweights as Siemens, ABB, and GE. There are also advances being made in the development of a world-class ethanol industry on the back of successful public-private partnerships. Brazil has committed to developing ethanol from sugarcane and has created more than 70 different varieties to find the perfect crop for producing the highest-quality fuel.

Food is another sector that bears closer scrutiny. I expect major Latin food companies to expand abroad, particularly in Asia, where competition isn't as stiff as in the United States and Europe.

Russia

The barebones web site for the Russian Venture Capital Association (RVCA) informs the Internet surfer that its 29 listed members include such financial stalwarts as Russia Partners, electronics manufacturer Intel, and a host of Russian government–managed venture funds.[6] Russia Partners, a pioneer in private equity investing in Russia and the Commonwealth of Independent States (CIS), as the former Soviet satellite states are now called, has over $1 billion of assets under management and is one of the oldest and largest private equity firms in Russia and the CIS.[7]

These guys are clearly heavyweights in the world of venture capital, with deep political connections and finance experience both in Russia and with their New York–based manager, Siguler Guff & Company. One would assume that such players would be a beehive of activity right in the midst of a multitude of investing opportunities. Russia is, at 17.1 million square kilometers, the largest nation in the world geographically and the ninth most populous, at nearly 139 million. Economically, it is apparently a different story altogether.

According to the CIA Factbook, the world's seventh-largest economy was one of the hardest hit by the 2008 global economic crisis. The Central Bank of Russia spent one-third of its $600 billion international reserves in late 2008 to slow the devaluation of the ruble. The government also devoted $200 billion in a rescue plan to increase liquidity in the banking sector and aid Russian firms unable to roll over large foreign debts coming due. The economic decline bottomed out in mid-2009, and the economy began to grow in the first quarter of 2010. Russia's long-term challenges include a shrinking workforce; a high level of corruption; difficulty in accessing capital for smaller, non-energy companies; and poor infrastructure in need of large investments.[8]

Another listing on the RVCA web site sheds some more insight on the Russian situation. The Federal Fund for Assistance to Small Innovative Enterprises, a nonprofit organization, was founded by a decree of the government of the Russian Federation in February 1994. Its mission was to fund projects that conduct public research for science. It has 1.5 percent of the federal budget at its disposal. It has had more than 24,000 projects submitted for funding. Only 200 have been funded in more than 17 years.[9] In a land with a rich history of technical and scientific research and innovation, either the government's standards are extraordinarily high or there is an extremely high number of questionable or unsuitable projects submitted. My opinion is that it is probably some combination of the two.

My friend Astrid Tuminez wrote a 2002 white paper while a director of research, alternative investments, at AIG's Global Investment Group, wherein she detailed some of the challenges in the Russian private equity market. These included, but were not limited to, a narrow deal pipeline, difficulties in the due diligence process, a difficult and unreliable legal environment, a limited and inexperienced entrepreneurial culture, inadequate financing options, and few exit opportunities.

Private equity begins with a deal pipeline from which investors can pick and choose situations in which they would like to invest. In Russia, it seems very difficult to find deals that simultaneously include solid management; transparent and credible financials; clean provenance; large and growing markets; a solid business plan; binding contracts with vendors, suppliers, and distributors; and clear potential exit strategies. When these deals do occasionally appear, private equity fund managers can find themselves in frustrating situations where their money is not wanted. For example, one private equity fund manager was interested in putting growth equity into a company that produced cooking oil and margarine and had over $200 million in sales, but the company in question was not interested in further growth. Such is the new Russian business mentality.

On the financing front, the problems of Russian banking cannot be underestimated and need not be elaborated further than by reverting to the comparison with the Wild West of nineteenth-century America. Suffice it to say that the absence or, at least, the grave scarcity of debt financing, equipment financing, lines of credit, or other types of short-term and medium-term financing make the burden of nurturing and growing companies too huge for anyone with a modicum of intelligence and experience to even attempt alone. Without a functioning banking system, there can be no sustained sources of funding for the small and medium enterprises that are needed for sustained Russian economic prosperity and growth. Private equity can propel some small and medium businesses forward, but it is woefully inadequate as the basis for a dynamic and diversified Russian economic base.[10]

What are the important factors to consider when dealing with Russia? Things do not seem to have changed very much since Dr. Tuminez wrote that paper. On the surface, Russia appears to be a "powerhouse" to the outside world. In my opinion, Russia is neither really appealing nor conducive to any significant investments. Many of my colleagues and professional peers agree. At a large private equity conference in Boston recently, Russia was ranked as the least attractive investment destination of the BRICs.

As David Roux, cofounder of U.S. private equity fund Silver Lake, observed about Russia: "It is a high-potential place but . . . it is easy to get your money in and almost impossible to get it out."[11] I could not agree more.

India

Another key market worth serious consideration is India. Indian companies today are aggressively seeking partners that can bring them sector knowledge, operating expertise, and access to new markets and technologies. The country has huge flexibility that is, in my opinion, a must for business to thrive. India is indeed the epitome of flexibility. Jeffrey Immelt, CEO and chairman of GE Worldwide, said in an interview with *Automation World* magazine, "This is the right time to invest in India, and we will be bold on the market here."[12]

The good news is that, unlike China, which faces structural change as it shifts from an export-driven to a consumer-driven economy,

India's growth has long been dependent on domestic demand, even as exports have risen. However, its major weakness remains infrastructure, with basic transportation, power grid, and irrigation systems lagging behind those of China. In their 2010 report on global private equity activities, Ernst & Young reported that the government plans to increase infrastructure spending by INR1.74 trillion ($38 billion). That is always welcome news in India.

The better news is that, unlike China and Brazil, which have witnessed an increase in acquisitions by local private equity firms, India attracts a greater proportion of foreign private equity firms. The country's legal and governance systems have indeed long attracted private equity investors from around the world. Since the opening of the economy in 1991, the country has seen huge improvements in both capital markets regulation and in corporate governance. The capital markets do indeed impose higher standards of governance on Indian listed companies, as judged by international benchmarks; and while the regulations per se are also of a high standard, enforcement has the potential to improve further. Most important, India's banks largely avoided the credit freeze that plagued developed countries, and access to capital has not been a significant issue.

Looking ahead, I believe India should continue to be a growth market, with minority investments the norm. However, buyouts, currently approximately 5 percent of all transactions involving Indian targets, may gain acceptance in the longer term, and this is very good news for investment groups seeking control. Exits should pick up over the next few years, as firms look to take profits on investments made between 2004 and 2006.

Overall, I think it is fair to say that the secular trend is for India's economy to grow during the period 2011–2013 at a significantly higher rate than the United States or economies of Europe. It is already ranked at 51 of 139 economies in the World Economic Forum's latest rankings and appears to be climbing. The road will be bumpy on occasion because development is not a neat process. However, it is this very growth, together with occasional disjunctions, that will continue to create unusual profit opportunities for investors.

China

Ignoring China is not an option. The only way any company can take advantage of its massive opportunities is by placing its China activities in a global context—as part of an integrated web of capabilities, including manufacturing, marketing and sales, innovation, new business model incubation, and talent development. China's GDP is growing around 10 percent annually, compared to 3 percent or so in the United States. The average mutual fund that invests in China and the nearby Asian Tiger nations has gained 17.5 percent over the past three years, far better than the Standard & Poor's (S&P) 500's 5.4 percent average.

China is facing several challenges with increasing inflation and the challenge of appropriate monetary policy settings. And while inflation remains a major concern, how the single-party socialist republic state ruled by a communist party deals with inflation should be very closely monitored. Linking the monetary policy of emerging markets to that of the United States could be one way of dealing with this issue, but it is largely impractical with what appears to be increasing support for the decoupling of the emerging and developed economies. It's fair to say that the emerging markets have also become addicted to undervalued currencies in order to improve their exports.

As noted earlier, Roubini is seeing China's centrally planned and controlled economy as coming in too steep and too fast. As China's government tries to boost growth through investment, they are causing excess capacity. Investment in fixed assets has climbed to about 50 percent of GDP, according to the NYU economist.

"Down the line," he said recently, "you are going to have two problems: a massive non-performing loan problem in the banking system and a massive amount of overcapacity is going to lead to a hard landing."[13]

It would also appear that all BRIC nations face several microeconomic challenges in the coming years. Of note is Brazil's public-sector debt, which accounts for 50 percent of GDP, Russia's increasing lack of transparency and embedded corruption, India's lack of infrastructure, and China's "one-child" policy likely to hamper future growth trends.

I strongly believe that China will definitely continue to grow over the next few decades. It will increase not only its economic power but also its geopolitical power in the world. It will be not only a large consumer market but a strong breeding ground for innovations. Twenty years from now, for a lot of global companies, China will be at the center of their strategies.

Most important, the Chinese have always been known as good entrepreneurs, and particularly good small-business people. This has been in the blood of the Chinese for maybe as long as the Phoenicians (Lebanese) have been trading.

So you've got entrepreneurial people at the grassroots level who are very independent minded. They're very quick on their feet. They're prone to fearless experimentation: imitating other companies here and there, trying new ideas, and then, if they fail, rapidly adapting, correcting, and moving on.

On the other side, the Chinese government has channeled its efforts deliberately: It has been building good infrastructure across China, enabling companies to do business in a very efficient and effective manner. The Chinese have put in place institutional money, from sovereign wealth funds to pension funds, to channel into the investment community within and outside of China.

Once again, ignoring China is not an option no matter the outcome of the U.S. situation.

The Middle East and North Africa (MENA)

I naturally embrace a link between business inclinations and personal relations. I was raised with this as a cultural norm. I know from experience that Arabs are not inherently dangerous partners and believe the American media has had a significant impact in promoting the negative ethnic stereotype that has caused U.S. businesspeople to hesitate to seek out business opportunities in the Middle East. The most ironic part of it is the total ignorance of economic theory on the part of the journalists who propagate the stereotype of the oil-rich Saudi sitting on stacks of petrodollars and counting out his gold coins. Nothing could be further from the truth.

The vast majority of business leaders and government heads in the Arab world are Western educated and understand that the only way to retain wealth is to put it to work to create more wealth. They understand that the oilfields are a finite resource that will someday be depleted, and they are anxious to diversify their economies. As their economy grows, so do the opportunities for investing in start-ups and providing expansion capital for established companies that are showing consistent profits and growth. The pro-business Arabs want what we all want: respect from our professional peers around the world. Yet the G-8 has not a single Middle Eastern country included in its ranks, but has Russia as a member. This can only be construed as an insult to the people of that region. What better way to confer respect than to do business with them, trade with them, and give them a seat at the table of international economic power. The creation of a democratic Middle East, economically linked to the United States, serves the strategic interests of both. It will never be achieved by military might. It can only be achieved by developing relationships in the marketplace. Nowhere on earth is the saying more appropriate or more true: people do business with people they know.

Today, the Middle East is a very different place than the one I left 25 years ago. A good friend and major power broker with whom I do business in the region loves to tell me, "This isn't your father's Middle East anymore." He is right. There is a new generation of activists and entrepreneurs emerging in the Middle East who are pro-American and pro-capitalist allies in places like the United Arab Emirates, Kuwait, and Lebanon. Hezbollah, Hamas, Al Qaeda, and the Syrian and Libyan regimes are no longer the norm but are becoming the exception and will soon be footnotes in the region's history.

Who are these pro-American, pro-business allies? I am talking about those people in charge of running the new and increasingly commanding pools of capital sources, such as the sovereign wealth funds and other private equity and investment groups shaping up in the region and who control over $1 trillion in wealth. Individuals like Prince Al Waleed bin Talal bin Abdelaziz Al Saud is surely a role model for many deal makers worldwide, but he is just one of an increasing group of Arab financiers and operators emerging throughout the globe. By the same token and on the institutional front, the Abu Dhabi Investment Authority manages today in excess of \$800 billion, more than the top 50 U.S. private equity funds combined.

It is a fact that since 2001, Gulf Arab investors have been increasingly looking to Asia to invest windfall oil revenue, eager to ride the rise of China and India and diversify away from their traditional ties with the United States.

Indeed, during the past decade, public and private companies in the world's largest oil-exporting region have wanted to take luxury hotel and resort brands to Beijing and Shanghai, invest in Indian power stations, and funnel billions of dollars into Pakistani real estate.

The United States, a traditional home for parking petrodollars, is in fact falling out of favor. Investors are counting the increased security concerns and risk that assets in the United States could be targeted since the September 11, 2001, attacks. These concerns are not just for actions by international terrorist groups but also, given the state of its economy and current political climate, actions being considered by the U.S. government. The direction in which the current administration's policies want to take the United States is becoming a growing topic of discussion among many of the leading merchant families throughout the Gulf.

Though we may have a short memory, major Middle East investors still recall how Dubai Ports World was forced to relinquish six U.S. assets that were part of its \$6.8 billion buy of British ports operator P&O in 2006 following a political furor stemming from concerns over national security. To the average American, it was an issue of national sovereignty and security at a time when we were still feeling hurt and vulnerable from the 2001 attack. To the people of Dubai, many of whom have lived and attended university here, it was a puzzling rebuke. They have a great deal of admiration and respect for America and felt their honor bruised by the incident. Once again, this was another example of the childish and irresponsible American media inflaming a sensitive issue instead of attempting to reconcile both viewpoints and build understanding.

There is no doubt that both the present and future U.S. administrations are and will be facing a tough set of problems in the region:

Iran's growing influence in the region, Hezbollah's dominance of the government in Lebanon, the perception of Western weakness induced by wars in Iraq and Afghanistan, and the continued stalemate between Israel and Palestine. There is also the perception of weak leadership in the West.

All our president had to do after taking office was focus on developing a new set of economic allies, while simultaneously dealing with the old set of political realities. He ended up doing exactly the opposite, initiating centrally controlled economic policies and giving away his charismatic advantage by bowing and scraping like a subordinate instead of a leader. Whoever has been advising him on Mideast affairs has been looking at the wrong intelligence, reading the wrong books, and has apparently never been to the Middle East.

As to investment opportunities in the Middle East region at large and despite all of the challenges the region faces, I strongly believe that its private equity industry will grow into a $5 billion industry, excluding infrastructure-related deals, by 2016. This bodes well for those who are willing to persevere through the crisis.

For those still clinging to their old traditions of doing business, you may find yourself totally shut out doing business in the new Middle East. Hopefully, there are enough Americans with common sense and the moral foundation to bring about a similar transformation in this country. Despite what the media talking heads tell you, the other nations of the world are waiting for the American people to wake up and shake off the parasitic political class that has attempted to subvert one of the world's leading economies. They have read our history books. They understand that the current administration's usurpation of constitutional power is not normal, but a historical aberration that must be eradicated. They have read our Constitution, and they are waiting for the American people to invoke the Tenth Amendment.

Notes

1. Chris Edwards, "U.S. Corporate Tax Rate the Highest," Cato@Liberty blog, Cato Institute, December 15, 2010. Retrieved from www.cato-at -liberty.org/u-s-corporate-tax-rate-the-highest/.

2. Xavier Sala-i-martin, ed., "The Global Competiveness Report 2010–2011," World Economic Forum, 2010. Retrieved from www.weforum.org/reports/ global-competitiveness-report-2010-2011-0, p. 23.

3. Jim O'Neill, "Building Better Global Economic BRICs," Goldman Sachs Global Economics Paper, 2001, 66.

4. Alex Frangos, "Goldman's Jim O'Neill on China's Slowdown, 'BRIC' lobbying," *Wall Street Journal Online—The Exchange Blog*, May 12, 2011. Retrieved from http://blogs.wsj.com/exchange/2011/05/12/goldmans-jim -o%e2%80%99neill-on-chinas-slowdown-bric-lobbying/.

5. Shamim Adam, "Roubini Says 'Perfect Storm' May Threaten Global Economy," Bloomberg.net, June 12, 2011. Retrieved from www .bloomberg.com/news/2011-06-11/china-economy-at-risk-of-hard-landing -after-2013-nouriel-roubini-says.html.

6. Russia Venture Capital Association (RVCA), 2011. Retrieved from www. rvca.ru/eng/default.php?mid=3.

7. Russia Partners, 2011. Retrieved from http://russiapartners.com.

8. The Central Intelligence Agency, World Factbook.

9. Development Fund for Small Innovative Enterprises in Science and Technology web site, 2011. Retrieved from www.fasie.ru/fund/about.aspx.

10. Astrid S. Tuminez, "Russian Private Equity: An Opportunity for Which the Time Has Not Yet Come," PONARS Policy Memo (272). AIG Corporation, 2002.

11. D. Busvine, M. Davies, and D. Nair, "Got Money? The Kremlin Can Help, *Globe and Mail*, June 13, 2011. Retrieved from www.theglobeandmail.com/ report-on-business/international-news/european/got-money-the-kremlin-can-help/article2058207/singlepage/#articlecontent.

12. Uday Lal Pai, "India Wants to Be Manufacturing Hub," *Automation World*, June 19, 2006. Retrieved from www.automationworld.com/webonly-2266.

13. Adam, "Roubini Says 'Perfect Storm' May Threaten Global Economy."

Chapter 10

The Tenth Amendment

The powers not delegated to the United States by the Constitution, nor prohibited by it to the States, are reserved to the States respectively, or to the people.

—The Tenth Amendment to the
Constitution of the United States of America

From the very beginning of the United States of America, there has been an ongoing debate about the role and power of the national government. Since the dawn of the twentieth century, we have been told that the federal government has the answers to solve all of society's problems, that if we just gave Washington, D.C., more of our money and more of our personal freedom, the problems of poverty, unemployment, and illiteracy would all be solved.

Alexander Hamilton is to be credited with establishing the fiscal policies that made it possible for this nation to grow quickly into an international economic force and for expanding and strengthening the

181

federal government's role and power to "regulate commerce." As I have shown, however, this is a two-edged sword. Over the past century, the Progressive ideology has dominated political theory in Washington, D.C. The federal government has assumed authority over many activities that previously were under the purview of the individual states. Various courts have issued opinions, which have upheld the federal government's appropriation of this authority per their subjective and often politically motivated interpretation of the law.

The framers of the Constitution attached the first 10 amendments to the Constitution because they knew that mankind has a tendency to be less than infallible and incorruptible. They also knew that money and power were addictive and tended to compromise reason. Not only did they list our rights, but the Tenth Amendment puts to rest the notion that the "necessary and proper" clause in Article I, Section 8, gives the federal government unlimited scope and authority. The "necessary and proper" authorization was clearly limited to the enumerated powers in Article I, Section 8. The Tenth Amendment reserves the powers that were not granted by the Constitution to the states or the people.

With the unfurling of historical events and the passing of time, it sometimes becomes apparent that legislation that once served the needs of a society no longer fills that role. Technological advances make the law obsolete. The evolving tastes, perception, or mores of a nation may change, and the law is deemed unjust or just unnecessary. Sometimes unintended negative consequences surface that make the original intent of the new law less important than correcting its unforeseen side effects. The Twenty-first Amendment repealing the Eighteenth Amendment's ban against alcohol is a perfect example. Americans weren't any more sober and socially upright under Prohibition; it gave us the Roaring Twenties, flappers, speakeasies, and gangsters. Government cannot and should not be expected to legislate based on a particular brand of morality; natural rights provide the foundation for our system of positive laws. It was we, the people, who decided that we were adults and were better judges of whether we should or should not drink.

If It's Broke, Fix It!

One of the advantages of living in a constitutional federal republic is that we have the ability, if not the duty, as citizens to repair or replace those acts of legislation under which we have agreed to live. We must act when it has become evident that said legislation no longer serves us as a people or advances the principles upon which this nation was founded, one of these being "the pursuit of happiness," which may only be secured through wealth creation. If it burdens the debt obligation of the government, it cannot be creating wealth. If it does not advance the cause of regaining American competitive dominance in the global marketplace, it is not creating wealth. If legislation and regulation were proposed that taught people how to fish instead of providing fish, then the unemployed would find a way to create jobs for each other. Wealth creation is mankind's natural objective when given the opportunity and the tools.

The question is not whether we should or should not regulate; it is how much should we regulate and who the regulators should be. We went overboard on deregulation under Reagan. Under Bush, many people lost in the casino. Now we have the Obama administration overreacting and overreaching with regulation that does the exact opposite of wealth creation. If we are to have change we can believe in, then we could start by replacing the majority of the lawyers in regulatory agencies with actual experienced, successful business veterans. They would have recognized the early warning signs of many of the financial debacles created by the bubble-bust cycle.

We must have laws and regulations, but, at the end of the day, we must ask ourselves where this course of action will lead us. It is not a zero-sum economic model; all sides win only if there are fewer people relying on government assistance and more people creating wealth. It is pragmatic to test every government activity against the standard of whether it creates wealth or inhibits wealth creation. Does it create more entrepreneurs, or does it increase risk and punish success?

How Is It Working for You?

While we are considering rejecting and repealing legislation, it is time we closely evaluate what government expansion of risk and abdication of responsibility have gained us. We need to take a look at every program, every department, every government agency, and all grants to all nongovernmental agencies. Do they promote life, liberty, and the pursuit of happiness? Do they promote a free marketplace? Do they promote the creation of wealth? My guess is that half of the current bureaucracies would not survive such an examination, but that should not stop the people from making the examination and asking for validation. This government was never granted the power, nor does it have the right, to expand ad nauseum.

We were born a nation of entrepreneurs. That is why so many people came to this country from so many different nations and cultures around the globe. The entrepreneur sees the opportunity, takes action, and successfully learns from the experience. They go on to create wealth. They become part of that demographic that is called "the rich." They, not the government, drive the economy and create jobs. Only a mind with an envious, greedy perspective would consider punitively taxing the rich as a viable solution to our fiscal miasma. This is a solution springing from the fount of ignorance and deemed wise only by fools.

There is a major difference between theoretical knowledge and experiential knowledge. Academics think they know how the economy should work; successful business owners know how the economy *does* work. They have been there and done it. Our government should be turning to those who have experiential knowledge when it comes to solving our fiscal problems. They would realize that many of their current policies may sound good but don't work in the real world and must be abandoned. They would spend less and live within their means. They would be promoting the creation of more entrepreneurs and business owners, instead of hiring more bureaucrats, consulting more academics, and enlisting more lawyers to harass and prosecute the true wealth creators of this nation. We need legislators to provide laws that protect and enable us, not coddle and control us. We need regulators who address specific issues and promote shared solutions and lessons learned, not launch investigatory probes that have no basis in fact and no probable cause. We have had almost 100 years of one theory of government, big enough to be involved in every aspect of your life, powerful enough to overwhelm you with enforcement of its will, and under a centralized control-and-command operational model. It isn't working. It is time to stop the madness.

You do not change the world with your ideas, but with your actions. Ideas may inspire, but someone has to take action before the change occurs. I encourage you to take action by doing nothing more than getting involved. Click on the web site for this book and you will find links to other people who share your desire for information, education, solutions, and testimonials. We are building a nation of people who want to see a prosperous and vibrant America again. We will support those whose ideas are oriented toward creating wealth, providing opportunity, and rewarding those who risk their capital to provide value to this world. These are some ideas that we believe merit consideration.

Repeal Bad Legislation

The Boston Consulting Group recently released a study showing that there were 5.2 million households in America that could be classified as millionaires.[1] I would love to see a candidate for national office, especially president, come out and announce that his platform was squarely oriented toward creating wealth, that in 8 to 10 years we would have 50 million millionaires in America.

One of the first ways of beginning that process would be to repeal all of the antiopportunity legislation that has been foisted on the American people in the past few years. Instead of Obamacare, we could repeal the McCarran-Ferguson Act and allow health insurance providers to compete openly for customers on a national basis. Break the stranglehold that health insurance providers have placed on the health care industry. Allow health care providers to compete in the marketplace, charging for their services what the market will bear instead of what the insurance company will reimburse. Return health insurance to the role of protection for unexpected or catastrophic medical expenses instead of a subsidy payment system. This would bring more market pressures to bear in the health care industry and bring costs down. If it were coupled with meaningful tort reform legislation that would curtail frivolous lawsuits and shift legal costs to the losing party, we could have world-class health care that was available and affordable.

Cutting Overhead

We need a top-to-bottom review of all cabinet-level departments to determine the purpose, mission, and efficacy of the organization. For instance, the Department of State under the leadership of Secretary Hillary Rodham Clinton has the mission to "advance freedom for the benefit of the American people and the international community by helping to build and sustain a more democratic, secure, and prosperous world composed of well-governed states that respond to the needs of their people, reduce widespread poverty, and act responsibly within the international system."[2] The State Department has an overall budget of $47 billion. That includes almost $33 billion in foreign assistance, $14 billion in operations costs to run our foreign embassies, and the billion dollars per year that gets spent through United States Agency for International Development (USAID) projects. There's room for savings here just by revising our priorities and making sure that money invested is used properly and not siphoned off by thugs and thieves in the countries we are trying to help. You can't buy friends and we should stop trying.

The role of the Department of the Treasury, according to their own web site, is to "maintain a strong economy and create economic and job opportunities by promoting the conditions that enable economic growth and stability at home and abroad, strengthen national security by combating threats and protecting the integrity of the financial system, and manage the U.S. Government's finances and resources effectively." I think we should demand the resignation of the current Treasury Secretary, Timothy F. Geithner, immediately. Never has reality stood in starker contrast to perception. If Geithner is supposed to be protecting the integrity of the financial system, why is he allowing Bernanke to run what is basically a counterfeiting operation at the Fed? Come to think of it, if that's Treasury's job, why do we need the Federal Reserve System at all? The Fed should be under the auspices and very tight control of the Treasury Department, subject to audit by the General Accounting Office (GAO) and held to the limited mandate of beneficial monetary policy and responsibility for a sound currency.

When it comes to the Department of Defense, I am in agreement with those who contend that it is time we take a break from being the world's policeman and bring the majority of our fighting forces home. The United States has over 1.3 million men and women on active duty, nearly 700,000 civilian personnel, and 1.1 million citizens who serve in the National Guard and Reserve forces deployed at more than 700 military installations in 63 different countries. Do we really need a global military presence in this technologically advanced age? How many billions of dollars could be trimmed simply by halving the number of installations we must maintain?

The Department of the Interior currently manages about 20 percent of the nation's land. Does the federal government really need to own that much land? Much of it is rich in natural resources that are not developed due to Bureau of Land Management regulations and other Department of the Interior policies. Auction these resources off to those who are best experienced at developing them responsibly.

The U.S. Department of Agriculture (USDA) has 17 different agencies and 15 different offices within the department, including an Office of Environmental Markets, which supports the development of emerging markets for carbon, water quality, wetlands, and biodiversity. I was not aware that there was a demand for a wetlands market, and I am not sure I understand how that fits under the purview of Agriculture as opposed to Interior. The agricultural secretary oversees an organization that employs more than 100,000 people and has an annual budget of approximately $95 billion. That is one employee for every 22 farms, at an average expenditure of $50,000 per farm. What is the USDA doing to protect and nourish the farming tradition? What are they doing to preserve the integrity of our food chain? What are they doing to protect Americans from the proven, impending threat of genetically modified crops? According to a recent article in *Popular Science* magazine, biotech companies will soon perform their own studies to determine whether their genetically modified seeds are safe for the environment, according to a new federal plan. That means companies like Monsanto, which provides about 90 percent of the world's transgenic crops, will help the government decide whether their own products should be approved. The USDA will let the firms do the research themselves and submit data to the government.[3] Isn't that the same logic the Securities and Exchange Commission (SEC) used to allow the banking industry to regulate their credit leverage ratios? Is it just me or are we now headed to a global food crisis due to government regulatory mismanagement?

The Department of Commerce is tasked with "improving living standards for all Americans by promoting economic development and technological innovation."[4] This department needs an overhaul to make it more responsive to its constituency. One of its jobs is gathering economic and demographic data that is used by entrepreneurs to develop marketing and business plans. It should be much easier to obtain this information than it currently is. The department also issues patents and trademarks, formulates telecommunications and technology policy, and promotes U.S. exports by assisting and enforcing international trade agreements. Also under its domain is the inexplicably noncommercial task of improving understanding of the environment and oceanic life. Are you kidding me? This should be changed to understanding the entrepreneurial environment and learning how to start and run a successful business. For an annual budget of $6.5 billion, I expect a lot more bang for my buck.

The Department of Education should be completely eliminated. It has failed, by every objective standard of measurement, in its mission to promote student achievement and preparation for competition in a global economy by fostering educational excellence and ensuring equal access to educational opportunity. This department is an embarrassment to this nation. The $68.6 billion in its annual budget should be divided up among the states in the form of block grants, distributed on a pro-rata-per-student basis with the task of secondary education being returned to local control. We have to do something radical about our failing education system if we are to compete in the global economy.

The mission of the Department of Energy (DOE) is to advance the national, economic, and energy security of the United States. It needs to spend more time doing that. Somewhere in the past 10 years, the DOE emphasis has shifted from the development of reliable, clean, and affordable energy to administering federal funding for scientific research for alternative energy technologies. The market, not the federal government, should decide which technologies are promoted. The DOE should be educating the public and promoting the relative safety and efficacy of current nuclear reactor technologies; we should be building nuclear power plants. What happened in Japan on March 11, 2011, at the Fukushima Daiichi nuclear power plant was due to old technology and faulty risk management planning. Today's nuclear technology is several generations more advanced than those reactor facilities. We should also be exploring and exploiting the oil fields that we have already identified in this country so we can end our dependence on foreign oil.

The Secretary of Health and Human Services oversees a budget of approximately $700 billion and approximately 65,000 employees. The Department's programs are administered by 11 operating divisions, including 8 agencies in the U.S. Public Health Service and 3 human services agencies, including the administration of Medicare and Medicaid, which together provide health insurance to one in four Americans. Why, again, do we need Obamacare? Why could we not achieve a better return on our health care dollar by simply improving the effective management of such a large organization? How much of the Health and Human Services portfolio could be privatized?

The Department of Homeland Security has turned into one of those government agencies whose name is the exact opposite of what it actually does. The multiple missions of the Department of Homeland Security are to prevent and disrupt terrorist attacks; protect the American people, our critical infrastructure, and key resources; and respond to and recover from incidents that do occur. First of all, as a business funder, I hear alarm bells when an organization has multiple missions. This indicates to me that what has been made into a conglomeration should be broken up into distinct operating units. The Department of Homeland Security consolidated 22 executive branch agencies, including the U.S. Customs Service, the Transportation Security Administration (TSA), and the Federal Emergency Management Agency (FEMA). The Customs Service is not allowed to prosecute effective control of our southern border. The politically correct TSA targets everyone *except* potential terror threats while it fondles, intimidates, and harasses the flying public. FEMA is still trying to recover from the total debacle of the Hurricane Katrina response. Again, the federal government should provide aid and logistical support during a crisis, but as the people of Joplin, Missouri, proved following the devastating tornado that destroyed a third of their community in the spring of 2011, it is the local people who can best coordinate the recovery response in their communities. The Department of Homeland Security is too large and too cumbersome to be effective, in my opinion. This organization needs a total restructuring of its operational procedures and a sweeping reformation of its attitude toward the people it is sworn to protect.

Department of Housing and Urban Development (HUD) could also be revamped. The federal government should only enforce fair housing laws. Homeownership is not a right, and the department's role in supporting homeownership for lower- and moderate-income families through its mortgage insurance and rent subsidy programs should be reevaluated for their effectiveness, with repetitive and overlapping programs trimmed back. Programs like community economic development, housing rehabilitation, public housing, and homeless assistance should be handled with block grants at the state and local levels, with the federal role being that of arbiter and enforcer of program standards and quality of service.

The mission of the Department of Justice (DOJ) is to enforce the law and defend the interests of the United States according to the law; to ensure public safety against threats foreign and domestic; to provide federal leadership in preventing and controlling crime; to seek just punishment for those guilty of unlawful behavior; and to ensure fair and impartial administration of justice for all Americans. With a budget of approximately $25 billion, the DOJ is the world's largest law office and the central agency for the enforcement of federal laws;

yet, it wouldn't prosecute the New Black Panthers for voter intimidation, it wouldn't prosecute the Association of Community Organizations for Reform Now (ACORN) for fraud, it wouldn't prosecute the Service Employees International Union (SEIU) for incitement, assault, and intimidation, and it could find no laws under which to prosecute anyone except Bernie Madoff and Raj Rajaratnam in connection with the recent financial crisis on Wall Street. Just recently, it was revealed that the DOJ approved a program that was administered by the Bureau of Alcohol, Tobacco, Firearms and Explosives (ATF) to allow high-powered weapons to be sold to Mexican drug cartels so they could be tracked back to the United States. Unfortunately, nobody in the brain trust who approved this scheme considered the fact that what would come back to the States would be bullets. The attorney general of the United States should be charged with manslaughter for the death of Border Patrol Agent Brian Terry and every other person killed in connection with weapons delivered to criminals under the auspices of the *Fast and Furious* program. This idea was insane in its concept and should never have been allowed to even be considered, much less implemented.

The Department of Labor oversees federal programs for ensuring a strong American workforce. These programs address job training, safe working conditions, minimum hourly wage and overtime pay, employment discrimination, and unemployment insurance. This is another agency that has lost its way. It is supposed to foster and promote the welfare of all job seekers, all wage earners, and all retirees of the United States by improving their working conditions, advancing their opportunities for profitable employment, and protecting their retirement and health care benefits. Instead, this department has become a de facto office for organized labor within the executive branch using the power of the federal government to give unfair advantage to labor organizers and restrict trade by companies that choose to operate in jurisdictions not controlled by organized labor. It has become that which it was formed to prevent—a racketeering operation. It clearly needs to be totally restructured and reorganized to be relevant in the global economy.

Speaking of organized labor, the Department of Transportation (DOT) has been thoroughly compromised in its mission to ensure a fast, safe, efficient, accessible, and convenient transportation system in this country. The DOT has 55,000 employees and a budget of approximately $70 billion, and our roads and bridges, constructed by union labor, are crumbling. Our rail system is slow, inefficient, and consistently loses money. Airlines are regulated into the ground, and it is getting harder and harder to get there from here.

Of all of the cabinet departments, the Department of Veterans Affairs should have access to the latest technology and most efficient service delivery models. It should have the highest-trained and most dedicated staff and the most modern facilities. It is the agency responsible for administering benefit programs for veterans, their families, and their survivors. It is a shambles and delivers substandard care and service to those who risked life and limb to defend this nation and protect the blessing of liberty. The Secretary of Veterans Affairs oversees a budget of approximately $90 billion and a staff of approximately 235,000 employees. This department definitely needs a professional service makeover.

Finally, there is the Environmental Protection Agency. This agency was created in an executive order issued by President Richard Nixon in December 1970. It was born as the enforcement arm of the National Environmental Policy Act of 1970, which requires the federal government to use all practicable means to create and maintain conditions under which man and nature can exist in *productive* harmony. I am told by close friends who have lived in America all of their lives that the environment today is exponentially cleaner than in the 1960s. One friend even told me that when it snowed in the industrial cities of the Midwest, the children could not eat the snow because it had black specks of soot in it. Snow was plowed off the roads and would evaporate as the weather turned warmer, leaving chunks of black dirt and pollutants, which would still be visible in early summer. The air is cleaner, the water is cleaner, and we are slowly but surely cleaning up the environmental pollution mistakes of the past; however, the EPA has taken its mandate to the extreme and abandoned any pretense of concern for productive harmony. It has taken on a zeal that has almost religious undertones in what appears to be an effort to shove aside the needs of man in order to restore the Earth to its pristine state. I think this agency needs to be reminded that its efforts are to be based on scientific constructs, not the theology of Gaia. The EPA is the epitome of over-zealous regulatory power run amok. Science is not based upon consensus of opinion regarding theory or hypothesis, but upon provable and demonstrable proof. If a theory or hypothesis cannot be objectively proven, it is just someone's opinion. You don't stop multimillion-dollar projects that will spur economic development because of someone's opinion.

Toward an Equitable Tax System

It is fairly obvious to most American citizens that the U.S. Tax Code has become a truncheon used to beat the American people into lock-step by an increasingly truculent political class. The actual legislative code is more than four times the length of the Christian Bible and is full of incomprehensible and contradictory exceptions and exemptions. It is an unjust piece of legislation that hinders and manipulates economic activity. It is enforced by an agency that is far too often the antithesis of the basic American principles of due process and equitable justice.

The time has come to replace this punitive tax system, which seeks to appropriate a portion of our income with a tax system that collects revenue on positive economic activity only. In that way, legislators would be less inclined to pass laws that inhibit economic growth or penalize success. Their actions would have a direct impact on the amount of revenues generated.

In July 1999, a conservative congressman from Georgia named John Linder introduced the FairTax proposal (HR 25). In 2005, Linder joined with syndicated talk show host Neal Boortz to write *The FairTax Book: Saying Goodbye to the Income Tax and the IRS*, which proposes that the current system be replaced by a single-rate personal consumption tax that would be collected only on purchases of new goods or services.[5] I like it because it provides people the option of opting out of taxable activity without inhibiting economic activity. It also fairly distributes the burden of supporting government across everyone who reaps the benefits of our society, everyone who chooses to purchase something new without regard to the source or amount of the customer's income or other personal information.

The FairTax gives everyone an automatic pay raise because of the elimination of all forms of income tax, including individual and corporate income tax, capital gains tax, and estate taxes. It is not a value-added tax (VAT). It is a replacement for the existing tax system with an embedded personal consumption tax of 23 percent of all goods and services sold at the retail level. It is not collected on the sale of used or previously owned items, only new transactions. And that includes government procurement of new goods and services. This would have the effect of being a competitive disadvantage to the government and cause them to divest themselves of businesses that could be run more effectively in the private sector.

Low- and middle-income families would be protected from being taxed on the basic necessities by the inclusion of a monthly prebate—a monthly stipend based on the government's published poverty levels for various-sized households, which would probably be credited to a person's purchasing card.

So, people would have all income and payroll taxes abolished; if you worked 40 hours for $10 per hour, your paycheck would be for $400, instead of the $292 it probably is now. The average 22 percent of business taxes that are currently embedded in everything we purchase would be eliminated. And everyone would receive a monthly payment to cover the sales tax up to the poverty level. For the low-income families, this plan would be all benefit and no burden.

This plan would also capture the shadow economy that currently pays no taxes at all. It wouldn't matter how or where your income was generated; if you purchase something new in America, you will pay the FairTax. Once enacted, the FairTax law would immediately repeal the Sixteenth Amendment, and the Internal Revenue Service would effectively become a bookkeeping department for the Treasury. The number of attorneys in Washington, D.C., would plummet because there would be no reason for many of the lobbyists on K Street to continue operations.

I believe it is infinitely better than any of the flat-tax proposals because Congress has shown that if given the choice between incrementally increasing the tax rate and dealing head-on with overspending issues, they will increase the rate. Plus, with the flat tax, we would still be competing with lobbyists and special-interest groups for the undivided attention of our duly elected representatives.

At 23 percent, the tax would be revenue neutral and Medicare and Medicaid would be protected. Americans would keep more of their money and could choose to spend it or invest it. Economists who have thoroughly examined the plan say it would result in a 10 percent growth in the economy within the first year of implementation.[6] When coupled with a Balanced Budget Amendment and the fact that manipulating the rate would have immediate repercussions with the electorate, the FairTax would ensure that the government lives within its means. We would regain our position of eminence among the world's economies.

End the Fed

Commerce is considered by classical economists to be a positive-sum game. The act of selling and buying always benefits both the seller and the buyer. It is unfortunate that popular culture has propagated the Marxist myth that one person gains in business at the expense of another, that capitalism is evil because it is a zero-sum game—somebody wins while someone else loses. When liberals make the argument that capitalism is the cause of all of our problems, they are either speaking out of abject ignorance or being totally disingenuous to protect their interests. We have not had true free-market capitalism in this country on any wide scale. Where we have had economic successes in this nation's history, it has been those times when people have done something outside of the government's involvement. Every time the federal government has been involved, it has created chaos, waste, and corruption.

Beginning in 1887 with the creation of the Interstate Commerce Commission (ICC), the federal government has taken an active role in overcorrecting for problems that it was largely responsible for creating. The ICC was created in response to the reckless behavior of the political entrepreneurs who were granted irresponsible largesse and perverse incentives to build the Union Pacific and the Central Pacific railroads across the nation. Construction was substandard, resulting in massive cost and scheduling overruns. Management of the lines was a dismal mix of gross incompetence and blatant fraud. Instead of prosecuting their cronies, Congress created the ICC to micromanage all rail operations across the country and to fix fares and freight rates. While this action may have been the proper medicine for the subsidy seeking swindlers who had run the UP-CP railroads into the red, it nearly destroyed the true market entrepreneurs like James J. Hill, who had built the Great Northern railroad into an efficient, prosperous operation without taking any government assistance at all. Laws that were passed to thwart monopolists were used to restrict Hill's enterprise. Congress responded quickly to the clamor of the public over the graft and inefficiencies of some of the railroad operators. The gain in social favor was temporary, but the loss of shipping with an efficient and prosperous railroad was apparently permanent.

Central planning inevitably leads to economic chaos and failure. Friedrich Hayek called the delusion that a single person or a group of government planners could possibly possess the knowledge to plan an entire economy a "fatal conceit." The overwhelming historical evidence is that the more freedom a nation has, the more economic opportunities will exist and the more dynamic that nation's economy will be. Likewise, the more regulations, controls, taxes, government-run industries, protectionism, and other forms of interventionism that exists, the poorer the country will become.[7]

This same principle applies whether we are talking about farm subsidies or banking, which brings us to the problem with the Federal Reserve System. The Fed is a privately owned central bank, modeled on the Bank of England, that was chartered in 1913 in response to public clamor over bank runs and credit deficiencies. Its stated purpose was to manage the government's monetary policies and hold inflation in check. In reality, the central bank shields the commercial banks in its cartel against true market competition and enables all banks to expand together so that one set of banks doesn't lose reserves to another and is forced to contract sharply or go under.[8] The Fed enables its cartelized commercial banks to inflate money and credit together by pumping reserves into the banks via demand deposits and bailing them out when they get into trouble. This creates a false sense of prosperity with easy credit, which leads to excessive risk taking and overleveraging—boom and bust. The only way to stop the cycle is to eliminate the cause: the legalized counterfeiting that constitutes and creates the inflation.

I strongly support liquidating the corporation that is the Federal Reserve and returning to a monetary system based on a market-produced precious metal, like gold, which is represented by a currency printed and managed by the U.S. Treasury Department as stipulated by our Constitution. The assets currently owned by the Fed should be liquidated and parceled out on a pro-rata basis to its creditors.

All we need is the will. The Keynesians who are vested in big government and a centrally planned economy will scream that the sky is falling and economic Armageddon is impending! It simply isn't true. The one world government proponents who have used central bank policies to undermine various national economies and bring them under the dominion of the central bankers in Basel will no doubt attempt to disrupt our efforts to regain our national independence. We should make it crystal clear that Americans are fed up with funny money, bailouts, and crony capitalism. Any efforts to disrupt our national economy by an outside agitator should be looked as a threat to our national sovereignty and dealt with accordingly with extreme prejudice.

People succeed or fail on the merits in America, not on who they know or whose reelection campaign they supported. This absolutely American principle must be reestablished and permanently fortified. There can be no more "too big to fail." If you are reckless, greedy, and arrogant, the American taxpayer should not bail you out.

Regime Change

The ultimate purpose for this book is to sound a call to arms and arouse every American to the fact that the freedoms and liberties we have enjoyed and taken for granted in this country are quickly and absolutely being usurped by the current administration. Whether you view this president as a socialist, communist, or just plain incompetent, he has filled his administration with people who have very different agendas for America. He has pushed through legislation that has sought to nationalize a significant portion of our economy and expanded the reach and intrusion of the federal government into every area of our lives. Not one of his proposals is grounded in a real-world grasp of fundamental economics, and most of his efforts seem to be aimed at destroying the free-market capitalist system that built this nation into the world-leading economy that it was until just a few years ago. His leadership style is based upon hubris that defies any reasonable or objective logic. He may talk a good game, but he has proven to be one of the most inept and insincere leaders in this nation's history.

This nation was founded on the principle of wealth creation. As a young Henry Clay said in the House of Representatives in 1812, "It [wealth creation] is a passion as unconquerable as any with which nature has endowed us. You may attempt to regulate—you cannot destroy it."[9]

That is supposed to be the federal government's primary objective. It is supposed to promote the creation of an environment conducive to the creation of wealth—not job creation, not bailouts, not subsidies, not expansion of the federal bureaucracy, and not providing lifetime support to those who choose not to take advantage of the innumerable opportunities that exist in this nation for them to create a better, more productive life for themselves.

It is not too late, but we are definitely at a crossroads. Either America returns to a nation where entrepreneurs and business owners can create wealth or capital will go where it is given more freedom. Obama's minions may rouse the victim underclass to support his policies and keep his cadre of leftists in office, but it will be a temporary, Pyrrhic victory. In an interview on Thames Television's *This Week* program in February 1976, then Conservative Party leader Margaret Thatcher said, "Socialist governments traditionally do make a financial mess. They always run out of other people's money."[10]

When capital flees America's shores and Obama is left with a nation of victims and government employees, it will not be long before his mendicants come knocking on the door of the White House demanding their monthly check.

The question will then be who is going to bail *him* out?

Notes

1. Boston Consulting Group, "Global Wealth Continues Its Strong Recovery with $9 Trillion Gain, but Pressures on Wealth Managers Persist, Says Study by the Boston Consulting Group." Press Release, May 31, 2011. Retrieved from www.bcg.com/media/PressReleaseDetails.aspx?id=tcm:12-77753.

2. U.S. Department of State web site. Retrieved from www.state.gov/s/d/rm/index.htm#mission.

3. Rebecca Boyle, "USDA Won't Regulate Genetically Modified Grass, Sparking Superweed Worries," *PopSci—Popular Science online,* July 11, 2011. Retrieved from www.popsci.com/science/article/2011-07/usda-wont-regulate-genetically-modified-grass-spurring-superweed-worries#.

4. White House web site, "The Executive Branch." Retrieved from www.whitehouse.gov/our-government/executive-branch.

5. Neal Boortz and John Linder, *The FairTax Book* (New York: HarperCollins, 2005), 73–80.

6. Ibid., 106.

7. Thomas J. DiLorenzo, *How Capitalism Saved America: The Untold Story of Our Country, from the Pilgrims to the Present* (New York: Crown Forum, 2004), 24.

8. Murray N. Rothbard, *The Case against the Fed* (Auburn, AL: Ludwig von Mises Institute, 1994), 70.

9. Gordon S. Wood, *The Radicalism of the American Revolution* (New York: Alfred A. Knopf, 1991), 326.

10. Transcript of Margaret Thatcher interview on Thames Television, February 6, 1976. Margaret Thatcher Foundation. Retrieved from www.margaretthatcher.org/speeches/displaydocument.asp?docid=102953.

Conclusion

U nlike many books out there dealing with gloom-and-doom scenarios and conspiracy theories, *Economic Warfare* is not about problems. It is about solutions.

This book is not about politics, parties, right or left affiliations, or jockeying for power. It is simply about learning how to beat the system at its own game, in a Machiavellian manner. Hopefully, it will become required reading at every business school and political think tank in the country for the next 100 years.

This book is also about how to deal effectively with the financial meltdown that appears to be ongoing, how to survive it, and, more important, how to prosper out of the situation and against all odds.

Looking back at the history of "wealth creation," the greatest fortunes of all times were created out of major breakdowns in the system or major voids that needed to be filled. Real fortunes are seldom created during times of normal economic activity, but in real troubled ones. We could not ask for a better opportunity than today's economic crisis for the sovereign citizens of the United States to rise like the phoenix from the ashes and show the rest of the world who we really are.

My aspiration for this book—along with the upcoming series of books I plan to write over this critical decade—is to empower the younger generations currently being groomed for wealth and power to start truly engaging in the political and wealth creation process this great country has to offer and to encourage them to stop relying on which of the big firms is going to hire them to fill their needs and execute on their hidden agendas.

Yes, this is about taking back America by force—political and financial force. Yes, this is a revolution of the best and brightest minds America has to offer to overtake big business and big government and dictate their own rules of the game using real intel in the process, not the dumbed-down propaganda fed to us by the nightly news or Big Brother's spokesperson of the day. Always remember: Business is War. At the end of the day, the one with access to the best intel wins. This applies as much to business and politics as it does to the military. Ask every single billionaire and military or political strategist out there. They will all confirm that as fact.

Once again, and it is absolutely imperative that you understand this fact: since Obama took power in 2009, the United States has gone on the most astounding spending and money-printing binge in the history of mankind. From the end of 2008 through the end of 2011, over $4.3 trillion will have been added to the national debt. That is the same as the annual gross domestic product of the third-largest economy in the world: Japan. Further, the Federal Reserve has increased the money supply by an equally astounding $1.5 trillion, engulfing the world in devalued dollars and thereby triggering inflation, disrupting the normal flow of capital, and promoting additional apprehension of the future.

Yet there does not appear to be any real effort to change course. Instead of and despite many underlying factors, such as a stubbornly high unemployment rate, declining real estate values, a potential stock market bubble due to too many dollars looking for a home, and inflation that the government refuses to recognize, there is no indication that Washington, D.C., is taking the current state of affairs seriously. If the United States collapses under the weight of its own debt, the world will be thrown into chaos, and many in the international marketplace recognize that very real possibility.

So where does this leave Obama?

It is a fact that the most frequent adjectives used to describe our current president today are *incompetent, amateurish, narcissistic, inexperienced,* and *haughty.* This is often followed, though, by a confession that many who supported him were impressed with Obama during his campaign and fell for his smooth delivery, rhetoric, and appearance.

Many Americans are stunned that so much damage could be done to our economy in such a short time, considering the sheer size of the U.S. economy. What's even much more disconcerting, though, is that throughout the world today, strategies and plans are being put in place concerning how to survive and prosper without the United States as the major global player if America does not come to its senses, reverse course, and change leadership. Never has worldwide esteem for the United States fallen to such a low point.

Personally, I can only tell those I deal with that I still have faith in the American people—their determination, their ingenuity, and their ability to finally wake up to reality and change course. I firmly believe that they will; and the world indeed needs the United States to be strong and resolute. I just hope we all come to our senses sooner than later and make the right decision come the presidential elections of November 2012.

The federal government of the United States of America was created—by those sovereign states—to oversee interstate economic activity and manage trade between the states individually or collectively with any foreign power. The central government was supposed to protect the integrity of the economy, not micromanage and manipulate it.

This government has abdicated its responsibilities toward the people in exchange for the largesse of the bankers. The bill has come due and the bankers are now demanding more than the people are capable of paying. It is time to ask the question: did we, the people, sign up for this with full knowledge and disclosure, or were we conned by a criminally corrupt political class?

Since the dawn of the twentieth century, we have been told that the federal government has the answers to solve all of society's problems. We have been promised, by supposedly serious men who have sworn an oath before God and man, that if we just give Washington,

D.C., more of our money and more of our personal freedom, the problems of poverty, illiteracy, racism, unemployment, crime, and corruption will all be solved. Today, each and every one of these problems is worse than it has ever been. The federal government and its blood-sucking bureaucracies do not have a solution to the problem, they *are* the problem.

Albert Einstein once said, "The definition of insanity is doing the same thing over and over again and expecting a different result." We, the people of the United States of America, appear to have gone insane. It is time to do something different. It is time to fundamentally change the way we do business in this country, starting with the way we govern ourselves and *our* economy. That will surely be a painful process, but the alternatives before us are slavery to the system or global war. It is time for new leadership in the United States—someone who truly understands and believes in American exceptionalism.

May you find within yourself the courage to reestablish your personal sovereignty and reclaim your inalienable right to life, liberty, and the pursuit of happiness; and may God bless the United States of America.

About the Authors

Ziad K. Abdelnour is an international deal maker, trader, and financier with more than 25 years of experience in merchant banking, private equity, alternative investments, and physical commodities trading. Since 1985, Mr. Abdelnour has been involved in more than 125 transactions worth in aggregate more than $10 billion in the investment banking, high-yield bond, and distressed debt markets and has been widely recognized for playing an integral role in those three key market sectors.

Mr. Abdelnour is currently President & CEO of Blackhawk Partners, Inc., a private equity "family office" that focuses on originating, structuring, and acting as equity investor in management-led buyouts, strategic minority equity investments, equity private placements, consolidations, buildups, and growth capital financings.

He serves on the board of TMax Capital, an investment management and specialty finance group that focuses on commodities securitization, proprietary structured products based on debt and assets, private equity placements, asset management, and other financial ventures that create synergistic value for its partners and portfolio companies. He also serves on the advisory board of DPG Investments, a recognized premier multistrategy global merchant banking, alternative investment, management, and advisory firm; and FlatWorld Capital, a global private equity investment firm led by a team of dynamic investment professionals and entrepreneurs with more than seven decades of experience in finding and structuring innovative and creative solutions to the challenges of global private equity investing. He is a regular panelist and speaker on private equity and venture capital topics at industry conferences nationwide.

He is also founder and president of the United States Committee for a Free Lebanon (USCFL), founder and chairman of the Financial Policy Council, member of the Board of Governors of the Middle East Forum, and former president of the Arab Bankers Association of North America.

Mr. Abdelnour holds an MBA in finance from the Wharton School of Finance at the University of Pennsylvania, and a BS in economics, summa cum laude, from the American University of Beirut.

Wesley A. Whittaker has been writing professionally for 35 years. This is his first nonfiction book.

Mr. Whittaker holds a BA in management and organizational development from Spring Arbor University.

Index